This portrait of the last Prince Bishop of Durham, William Van Mildert, and his associates in the influential High Church 'Hackney Phalanx', illuminates a little-explored area of Anglican history. Drawing extensively on original correspondence, Dr Varley outlines the perceptions of the Phalanx in the struggle they were engaged in, the vision of the Church of England which inspired them, and the part they played in the immediate post-1833 reappraisal of Church–State relations. The author shows how the Phalanx, reacting to Evangelical and Radical initiatives, launched important new ventures in urban Church extension, overseas mission, and Church-sponsored public education, and these public achievements are set against the group's unsuccessful struggle to defend the traditional ascendancy of the Church of England and its relations with the nascent Oxford Movement.

THE LAST OF THE PRINCE BISHOPS

THE LAST OF THE PRINCE BISHOPS

William Van Mildert
and the High Church Movement
of the early nineteenth century

E. A. VARLEY

CAMBRIDGE
UNIVERSITY PRESS

Published by the Press Syndicate of the University of Cambridge
The Pitt Building, Trumpington Street, Cambridge CB2 1RP
40 West 20th Street, New York, NY 10011-4211, USA
10 Stamford Road, Oakleigh, Victoria 3166, Australia

© Cambridge University Press 1992

First published 1992

Printed in Great Britain at the University Press, Cambridge

A catalogue record for this book is available from the British Library

Library of Congress cataloguing in publication data

Varley, E. A.
The last of the prince bishops: William Van Mildert and the High Church movement
of the early nineteenth century / E. A. Varley.
p.   cm.
Includes bibliographical references and index
ISBN 0 521 39093 1 (hard)
1. Van Mildert, William, 1765–1836.
2. Oxford movement – England.
I. Title.
BX5199.V29V37   1992
283'.092 – dc20   [B]   91–30016   CIP

ISBN 0521 39093 1 hardback

To Sheridan Gilley
with humble thanks

. . . our champions and teachers have lived in stormy times; political and other influences have acted upon them variously in their day, and have since obstructed a careful consolidation of their judgements.

J. H. Newman, *Lectures on the Prophetical Office of the Church*

Every great movement, like every great personality, has an inclination to put its neighbours in the shade, and concentrate all attention on itself. It can easily cast its shadow behind itself on the pages of history. A period, which was not worse than many others, is often unjustly criticised through the proximity of a time of uplifting and of heightened life. In a special degree was this the case with the first third of the nineteenth century in the history of the English Church.

Y. Brilioth, *The Anglican Revival*

Contents

xi

Preface

Many hands have helped to make this light work.

The Dean and Chapter of Durham, by inviting me to deliver the 1986 Durham Cathedral Lecture, first spurred me to dust off my doctoral thesis, begin repairing its numerous faults and omissions and condense it savagely in order to concentrate on Van Mildert's Durham episcopate.

My editor at Cambridge, Alex Wright, continued the crash diet, insisting that the thesis text slim off nearly half its original poundage. His interest and guidance have helped me dig through to the meaning of what I had written, and also provided the incentive to extend my researches, principally among the Jenkyns Papers. Through the stressful process of hacking out writing time from the overfull diary of a Diocesan Adult Education Adviser and Anglican committee person, I have rediscovered Van Mildert with great pleasure – particularly the parts of his life when he too was trying to fit scholarly activities into the spare time he didn't have.

Among those who have helped me with advice, information and suggestions I owe a particular debt to Arnold Bradshaw, Vice-Master and later Master of Van Mildert College, who, with great generosity, made available to me the fruits of his own researches on the uncatalogued Van Mildert Archive, then held at Van Mildert College, since transferred to Durham University Library. Mr Bradshaw lent a sympathetic ear at several strategic points in the original research, helping me to put the material in perspective, and his support has been a much valued stimulus to my work.

His predecessor as Master of Van Mildert College, Dr Paul Kent, took a close interest in my researches, providing me with useful introductions and nuggets of information picked up from his own broad-ranging reading. Other colleagues in the Van Mildert Senior

Common Room have also been kind enough to discuss the work with me; I am especially grateful to the present Vice-Principal, George Patterson, for help with the background to the 1831 Miners' Strike.

During my original researches, the then Van Mildert Professor, Canon Stephen Sykes, helped me with a number of suggestions, including pointing me to the Jenkyns Papers. I am also particularly indebted to Gerald Bonner for his guidance in learning to appreciate the ambience of Van Mildert's age.

Alan Heesom gave me valuable advice on the question of Van Mildert's rôle in the founding of Durham University. S. B. Black kindly provided information on Van Mildert's Farningham incumbency from her researches in the parish records, held at the Kent County Record Office in Maidstone. Canon D. G. A. Hinge, Rector of Etherley, helped me clarify the 1834 carving-out process which created his parish within 'the Chapelry of St Helen's Auckland in the parish of St Andrew Auckland', and introduced me to the useful parish history by Peter Kilmister.

The staff of Durham University Library's Palace Green section have assisted me in innumerable ways with their usual friendly efficiency; so have the Dean and Chapter Library staff, who clarified various local historical points for me. To Roger Norris, the Deputy Chapter Librarian, I owe many good things. The Durham University Department of Palaeography and Diplomatic pointed me to a number of interesting materials. Northumberland County Record Office provided information on early nineteenth-century use of Bamburgh Castle.

In Oxford, the authorities of Christ Church and The Queen's College kindly allowed me to consult their records; the Bodleian gave me access to the Norris Papers and to some of the rarer of Van Mildert's printed works. Dr Bulloch and her colleagues at Balliol College Library generously made welcome, during the 1989 Long Vacation, not only my grubbings among the Jenkyns Papers but also my four-month-old research assistant.

The Cambridge University Library Manuscript Room staff's help included retrieving a thesis from the depths of the bindery; and back in 1979 the Lambeth Palace Library staff guided me to treasures in a number of the manuscript collections housed there. The archivist at Grocers' Hall provided useful information on Van Mildert's election as Chaplain to the Grocers' Company, and the archivist of St Paul's

Cathedral courteously regretted his inability to clear up the Lady Moyer's Lecture mystery.

The help of family, work colleagues and other friends, and the patience of my long-suffering children, have made this book possible. Too many to name have chewed ideas over with me, suggested sources of information and shed new light on the nature of early nineteenth-century High Churchmanship.

I am also indebted to colleagues on the Church of England General Synod and assorted ecclesiastical committees for enlarging my understanding of how the Church of England works. While there were no official synodical structures in Van Mildert's day, the great majority of Hackney committee-work was undertaken by laity, clergy and bishops 'travelling together', and their labours marked a stage in the long preparing of ground that eventually produced formal synodical government. Among modern practitioners of the spirituality of devoted committee-work, I have learnt most from Mr Oswald Clark's deft and faithful stewardship of Anglican organisational process – 'the same yesterday, today and forever'.

Above all, any merit in this book is due to Dr Sheridan Gilley, who in 1978 accepted the challenge of trying to turn a renegade Maths teacher into a church historian. He has shared with me his own deep-rooted scholarship in the period and theological mindset of the Hackney renewal movement; he has taught me his love of high Anglican tradition and his meticulous concern to do justice to the commitment and priorities that motivated its late eighteenth- and early nineteenth-century defenders. Misapprehensions and inaccuracies are all my own work.

Introduction

R. W. Church, Dean of St Paul's, spent the last months of his life working on *The Oxford Movement*, his retrospective on the eventful period 1833–45. He died without completing it, but friends saw it into print in 1891. Church told Lord Acton he aimed

> to preserve a contemporary memorial of what seems to me to have been a true and noble effort that passed before my eyes, a short scene of religious earnestness and aspiration, with all that was in it of self-devotion, affectionateness, and high and refined and varied character, displayed under circumstances which are scarcely intelligible to men of the present time; so enormous have been the changes in what was assumed and acted upon, and thought practicable and reasonable, 'fifty years since'. For their time and opportunities, the men of the movement, with all their imperfect equipment and their mistakes, still seem to me the salt of their generation . . .

Dean Church was speaking of the Tractarians; his words apply with almost the same force to their immediate spiritual forebears, the early nineteenth-century High Church renewal movement remembered as the 'Hackney Phalanx'.

Church would deny the application. For him, 1833 found the 'official' Church leadership 'stunned and bewildered by the fierce outbreak of popular hostility', unready for the crisis. 'They scarcely recognised the difference between what was indefensible and what must be fought for to the death; they mistook subordinate or unimportant points for the key of their position: in their compromises or in their resistance they wanted the guidance of clear and adequate principles, and they were vacillating and ineffective.' The few 'men of active and original minds' who held the true Faith were ineffectual: 'Sound requires atmosphere; and there was as yet no atmosphere in the public mind in which the voice of this theology could be heard.'[1]

The time was, in other words, long overdue for the trumpet-blast of J. H. Newman riding to his beleaguered Mother's rescue.

C. P. S. Clarke's 1932 *The Oxford Movement and After* struck the same note even more emphatically. The Oxford Men's predecessors were there; they held the right theology; but they made nothing of it. 'The question might well be asked, why there was not a Hackney instead of an Oxford Movement, and why tracts and sermons emanating from Hackney instead of Oxford should not have revolutionised the Church.' Clarke's answer was that the Hackney men were too boring ('the High Church services were unutterably dull'), too complacent ('Though they held their own opinions tenaciously, they made little attempt to propagate them') and too comfortable ('they furnished few examples of conspicuous self-denial to kindle the imagination and touch the conscience of humble folk').[2]

This was substantially Newman's own judgement. The *Apologia Pro Vita Sua* damned his predecessors with the faintest possible praise: 'high Church dignitaries, archdeacons, London rectors, and the like, who belonged to what was commonly called the high-and-dry school', and whose '*beau ideal* in ecclesiastical action was a board of safe, sound, sensible men . . . The great point at the time with these good men in London, – some of them men of the highest principle, and far from influenced by what we used to call Erastianism, – was to put down the Tracts.'

While Yngve Brilioth's 1925 study *The Anglican Revival* protested that it was unfair to brand the pre-1830 Church of England as moribund simply because of the dazzle from Oxford Movement pyrotechnics, most historians with High Church sympathies have been content to follow Newman and classify the Hackney men as Right but Repulsive, and pass rapidly over their achievements on the way to richer Tractarian pasturage.

Liberal historiography has rubbished them for other reasons, granting them at most a certain misguided conscientiousness. V. F. Storr's 1913 *The Development of English Theology in the Nineteenth Century* consigned them to the dustbin of history as the last flotsam of an ebbing eighteenth-century tide, defending an indefensible static view of Christian doctrine as once for all given and completed. Having failed to discern the true Evolutionary faith aborning, they were Wrong and hardly even Romantic.

G. F. A. Best, whose 1964 study of Queen Anne's Bounty and the Church Commissioners, *Temporal Pillars*, brought to light important layers of detail for reconstructing the Hackney Phalanx's work, devoted a 1963 published article to the 'mind and times' of the principal Hackney theological luminary, William Van Mildert. After a painstaking demonstration of Van Mildert's personal integrity, Best savaged him for culpably failing to be convinced by progressive liberalism. The article blamed the defensive cast of Van Mildert's theology, combined with his propensity for explaining political and doctrinal views which he found distasteful as diabolically inspired, for so blinding him to the work of the Holy Spirit in his own generation that he rejected 'the germs of almost every idea that Protestant and liberal Catholic theologians have called into service, over the past century or so, to make Christianity believable in the modern world'.[3]

Reactionist historiography has produced more sympathetic appraisals of the Hackney group. E. R. Norman gave a paragraph of his 1976 epic *Church and Society in England 1770–1970* to demythologising Newman: 'The Church was not spiritually ill-adapted to meet the challenges of a new age – as High Churchmen of the Tractarian School were at some pains to suggest . . . the spiritual life of the Church in the early years of the nineteenth century had an impressive integrity, and the aspiration to extend Christianity to the masses was an external indication of a considerable religious vitality. Despite all the assertions to the contrary, there was a sense in which the Oxford Movement was not so much a protest against a totally arid religious terrain as itself a manifestation of an existing religious renaissance.'[4] J. C. D. Clark's *English Society 1688–1832* (1985) reconstructed the theological and political positions taken by the eighteenth-century Hutchinsonians, the Hackney group's fathers in faith, and detailed the High Church case in the politico–theological struggles around the 1828–32 crisis of the English confessional state.

With the single exception of A. B. Webster's *Joshua Watson: The Story of a Layman, 1771–1855* (1954), a thematic treatment of the major Hackney public initiatives, there have been no studies centred on the Hackney Phalanx since Edward Churton chronicled them in his 1861 *Memoir of Joshua Watson*. P. B. Nockles' 1982 doctoral thesis 'Continuity and change in Anglican High Churchmanship in Britain, 1792–1850' examined Hackney's theology in the context of its antecedents and descendants; R. K. Braine, in 1989, explored the kindred but non-identical theological stance of Herbert Marsh.

Besides G. F. A. Best's exuberant 1963 hatchet job there have

been two biographical studies of William Van Mildert. Immediately
after his death in 1836, his cousin-nephew Cornelius Ives, a rural
Northamptonshire incumbent and amateur littérateur, produced a
biographical essay to preface the posthumous Collected Works. Ives,
'comparatively young in years' and 'prevented by remoteness of
situation, and a retiring disposition, from enjoying many opportunities of converse with his revered Relative, or with other public men',
protested he had agreed to write only 'in consequence of . . . an
assurance that probably no one else could be induced to undertake
the work'. The *Memoir* contains quantities of mostly superficial
family information, much of it concerned with Van Mildert's
health; some valuable correspondence; and a bald outline of his
career.

In the 1940s the Revd R. A. Cochrane set out to compile a
modern biography of Van Mildert. His researches produced much
useful archival material, all of it reproduced in his 1950 B. Litt.
thesis – a godsend to later students.

Not enough of Van Mildert's personal writings have survived to
make a full biography feasible. Some of his correspondence has been
mutilated, apparently by dutiful descendants; Ives' comment, that
given his 'highly sensitive constitution' it was 'not . . . to be thought
strange, if occasionally he manifested a spirit not incapable of being
agitated, or excited', hints tantalisingly at a private person very
different from his serene and magisterial public persona. The few
personal letters that survive reveal a playful, self-mocking wit and a
genuine diffidence about his personal adequacies. He once sent
Joshua Watson the manuscript of a lecture for 'last revision' with the
comment: 'I have endeavoured to clear it as much as possible of
exceptionable matter, and have revised it throughout. On looking
over it again I am somewhat more at ease about it than I was, when
in a sort of panic I sent it to you . . .'[5]

The present study attempts to reassemble the scattered pieces of
the Phalanx jigsaw, reconstructing the life and struggles of Van
Mildert and his friends so far as possible in their own words. To
demonstrate that they were Tory High Churchmen is trivially easy.
I have tried rather to find out how *they* saw their life's work. What
did they think they were defending, and against what, and why?

Like Van Mildert's own memorial to Daniel Waterland, this is
not a purely antiquarian exercise. My perception is that the issues
Van Mildert took to heart and fought for are mostly live and

current. Even his insistence that local mission would be harmed by violating the connection between Church endowment and the particular locality that endowment was given for, has recently been restated by some members of the Archbishops' Commission on Rural Areas.

The question of what makes Christianity 'believable in the modern world' is a complex and controversial one. For Van Mildert, its believability rested on the reliability of the Scriptures and of the living tradition through which the Church interprets them, guaranteed by the unchanging faithfulness of God. That is still the manifesto of significant elements in the modern Church of England.

Theories of knowledge have moved on beyond the eighteenth and nineteenth centuries' reassessments of empirical science. Enlightenment rationalism and General Evolution no longer seem to be the Church's only tools for producing a believable theology. The debate opened by Lesslie Newbigin's *The Other Side of 1984*, arguing that, for fruitful encounter with other great world religions, the Church must not be afraid to develop a theology resting on the fact of faith, is one in which Van Mildert would have valuable insights to contribute.

His understanding of the nature and purpose of the Church has contemporary edge. Van Mildert's insistence on the inseparability of temporal and spiritual concerns remains a corrective against temptations for the Church to accept exclusion from 'politics'. To Van Mildert, the Established Church's calling was to keep the State faithful, struggling to bring the nation's communal life more closely under the Kingship of God. His conviction that the Church of England is answerable for the whole nation and not merely her own active membership also addresses current issues.

Van Mildert was of medium height, with a slight spare frame and a 'strongly expressive' face; 'quick and active, but of a remarkably erect gait, never undignified, and well able, when it behoved him, to assume a highly imposing step and mien'. He emerged for me as a lively, generous and vulnerable man whose insensitivities no less than his considerable strengths grew out of his fierce, protective love for the Reformed and Catholic Church of England.

Despite his genuine respect for Roman catholic tradition, the need he felt on ecclesiological grounds to resist the removal of Roman civil disabilities made it politically impossible for him to do full justice to the elements of 'Popery' which he himself found valuable. This, surely, is the reason 'why there was not a Hackney instead of an Oxford Movement'. After Catholic Relief was finally lost, the way was clear for the reappropriation of Anglicanism's Catholic inheritance to accelerate away, along a path Van Mildert and his friends had already done much to clear.

CHAPTER I

The little Dutch curate

The extraordinary career of the last Prince Bishop of Durham, like almost everything else about the early nineteenth-century High Church movement, had its roots in the eighteenth-century circle surrounding William Stevens: an alliance of prosperous lay churchmen from mercantile, financial and legal backgrounds and campaigning High Church clergy.

Many of Stevens' circle were actively involved in the politico–theological contests of the eighteenth century. His cousin George Horne, President of Magdalen College, Oxford, and his close friend William Jones, perpetual curate of Nayland, Suffolk, played a leading part in the controversies inspired by the maverick biblical scholar and polemicist, John Hutchinson.[1]

Hutchinson's idiosyncratic approach to decyphering the true meaning of the Hebrew Scriptures was merely laughable to mainstream Hebraists, but his work also had live political implications. Horne and Jones vigorously defended Hutchinson's insistence on the centrality of Revealed Truth to all human knowledge and the absolute dependence of man on God. They also endorsed his affirmation of the biblical basis for a high doctrine of kingship, duelling in print with the Whig Hebraist, Benjamin Kennicott, who accused them not only of using 'the pretence of glorifying revelation' as an excuse to 'insult and trample upon reason' but also of Jacobite sympathies. The Jacobite tag was unjustified, despite Horne's friendship with Samuel Johnson.[2] Stevens and his circle held firmly to doctrines of divinely ordained kingship and passive obedience, but invoked them in support of the Hanoverian dynasty.

The work of J. C. D. Clark suggests that this was not an uncommon stance: 'Though the full doctrine of indefeasible right as taught by the Church of England between 1660 and 1688 was not deployed in [the Hanoverians'] favour, nevertheless the doctrine of "divine

7

right by Providence" was; it, equally, had wide-ranging and almost identical implications for the proper behaviour of subjects.'³ Despite their theological sympathies with Non-Jurors such as Leslie, Hickes and Law, whose writings both Horne and Jones brought into regular use against the 'infidels and dissenters' of a later age, Stevens and his associates took the opposite view of the allegiance issue.

The key to holding this position with integrity was a powerful insistence on the corruptness of the 'Romish Church'. Stevens' younger friend Charles Daubeny, later Archdeacon of Salisbury, argued with passion in his *Guide to the Church* (1798) that the Church of England was compelled to separate from the Roman Communion, and did not thereby commit the sin of schism, because Rome had corrupted the pure apostolic faith. High Anglicans could interpret the Glorious Revolution in a similar light: Providence had intervened to preserve the English Establishment by replacing those whose Papist corruptions rendered them unfit to rule.⁴

Stevens and his circle retained a sense of kinship with those High Churchmen who had felt compelled to remain loyal to the Stuarts: John Bowdler's family offered practical support to the last of the English Non-Jurors, and later the whole group took up the cause of the disestablished Scottish Episcopalians. Their compassion extended naturally to French Catholic clergy exiled for opposition to the Revolution.

One prominent member of the group, Jonathan Boucher, had personal reasons for tenderness to dispossessed clergy. Boucher, a former friend and tutor of George Washington, was Rector of St Anne's in Annapolis until expelled for his fiery opposition to American Independence. His abrupt return to England meant ten years living in poverty, discreetly supported by Stevens' circle, until the Hebrew and Greek lexicographer John Parkhurst (another Stevens ally) presented him to the vicarage of Epsom.⁵

Stevens himself was a successful Southwark hosier who devoted much of his time to Church and charitable work. He was 'silent and reserved' among strangers, and never married; but among friends or with 'good young people' he blossomed.

Renowned for his generosity (he claimed to be too lazy to refuse people who asked him for money), Stevens is said never to have given away less than half his income to those in need, with a particular concern for impoverished clergy and their families. He was appointed Treasurer of Queen Anne's Bounty in 1782, and held the post until his death, when it passed to his friend and business partner, John Paterson.

Stevens studied Latin, Greek, Hebrew and French in his spare time. His main love was biblical scholarship: 'wherever he went to visit in the country, he carried with him his Hebrew Bible and Greek Testament – and uniformly read the lessons for the day, before he left his chamber, in their original language'. Devout and punctilious in his religious observances, he attended two services every Sunday, 'even to the day of his death', and 'never missed an opportunity of receiving the Holy Sacrament'. Unusually for his time, Stevens regularly attended weekday Mattins and Evensong: meeting a friend at Evensong in an almost deserted church one weekday, he whispered as they left, 'Never mind: if you will not tell of me, I will not tell of you.'

Stevens took a high view of the Real Presence, writing wistfully to a friend in 1800, 'I have read of a practice, which obtained, at one time, of the priest using no other words at giving the bread, than, "The body of the Lord;" and, on giving the cup, "The blood of the Lord:" and I like it much; but, I suppose, it would be thought Popery.' He had an aversion for changing ancient customs, 'though sanctioned by high authority', and 'never omitted to stand when the praises of God were sung, even though in a congregation, where he might be the solitary instance of this decorous and becoming usage'.[6]

In many ways, Stevens' personality and concerns established the hallmarks of the early nineteenth-century High Churchmen. The commitment to charitable giving, with a particular emphasis on the needs of the parochial clergy; the principle of working wherever possible with quasi-official institutions and episcopally governed structures; the deep and passionately felt concern for 'sacred learning'; the devotion to Word, Sacrament and Office; and the preference for working in an informal alliance of friends and family bound by close ties of mutual affection, were all later echoed by his younger associates.

Among the fringe figures of Stevens' circle was Thomas Calverley, a chemist of about Stevens' own age and an intimate 'since their earliest youth'. Stevens habitually spent long weekends at Calverley's house, and even after his friend's death in 1797 continued for the rest of his life to pay regular visits to Calverley's wife and son.

Although there is no direct evidence, it is at least possible that, through this relationship, Stevens became acquainted with Calverley's friend Cornelius Van Mildert and his son William, a contemporary and friend of Calverley's son Thomas. Whether or not William Van Mildert met Stevens personally at this point, it is clear that the beliefs and values of Stevens' circle heavily influenced Van Mildert's childhood.

A younger son whose initial capital was only about three hundred pounds, Cornelius Van Mildert established himself as a distiller but made no great commercial success of it, and towards the end of his life made some new excise regulations the excuse for early retirement. Cornelius Ives, William Van Mildert's biographer, who, due to the successive unions of the two families, was both William's cousin and his nephew, describes Cornelius Van Mildert's income as 'only a respectable competency'; at his death in 1799, his son inherited the princely sum of £62.9s., less 5s. stamp duty.

The family was of Dutch origin, part of the immigrant mercantile community that established itself in London after the accession of 'Dutch William'. Cornelius' grandfather Daniel emigrated from Amsterdam with his father somewhere between 1662 and 1687. Daniel, 'naturalized in England', lived at Homerton as 'a Gentleman'. He served the Dutch Reform Church at Austin Friars as deacon and on several occasions as spokesman.

Cornelius' father Abraham married within the Dutch community in 1709 and was a deacon of Austin Friars in 1711, but thereafter the family seems to have become more determinedly British. In 1748 Cornelius' elder sister married William Ives, whose family had held the estate and rectory of Bradden in Northamptonshire since 1677, and this marked a decisive assimilation to the Church of England. Cornelius himself was a devout Anglican.

William was interested in his Dutch origins, making careful genealogical notes and in 1792 travelling the Low Countries on a kind of ancestor-seeking pilgrimage; but he very emphatically regarded himself as an Englishman.[7]

Cornelius' wife Martha was the daughter of William Hill, a prosperous Vauxhall businessman. Her brother William died worth £12,000; his influence with the Grocers' Company gave decisive help to his nephew's career.

The Van Mildert distillery was in Blackman Street, Southwark. The family lived at Newington, where William was born on 6th

November 1765, his parents' fourth child and second son. He was baptised on 8th December by the Rector of Newington, Dr Samuel Horsley, a theologian and scientist who was to enjoy a brilliant career as the most influential High Church bishop of his day; his impact on Van Mildert was to be profound and lifelong. Horsley's chief patron was his Cambridge contemporary Lord Chancellor Thurlow. According to anecdote Thurlow came across Horsley's Letters to Priestley by accident, having asked a friend to lend him something to read on a journey; detected a mind 'of a kindred stamp, and Horsley's fortunes were made'.[8] Thurlow was a great bishop-maker, whose younger brother Thomas became Bishop of Lincoln in 1779 and Prince Bishop of Durham in 1787.

On the scanty evidence available, the Van Mildert home was loving and secure. A servant, Ann Williams, commended in Cornelius Van Mildert's will for her 'long and faithful service', was still with the family when Martha Van Mildert made her will in 1825, and a memorandum drawn up during Martha's last illness asked her unmarried daughter Catherine to keep 'Williams and Clare' in employment.

William Van Mildert met death early, losing his eleven-year-old brother Cornelius when he was six. His other brother Dirck and two of his sisters died in infancy. This was not unusual for the time: of his father's ten siblings, two were stillborn and four more died before reaching their first birthday.

Health was a favourite preoccupation of the age, a rule to which the Van Milderts were no exception. His childhood shaped by his parents' weak health, Van Mildert enjoyed a 'highly sensitive constitution, of both mind and body', disposing him to 'maladies . . . of an irritable cast', and ill-health dogged him in one way or another all his life. A severe childhood attack of smallpox left him 'liable to inflammation in the eyes, if exposed to cold or rain', and in early adulthood he developed 'an inherited tendency to haemorrhage of the lungs, or throat', which 'repeatedly showed itself, to a degree to excite considerable alarm'.[9]

Four sisters survived infancy: Anne (or Anna) and Martha, older than William, Catherine (Kitty) and Rachel younger. Tragedy struck again in 1795 when Rachel died aged twenty-seven: 'poor Rachel is much as before,' Van Mildert wrote to his cousin-in-law Thomas Grant shortly before her death, 'only weaker and weaker'.[10] There were no Van Mildert cousins, both Van Mildert uncles having died without issue; but William and his sisters were on good terms with their uncle William Hill, his wife and daughters, and enjoyed a close relationship with their Ives cousins Cornelius, Anne (Nancy) and Eliza.

The Ives children were taught to read and write at home before being sent to school at the age of about eight, and Van Mildert no doubt followed a similar pattern. He attended St Saviour's School, Southwark, winning the school silver medal for merit in 1776.

When he was about thirteen, Van Mildert asked his father to apprentice him to Thomas Calverley. Calverley, however, refused, on the ground that he intended to retire from business soon. The attraction was Calverley, not pharmacy. Rather than exploring other similar possibilities, Van Mildert 'at once avowed his inclination to pursue his studies, with a view to become a clergyman'.

His father's reception of this announcement may have been less than rapturous. Clergy stipends were frequently small, and preferment uncertain; a recent study has shown that at the end of the eighteenth century, some 55% of those ordained in the Church of England remained curates for the bulk of their careers, and only about 20% found a benefice within five years of ordination. In 1803 the Revd William Jones of Broxbourne noted bitterly in his diary:

> As to those who court this genteel profession, with no other prospect but of being 'journeymen' – 'soles' not 'upper-leathers' – which is (being interpreted) poor curates – they are truly to be pitied. If they regard present circumstances, without 'having respect unto the recompense of future reward', they would, I am sure, do better for themselves, and for their families, by making interest for upper-servants' places in a genteel family, than by being mere 'soles or understrappers' in the Church.[11]

To make a comfortable career a clergyman needed private means or influential patronage, and Cornelius Van Mildert was in no position to provide either. Poor health, contemplative habits and an unambitious temperament meant that, in Ives' words, 'although he obtained the esteem of all who knew him, as a man highly moral and religious', Cornelius 'never formed an extensive or lucrative connection'.

Horsley, now well launched on his own distinguished and pluralistic career with the rectory of Albury and a prebend of St Paul's added to his rectory of Newington, was consulted about Van Mildert's clerical ambitions. He was not in favour, remonstrating against 'diverting the boy from trade'. Van Mildert carried the day, however, and was duly sent to public school to be groomed for Oxford, the respectable route to ordination. Ives relates what looks like a family legend that Westminster and St Paul's were considered, but neither sympathised with the need for Van Mildert to protect his weak eyes by staying at home in bad weather. Merchant Taylors' proved more accommodating.

Van Mildert entered Merchant Taylors' in 1779, a year after the death of the reforming headmaster James Townley. Among Townley's achievements at the school was the institution of 'repetitions every three to four months of select passages from the Bible in Hebrew and from English, Latin and Greek writers'; Hebrew had formed part of the Merchant Taylors' curriculum from the school's beginnings. Townley also added geography, and tried unsuccessfully to add mathematics, to the school curriculum.[12]

At Merchant Taylors', Van Mildert showed some flair for 'English exercises, both prose and verse'. Writing verse became a lifelong hobby. In his last years at school, Van Mildert helped his friend Thomas Percy, nephew of the Bishop of Dromore, to set up a literary society named The Council of Parnassus, which in 1784 published a decidedly precious slim volume of *Poems by A Literary Society, comprehending Original Pieces in the Several Walks of Poetry.* Printed by J. Nichols, it retailed for one shilling. Its 'Prefatory ADVERTISEMENT' dedicated it to the needs of the poet who, in 'an age in which criticism, and a refined taste for POETRY, shine forth in the zenith of Attic perfection', had not yet written enough to fill a book but deemed his work 'superior to the trivial and worthless pieces exhibited in the generality of Magazines'.

The Poems, rife with Strephons and Delias, fragrant mossy banks, undigested classical imagery and admirable sentiments, are not among the great lost treasures of literature. Van Mildert's four pieces avoid the worst excesses of his fellows and show a certain breadth of technique (if not much else). He was fond of mild satire, the mildness of which was certainly deliberate: in the undated essay 'Observations upon the Works of Horace', he noted approvingly that the Satires, 'whilst they lash in the severest manner the vices and follies of his age, are free from that malice and personal sarcasm, which too frequently is made the principal object in satirical compositions'. Van Mildert's sonnet 'On reading Churchill's Poems', dated 9th June 1785, condemns the vitriolic satirist to see his 'Muse's Trophies fade/Wither'd and shrunk in Slander's baleful shade', preferring those 'other Bards' who 'to Vice and Folly's View/Bid Satire shine in Humour's mild attire'. In the 1784 collection, his satire 'Miss DIANA TOOTHLESS' Petition' presents a marked contrast to 'Methodism, a Satiric Poem' by W. B. P., in which the Methodist preacher goes drunken into the pulpit, fornicates with most of the female members of his flock and steals purses, while the worshippers are graced with such names as Avaro, Iniquo and Libido. In Van Mildert's piece, a little gentle fun is poked at pious old ladies and curates.

Despite his literary laurels Van Mildert was not awarded one of the school's thirty-seven appropriated fellowships at St John's College, Oxford, although his friend Thomas Percy was luckier. This, Ives explains, was due to his having entered the school at the advanced age of fourteen, not to any 'moral fault, nor any defect of learning . . .' He was now too old to wait on for a second try, so on 21st February 1784 entered as a commoner at The Queen's College. His reasons for choosing this college, most of whose ties were with Cumberland, are unknown. Thomas Calverley, to whom he remained close, went to Oriel.

From the relevant entries in the Queen's College Batells Book, Van Mildert seems to have avoided extravagance without living in undue austerity. Regular termly payments of half a guinea to the hairdresser – not a college fixed charge – suggest a certain regard for his appearance but, unlike some of his contemporaries, he never ran up bills to tailor, shoemaker, breeches maker, hatter, sempstress, shoecleaner or even laundress. His chamber, at £1.15s. per term, was neither the cheapest nor the most expensive of the rooms available to commoners. His only recorded piece of self-indulgence over the three years was the reckless expenditure, in Michaelmas term 1785, of £1.9s.10d on fruit and cream.[13]

No records were kept of his academic progress. In the unreformed Oxford of the late eighteenth century, university examinations had become a series of formal set-pieces, with 'arguments' often handed down from generation to generation of undergraduates on slips of paper, and how hard an undergraduate worked was very much his own affair.

Teaching was college-based. The diary of John James, who went up to Queen's in 1778, gives a very full picture of the teaching offered at this period. James attended his tutor Thomas Nicolson's

Logic lectures for three years and was unimpressed: 'The Doctor construes a few chapters [of Sanderson's Logicae Artis Compendium], which the next lecture we repeat to him. He does not explain a single term, and were I only to rely on the instruction I receive from him, I should find myself very deficient.'[14]

James, an able and determined student who in 1782 won the Chancellor's Prize for Latin verse, did not rely on the lectures, but pursued a formidable course of study laid out for him partly by his schoolmaster father, partly by Dr Nicolson, partly by his own inclination. His letters refer to works by Lucian, Terence, Aristophanes, Anacreon, Xenophon, Sappho, Homer, Cicero, Livy, Plato, Horace, Virgil and Herodotus, as well as the New Testament in Greek and, in his fourth year, parts of the Old Testament in Hebrew.

Besides the Logic lectures, Nicolson also lectured on Ethics, but an attempt to institute a mathematics class failed for lack of support. A number of the professors lectured; some, for instance the astronomer Thomas Hornsby, regularly drew large classes.

Van Mildert's tutor was Septimus Collinson, who in 1793 became Provost of Queen's. Collinson 'belonged in spirit to the eighteenth century . . . enjoying his comforts and preaching good sermons in a Cumberland accent so strong as to be scarcely comprehensible'. His 'letters on the Thirty-nine Articles' were generally esteemed, although never published, and in 1798 he became Margaret Professor of Divinity. Ives notes that Van Mildert always spoke of his former tutor 'in terms of affectionate esteem', and when in 1793 Van Mildert wrote to remove his name from the College books, Collinson's reply, strikingly warm and charming, concluded 'your very affectionate friend'.[15]

According to John James, Collinson recommended his pupils to 'obtain some knowledge of [chemistry] previous to the study of natural philosophy'. James complied, finding the chemistry classes full of 'clergymen, or men intended for the Church'.

Van Mildert probably took Collinson's advice, for he went up to Oxford with a professed interest in natural history, especially the study of fossils. This may have been due to the influence of Horsley, who 'thought that every clergyman had an obligation to possess a knowledge of science and to encourage its development in the universities. Horsley himself was a mathematician, a physicist, an astronomer . . .' Jones of Nayland also took a strong interest in fossils, for the good Hutchinsonian reason that they provided evidence of the Flood: Hutchinson himself and many of his followers were 'diligent collectors of fossil bodies'.[16]

Fossilology was in any case a respectable and gentlemanly pursuit, if not yet as popular as it was to become in the early nineteenth century. The great geological controversies lay in the future: Neptunists and Vulcanists had yet to clash, the date of the world's creation remained in 4004 B.C. where the calculations of Archbishop James Ussher had set it, and the historicity and universality of Noah's flood had as yet few serious challengers.

The intrepid fossilologist took 'two or three walks to Shotover, and Heddington [sic] Quarry', but 'had the ill luck to be caught in a violent Rain, which entirely prevented me from making any researches'. Instead he purchased specimens from a labourer at Headington Quarry who hawked them round the colleges.[17]

Students at Queen's could learn French: there was 'one master, Chamberlain, very clever, and a native of France'. Since Van Mildert read French when he embarked on his Boyle Lectures in 1802, and since modern languages were seemingly not taught at Merchant Taylors' in his day, he may well have taken this opportunity.

Outwardly at least, all Oxford studies took place in a religious matrix. The great majority of dons were in Anglican orders; daily attendance at College chapel was compulsory (John James, himself an embryo cleric, thought his tutor's insistence on this point excessive); Holy Communion was 'regularly if infrequently celebrated' in college chapels; and each student had to subscribe the Thirty-nine Articles not only, as at Cambridge, on presenting himself for his degree, but also at matriculation. An Oxford or Cambridge degree was automatic qualification for Anglican orders. A steady 50% of Cambridge undergraduates were afterwards ordained: the Oxford figure was even higher.[18]

In Van Mildert's undergraduate days some study of the New Testament in Greek was evidently customary, and the more highly motivated students tackled the Old Testament in Hebrew. Van Mildert, according to Ives, 'was of regular and studious habits, and from the first applied himself more particularly to theology'. The foundations of his later legendary familiarity with Anglican theology were presumably laid during his undergraduate days. He may have followed some such plan as that laid down in Waterland's

Advice to a Young Student, which exhorted undergraduates to study English sermons, 'the easiest, plainest, and most entertaining books of divinity . . . [which] contain as much and as good divinity as any other discourses whatever', church history, doctrinal controversies, Pearson on the Creed and Burnet on the Articles, besides 'the reading the best English writers, such as Temple, Collier, Spectator, and other writings of Addison, and other masters of thought and style'. Van Mildert's works witness to a theological diet very much as Waterland prescribed.

Late eighteenth-century Oxford examinations were undemanding: John James regarded his as irritating interruptions to his studies. Over the three years, a number of formal disputations in grammar or logic were required. Finally came the viva voce examination, covering (in theory) grammar, rhetoric, logic, ethics, geometry, Greek classics and Latin, before three Regent Masters who were supposedly nominated in rotation by the Senior Proctor but often recruited by the candidate himself, and took their responsibilities no more seriously than tradition demanded. James' examination, fixed for a Monday, was postponed to the Friday 'for want of Masters'. He answered the examiners' questions and construed 'a few lines in my classics' with ease, dismissing the whole business as 'trifling and farcical'.[19]

If this atrophied parody of mediaeval scholarship too often produced, as James complained, only 'bad Latin, bad arguments, and bad philosophy', ignoring most areas of contemporary learning, the intellectual degeneracy of late eighteenth-century Oxford can be overstated. James' own studies demonstrate that the bright and highly motivated student, willing and able to work on his own without the spur of rigorous examinations, could follow a challenging course of study in classics, classical philosophy, natural sciences or divinity. Unreformed Oxford could still produce a classicist of the calibre of Thomas Gaisford, or a scholar as familiar with the byways of divinity as Van Mildert himself. It was not only the disciplines on which Oxford was notoriously weak, such as mathematics, which however lacked a quality of inspiration. The indifference to Van Mildert's embryonic interest in geology was symptomatic of a wider disinclination to be excited by the new and unexplored. At this period the University of Oxford neither was, nor aspired to be, a focus of intellectual advance. At a time when both the quality and the quantity of British scientific research showed a marked rise, 'the

functions that the universities might have performed were undertaken in scientific societies and private institutes which grew up in
the last quarter of the century', notably in London, Edinburgh and
Birmingham. In philosophy also, new movements were afoot which
found little sympathy in Oxford. The values of the University were
those of conformity not criticism; fidelity not originality the desired
academic virtue:

> If, in fact, both universities were less torpid in the eighteenth century than
> their critics then and later would have us believe, it is yet plain that their
> spiritual and intellectual temper became perceptibly lower. They had been
> left high and dry by the more important philosophical and intellectual
> developments of their age.[20]

Closely linked with this conformity to academic tradition was an
increasing attachment to the political status quo. As the eighteenth
century neared its end the University of Oxford set aside its
prolonged flirtation with Jacobitical treason, re-emerging as 'a
bastion of the protestant order in church and state, a pillar of the
establishment in the broadest sense'. The last acknowledged Pretender died in April 1788, but his cause had already been dead in
Oxford for some time. Horace Walpole observed that 'even the
University of Oxford had almost ceased to toast the Pretender by
1771', and George III's highly successful visit in August 1786 made
the University's new loyalty abundantly plain. If full-blown indefeasible Divine Right had been laid quietly aside, yet its trans-
formation products, Divine Right by Providence and the Divine
Utility of the Constitution, were to bind Oxford tightly to the
established order in Church and State through the years of political
turbulence ahead.[21]

Oxford men may no longer have drunk the health of the Pretender, but they found plenty of other reasons for drinking. Large
amounts of alcohol were consumed both by students and by dons.
The University's reputation as a place of dissipation and extravagance may have contributed to the fall in undergraduate numbers
during the eighteenth and early nineteenth centuries.

There were other factors, among them Oxford's insistence on
signing the Thirty-nine Articles at matriculation, which increased in
significance as Dissent spread. As early as 1772 a proposal to abolish
the subscription requirement was put up to, and roundly defeated
by, the House of Commons. Subscription was generally popular in
Oxford: proposals in 1787 and 1789 to repeal the Test and Corpor-

ation Acts caused an upsurge of opposition and general High Church sentiment in the University.

Numbers fell most sharply at both ends of the social spectrum. By 1785–6 only five per cent of matriculants were the sons of peers, baronets or knights: the more influential aristocratic families increasingly preferred sending their sons to travel abroad with a tutor or to study at Continental universities. At the same time, the number of undergraduates from lower-class homes fell sharply as the cost of University study rose and the scholarships originally intended for poor students were increasingly appropriated by the wealthy and influential. The main motive for study at Oxford by members of the lower social groups was entry into the Church; but the prevalence of pluralism meant a diminished number of opportunities, and moreover

the lower classes were being squeezed out of jobs in the church, as the latter became a more socially respectable and economically attractive profession . . . The proportion of B.A.s drawn from the ranks of esquires and above rose during the eighteenth century from five percent to thirty percent, the great majority of whom were aiming at a career in the church.[22]

The Oxford of Van Mildert's undergraduate days was a society of growing social and vocational homogeneity, where the sons of prosperous businessmen or minor gentry formed an increasingly important social category, and intending clergymen much the largest vocational group. Under the circumstances, his experiences were unlikely to make him question the rightness of the social hierarchy to which he belonged, or the ecclesiastical hierarchy he aspired to enter.

Van Mildert evidently enjoyed his three years. 'He was fond of the elegancies of social life, and had a taste for polite accomplishments. Besides music, drawing and poetry were his recreations; in both of which he seems to have been respectable as an amateur.' His uncle William Hill sent him at least one food hamper; the Ives family entertained him at Bradden, and he was no doubt present when in July 1787 his sister Anna married his cousin Cornelius Ives. He wrote birthday poems to his cousin Eliza Ives in 1782 and 1783, but if this represents a teenage romance, nothing came of it.

Van Mildert took his B.A. on 23rd November 1787, and went down at the end of the Michaelmas Term. After satisfying the Bishop of Oxford's Examining Chaplain he was ordained deacon in May 1788. Being examined for Orders was not an utter formality: in

1783 one of John James' fellow-examinees failed because, 'transcribing from an old bit of dirty paper which, not being able in some places to understand himself, he got a neighbour to explain to him', he 'shewed up an affair that neither the examiner nor himself could construe'. James was required to write a theme on 'An humana ratio sit per se sufficiens ad salutem consequendam? NEG.', to 'read a verse or two in the Greek Testament for form's sake', and to be an agreeable companion at dinner.[23]

Van Mildert evidently impressed the Examining Chaplain, Houstonne Radcliffe of Brasenose, who two years later gave him a reference for his third curacy. He was ordained as curate of Sherborne (Shirburn) and Lewknor, two villages near Watlington.

While Van Mildert pursued his studies, William Stevens and his friends were taking up the cause of the disestablished and financially devastated Scottish Episcopal Church.

When Britain and America made peace in 1783, the American Anglicans at once set about securing an independent episcopate in the apostolic succession. In April 1783 the clergy of Connecticut elected as Bishop Dr Samuel Seabury, a former SPCK missionary well known to Stevens, and sent him to England for consecration. The English episcopate demurred, ruling indispensable 'the oath of royal supremacy in the consecration', which Seabury was unable to take. In August 1784 he applied instead to 'the good bishops in Scotland', suggesting that perhaps Providence had 'supported them and continued their succession under various and great difficulties, that a free, valid and purely ecclesiastical episcopacy may from them pass into the western world'.[24] The Scottish Primus and two brother bishops consecrated Seabury at Aberdeen in November 1784.

The affair made Stevens aware for the first time of the survival, and hardships, of the Scottish Episcopalians. He responded with characteristic generosity.

After Prince Charles Edward's death at Rome on 31st January 1788, the Scottish Bishops swore allegiance to King George. Early in 1789 the new Primus, Skinner of Aberdeen, with two fellow-Bishops journeyed to London seeking financial relief for their Church. A Relief Bill passed the Commons but was adjourned in the Lords at the urging of Lord Chancellor Thurlow.

Stevens with two friends, the young lawyer James Allan Park and

Dr Gaskin, Rector of Stoke Newington and SPCK Secretary, formed a 'voluntary Committee for managing in England the Affairs of the Scotch Episcopal Church'. Horsley, now Bishop of St David's, championed a fresh Bill through the Lords, and it received Royal Assent in June 1792. The Act removed the prohibition of Episcopalian clergy to minister in Scotland, provided they subscribed the Thirty-nine Articles, but disbarred them from holding preferment or officiating in England. Thurlow bore Horsley no grudge, securing his translation to Rochester in 1793.

Stevens, Gaskin, Park and their friends John Richardson and John Bowles afterwards served on the English committee of the Duke and Duchess of Buccleugh's fund for augmenting the incomes of Episcopalian bishops and clergy. Its success was decidedly modest.

Van Mildert preached his first sermon on 1st June 1788 at Pyrton, the next hamlet to Sherborne. His text was a William Stevens favourite: Ecclesiastes 1.14, 'I have seen all the works that are done under the sun, & behold, all is vanity and vexation of spirit.' Heavily redolent of the Schools, the sermon analysed the proposition that Wisdom, Pleasure, Power and Riches can lead to human happiness, successively discounting Wisdom, Pleasure and Power as 'vain' because their finitude made them incomplete. Dismissing the miser's delight in merely possessing Riches, Van Mildert inferred that wealth's only value was procuring other means to happiness. He could then produce the rabbit from his hat: 'But we have already seen that neither Wisdom, Pleasure, nor Power, have that in them which can constitute real happiness. If, then, Riches have no other claim than that which arises from the purchase of these, their pretensions to felicity must of course fall to the ground.'

Christianity, he concluded, offered, to those who had made correct use of their earthly blessings, eternal enjoyment of transcendent equivalents: true and complete knowledge, 'joys without ceasing, & pleasures at God's right hand for evermore', unassailable heavenly riches and, for the virtuous possessors of earthly power, 'a crown of glory that fadeth not away'.

Earning these rewards turned on obedience. Chastity went unmentioned, the pursuers of earthly pleasure being eirenically described as 'the gay & chearful'. Poverty Van Mildert did not regard as a virtue: 'everyone must allow that Riches are in themselves things totally indifferent, only productive of good or evil according to the uses to which they are applied', although 'the poor man might comfort himself by observing that the rich are overwhelmed with thought & anxiety, & sinking under the fatigue of the duties of their situation'.[25]

Van Mildert was proud of this *opus*. He preached it from five pulpits that year and two the next, including Horsley's at Newington.

In 1789 he moved to the diocese of Canterbury to become curate of Newchurch and Bonnington, two villages on Romney Marsh. He took lodgings in the town of Ashford, home to a number of clergy from the surrounding area. He had preached his Ecclesiastes sermon at Ashford in November 1788, which suggests he already had friends among the clerical colony.

Van Mildert's new parishioners experienced the sermon on 9th August 1789. On 10th December he was ordained priest by Beilby Porteus, Bishop of London, on letters dimissory from Archbishop Moore. Before the end of the year he conducted one wedding at Newchurch and two at Bonnington.

The situation had drawbacks. Bonnington was some six miles from Ashford, Newchurch nearer ten: inconvenient distances, especially in bad weather. 'Intercourse with his parishioners, for the purpose of enlightening their minds' proved difficult and unrewarding, and he feared mental and spiritual atrophy. Besides, the marshes deserved their unhealthy reputation: malaria was prevalent on Romney Marsh well into the nineteenth century. Van Mildert decided to seek a more salubrious post.

In 1790, with testimonials from his father's friend Robert Finch[26] and from Houstonne Radcliffe, he became curate of Witham, near Colchester.

The Rector of Witham, Andrew Downes, was grandson of a Bishop of Derry and son of a Bishop of Raphoe. He resided in the parish, but having a 'weak constitution' left most parochial duties to his curate. During five years at Witham, Van Mildert took sixty-two of the seventy-five weddings 'and probably a similar proportion of the two hundred and fifteen Baptisms, and of the two hundred and four burials'.[27] Downes never preached, so Van Mildert delivered two sermons every Sunday – although he seems to have spared Witham the Ecclesiastes epic.

According to Ives, he initially produced two original sermons each week; but Downes soon 'advised him to abate somewhat of so arduous an undertaking; thinking it likely, not so much to improve, as to exhaust his mind, and prevent him from advancing in theological knowledge'.

Van Mildert complied; to judge by his own later advice to young clergymen, he filled the gap with material abridged or compiled 'from the most approved authors, especially from some of our older divines' and selections from 'the Homilies of our church', divested of 'quaintness of style, and of any peculiarities adapted only to the times in which they were written'. By the time he left Witham, Van Mildert's collection of manuscript sermons numbered at least two hundred.[28]

During these years, Van Mildert worked hard at divesting his own style of quaintnesses. All his manuscript works of this period show signs of at least one rigorous editing. For the rest of his life he remained critical of all that he wrote, making stylistic corrections even to his private correspondence.

Theologically, Van Mildert's early sermons stood squarely in the Hutchinsonian tradition of Horne, Jones and Boucher. He insisted on the rightness of social subordination and the absolute dependence of man on his Creator, urging a vision of the Kingdom as emphatically discontinuous with present reality and explicitly denying notions of moral progress. His Ascension Day sermon, preached for the first time in May 1792, gave an early airing to a key theme of his Boyle Lectures by restating Leslie's anti-Deist argument that the miracles performed by Jesus and his disciples, and the miraculous events surrounding the Saviour's life, constituted an incontestable divine endorsement of the whole Christian revelation, compelling belief in Jesus' divinity and acceptance of all His teachings.

Like Horne, who argued in a response to Locke that God had provided for the peace and order of mankind 'by ordaining, first in the case of Adam, and then again in that of Noah, that the human race should spring from one common parent',[29] Van Mildert took the literal historicity of the Bible as axiomatic. The proponents of this doctrine were to find themselves increasingly on the defensive as the nineteenth century advanced, and in his maturity Van Mildert gave more careful attention to the nature of the inspiration of Scripture.

Interestingly, while at Witham Van Mildert was involved in running a Sunday School. The Sunday Schools movement gained momentum in the mid-eighties from the advocacy of Thomas Stock, master of the Cathedral School and Rector of St John's, Gloucester, and of Robert Raikes, editor of the *Gloucester Journal*. The movement had an ecumenical flavour: the principal co-ordinating body, the Sunday School Union, formed in 1785, boasted a 'mixed committee of Churchmen and Dissenters'. The Sunday schools also had High Church supporters: George Horne hoped that 'the late practice of gathering such multitudes of children together in our sunday schools, and accustoming them early to the service of the church' might produce a generation more zealous in devotions than his own.[30] The Witham Sunday School was run by a Mr Kynaston; its theological complexion is not known.

Van Mildert also became friendly with the family of General Douglas, whose 'good, substantial country house' was among the notabilities of Witham. The General, Hanoverian son of a noted Jacobite, died in 1778 after a long military and Parliamentary career under the patronage of his kinsman Charles, third Duke of Queensberry.[31] His remarkable will bequeathed the house to Robert, youngest of his five surviving sons, but gave his sons Philip and Alexander and daughters Katherine, Elizabeth and Jane the right to live there too. The other sons had gone further afield: Archibald to Dublin, William to India with the East India Company, where he was made Judge in 1790.

Philip, seven years Van Mildert's senior, and Robert, Van Mildert's exact contemporary, were both in Holy Orders: Philip was Joint Tutor of Bene't (Corpus Christi) College, Cambridge, Robert curate of Knightwick in Worcestershire. Alexander, a career naval officer, died at Plymouth in 1793.

Van Mildert became a regular visitor to the house. By the autumn of 1791, the Witham grapevine hummed with the news that the curate was courting Jane Douglas.

In September Van Mildert wrote to tell Philip that Jane had accepted his proposal, and to ask his consent to their marriage. Philip's reply breathed tactful discouragement. He described the news as 'entirely unexpected'. He was aware of rumours but, 'not having received the least hint, either from you, or my sister, that there was any foundation for them', claimed to have paid no attention. He protested his attachment to Van Mildert as a person:

I had long regretted the want of a companion at Witham, & . . . since your arrival there I have experienced not only the pleasure of an acquaintance but the recourse of a valuable friend. I know indeed of no person to whose Manners, Disposition & Principles I could less object than to your own, or to whose connection with our family in case of a Competency I could give my consent with less reluctance or Hesitation.

The problem was purely financial. Philip felt that nothing below £400 per annum could properly 'be called a Competency', and did not see how Van Mildert could find even this minimum. His private means were small; he would need to find preferment in the Church: 'Your views of obtaining this by the Interest & Exertions of your friends, – however justly founded, – you must still allow to be precarious.' Jane had little money of her own and 'no prospect of increasing it either from near or distant Relations'.[32]

Van Mildert and Jane apparently became engaged almost at once, despite Philip's warning against 'an Engagement which may never be fulfilled'. Their engagement lasted for the rest of Van Mildert's stay in Witham: they were not so rash as to marry while he remained a curate. During this time he made at least one journey to Scotland, no doubt to meet some of Jane's Scottish relations. He also received at least one invitation to preach at Bene't.

If Van Mildert's wooing of Jane dominated his private life, public life was dominated by events in France. In 1791 Horne, now Bishop of Norwich, feared that the 'rising storm' would 'tear us away from our comforts, our possessions, our liberties, and our lives'.[33] The French Revolution gave the imaginations of a whole generation a shock from which, for better or worse, they never recovered. In 1838 Bishop Maltby of Durham, who was not a conservative churchman, still blamed the 'ignorance, bigotry and uncharitableness' of contemporary opinion on the continuing influence of 'the war of the French Revolution', adding 'That unhappily turned every thing into bitterness; in Religion as well as Politics.'[34]

The Reign of Terror had considerable impact even in circles sympathetic to revolutionary principles. Robert Hall, the eminent Baptist preacher who 'in his youth, defended the French Revolution, and rebuked a preacher who advised all ministers to have nothing to do with politics . . . lived to be of another opinion and to speak of the vanity and ferocity which spring from sceptical infidelity'.[35]

Van Mildert had never sympathised with revolutionary principles. His childhood was spent in the neighbourhood of St George's

Fields, a favourite point of assembly for protest mobs, which on 2nd June 1780 saw the mass parade of the Gordon Rioters.[36] In the American Revolutionary War, which broke out shortly before his tenth birthday, his sympathies were entirely with men like Jonathan Boucher.

Van Mildert's youthful attitude to revolutionary theories appears in his poem 'Janus Clusus' (1783). Written at the end of the American War, it describes the London mob's reception of the news of peace. On 6th October, the night before the ceremonial proclamation and the opening of the gates at Temple Bar, 'several persons were very ill treated by a numerous mob, who put the constables at defiance . . . the Deputy City Marshal, in endeavouring to keep the peace was grossly abused, and knocked down, with two of his men'.[37]

The poem has a vividness rare in Van Mildert's verses, suggesting that he felt strongly about the topic:

> There tost in the air see a dead Dog approaches,
> Here crowded and falling advance broken Coaches;
> Broken Shins, broken Arms, shattered Heads, bloody Nose,
> And Battles the Nation to Peace shall compose . . .
> Hail, Liberty, Liberty! hail, happy Souls,
> Whom Justice, nor Law, nor Good Order controuls![38]

To Van Mildert, Revolution was already a synonym for lawless violence. On the doctrine of Equality, he agreed entirely with Horne:

A natural equality amongst mankind is contrary to the actual condition of human nature. Women are not equal to their husbands, children are not equal to their parents, the foolish are not equal to the wise, the idle and dissolute are not equal to the sober and industrious. They cannot have equal rights, because the rights of man in society, so long as we admit that there is a divine law, and a moral government of the world, are the rights of duty, and virtue, and religion; and no other rights can subsist in a state of civilisation. The society which admits the rights of violence and rapine, is *felo de se*.[39]

Van Mildert expressed similar views in a 'Ballad' entitled 'Rights of Men', attacking the teachings of 'wise Thomas Paine'.[40]

If Van Mildert and his associates lacked sympathy for radical ideas, they indignantly denied being foes to Liberty. Daubeny warned that 'it is a matter of importance, to prevent people from running away with words; because there is a certain unaccountable magick in the sound of some words . . .'[41] For them Liberty meant secure enjoyment of the rights given by the English constitution.

The French Revolution confirmed their worst suspicions about the nature and ultimate aims of political radicalism. Boucher's *A View of the Causes and Consequences of the American Revolution* (London, 1797) attributed a large rôle to religious dissent in fomenting rebellion, but the French Revolution elevated anti-clericalism into a principle and a policy. Even *The Times*, which greeted the September 1789 order for the surrender of church plate to be melted down for coinage as 'a bold and wise regulation [which would] . . . hurt no individual', adding that 'as the nation has for centuries been the slave of the Church, it is but fair that the latter should now repay the obligation', had by 1792 changed its opinion:

What an eventful period is this! What an awful perspective! . . The phial of wrath is poured out from the hands of the avenging Angel, and one of the greatest WOES mentioned in the REVELATIONS is on the point of being accomplished. A solemn lesson this to surrounding nations! read to them with all the solemnity of a voice from Heaven![42]

The events of 1793–4 surpassed all prediction. Much of the horror directly affected the Church. Church property was looted, church buildings desecrated, smashed up, even demolished; bishops and clergy were driven into exile, imprisoned, killed. From Paris came accounts of sacrilegious orgies, with 'naked dancers and drunken children in the ruined churches and among the gravestones'. Attempts were made to promote a non-Christian state religion, begotten on Deism by neo-classicist nature worship: 'Robespierre's new civic religion of the Supreme Being, complete with ceremonies, which attempted to counteract the atheists and carry out the precepts of the divine Jean-Jacques'.[43] The belief that revolutionary notions posed an authentic threat, not merely to the privileges of an Established Church but to Christianity itself, suddenly seemed more plausible.

Faced by such events, many commentators employed the language of apocalyptic. 'Predictions of the Antichrist rising from the chaos of revolution were plentiful in the 1790s, and the emergence of the apparently invincible Napoleon certainly strengthened the argument . . . the approaching end of a century was itself an apocalyptic stimulant that took on added significance in such times.'[44]

Even so level-headed a prelate as Beilby Porteus, who refused point blank 'to pronounce, whether we are now approaching (as some think) to the Millennium, or to the Day of Judgment, or to any other great and tremendous and universal change predicted in the sacred writings', was convinced in 1794 'that the present unexampled state of the Christian world is a loud and powerful call upon all men, but upon US above all men, to . . . prepare ourselves, as well as those committed to our care, for every thing that may befall us, be it ever so novel, ever so calamitous'.[45]

Apocalyptic speculation both nourished, and was nourished by, the explosion of British missionary activity, beginning with the founding of the Baptist Missionary Society in 1793, as French seapower and colonial dominion were trimmed by the Revolutionary and Napoleonic Wars. Jones of Nayland took an interest in the eschatologically significant question of the conversion of the Jews, and hoped that the reception in 1799 of three Jewish converts into the Church of England might be 'the first fruits of an harvest not far off'.[46]

Theologians of varying weight and ecclesiastical allegiance produced an enormous volume of eschatological writings. Horsley's apocalyptic speculations, elaborated by G. S. Faber, Vicar of Stockton-upon-Tees, achieved an international reputation.[47]

Stevens' group actively supported the exiled French clergy. Horsley wrote commending them to the charity of his St David's clergy: they had been exiled for opposing 'conditions with which conscientious men could not comply', the victims of 'inveterate and avowed enemies of God, and of his Christ: who, having succeeded in their nefarious project, to destroy their national church, under the pretence of making room for an universal toleration, do in fact persecute every thing but atheism'.[48]

Daubeny, collecting in his parish, was shocked to find

an almost general disinclination among dissenters from the Church to contribute. At length one, more open than the rest, furnished the following reason for it; by telling me that 'Christ never died for those priests; and therefore he had no feeling for them, or concern about them.' Another, who had learnt his Christianity in the same school, upon my application to him on the same occasion, immediately exclaimed, 'What, Sir, to a *Roman*? give to a Roman! one that lives in such errors; if I had ten thousand guineas, I would not bestow a single mite upon him!'[49]

Besides succouring the casualties, Stevens and his friends took a prominent part in the propaganda war, defending a high view of the relationship between national church and national government against 'French' contractarian notions.[50] They based this on the benefits to the State of being grounded in a proper submission to the lordship of God, vigorously denying that the Church was in any sense a department of government. 'Making establishment necessary to the existence of the Church, as many are apt to do, is a grievous mistake', Stevens wrote to Bishop Skinner of Aberdeen, who, as Primus of a disestablished Church, no doubt agreed (if perhaps wryly); 'but to be sure it is a convenient appendage; and there is no harm in Kings being nursing fathers, if they will nurse it properly'.[51]

Horsley, in his Charge to the St David's clergy, while denouncing the kind of 'high-churchman . . . who claims for the hierarchy, upon pretence of a right inherent in the sacred office, all those powers, honours, and emoluments, which they enjoy under an establishment; which are held indeed by no other tenure than at the will of the prince or by the law of the land', allowed the State neither right nor power over the Church's essential being: 'he who thinks of God's ministers as the mere servants of the state, is out of the church – severed from it by a kind of self-excommunication'.[52]

Here in germ was the conception of the nature of the Church developed more fully by the Oxford Movement in response to the 'National Apostasy' of 1833.

In July and August 1792, as the Revolutionary Wars opened in continental Europe, Van Mildert made his first and only trip abroad, touring the Low Countries with five companions. The party set out from Ashford, making it likely that some at least were friends from his previous curacy.[53]

In accordance with the rules for continental journeys, the six companions industriously pursued culture. They enjoyed the German Comedie in Amsterdam, even though only one member of the party spoke German: 'The acting was excellent, & the piece very lively & spirited, possessing much of that broad farcical humour which is in general so acceptable to the taste of John Bull.'

While in Amsterdam they also visited the principal hospital, the 'Spin-house, or house of industry for vagrants, thieves & prostitutes' and the 'Rasp House, or Bridewell'. Van Mildert's strictures on the Rasp House – 'a miserably close confinement, exhibiting nothing but filth and wretchedness' – suggest an outrage more aesthetic than moral. The griefs of the poorest never cut Van Mildert very deeply;

perhaps his own qualitatively different experience of 'poverty' insulated him against any real understanding of their plight. His comments on the 1831–2 Sunderland cholera epidemic reflect the callousness of incomprehension: 'its fatal effect is almost exclusively among the most squalid of the Poor, whose wants I fear, have hitherto been much neglected. But . . . I trust that good may result from it, in improved habits of cleanliness and sobriety among the lower orders.'[54]

The great political events of the day receive one brief mention. Van Mildert and his companions shared the boat from Dover to Ostend with 'three or four French Aristocrats who having been stripped of their property in France, were proceeding to Flanders to join the emigrant party'.

Early in 1795, Van Mildert's cousin/brother-in-law Cornelius Ives offered him the Ives family living of Bradden, Northamptonshire. The decision to accept was not an easy one. Bradden fell well short of Philip Douglas' stipulation: Van Mildert's biographer, himself Rector of Bradden, explained frankly that its value 'was then considerably under two hundred pounds a year, and there was need to build on it almost a new house, at an expense of nearly a thousand pounds'. Nevertheless Van Mildert accepted. He saw 'only an uncertain prospect of any thing more eligible being offered to him', and was formally instituted on 24th April 1795.

Somehow 'the little Dutch curate' persuaded Philip Douglas to view this very minor stroke of good fortune as sufficient. He and Jane were married on 22nd December 1795.

Work on the Bradden parsonage was duly begun. It ran over budget, perhaps because of Van Mildert's preference for high ceilings and for a slate rather than a tiled roof, and he had nothing from it but the expense. He was Rector of Bradden for little more than a year.

The following July the important London living of Bow fell vacant. Presentation was with the Grocers' Company. Uncle William Hill exerted his influence, the only other candidate withdrew before the election, and Van Mildert became Rector of St Mary-le-Bow, Cheapside.[55]

From the time of his return to London, Van Mildert's membership of William Stevens' circle is a matter of record. Besides established friends such as Jones, Boucher and Daubeny (Horne had died in 1792), Dr Gaskin of the SPCK, John Bowdler, and the campaigning lawyers John Bowles and John Reeves, Stevens attracted a group of lively younger men: James Allan Park and John Richardson, both later to be made Justice of the Common Pleas; John James Watson, Boucher's curate at Epsom; Henry Handley Norris, only son of a wealthy London merchant, who had taken Holy Orders against his father's wishes from a conviction 'that the dangers of the time, and the conflicts to which the Christian cause was subjected . . . were only to be effectually met by a spirit of earnest self-devotion, and large sacrifices of private wealth, and liberty, and ease';[56] and Watson's brother Joshua.

Joshua Watson, six years Van Mildert's junior, was a partner in his father's firm of wine merchants (now piling up a considerable fortune from wartime government contracts), and a great favourite of Stevens, who saw him as a younger edition of himself. Norris, recruited by Watson in 1794 while fundraising to give a public dinner on the King's birthday to 'a company of the Shropshire militia . . . quartered at Hackney', found him immediately congenial:

In him is centered every requisite to complete the character of a pleasant companion and sincere friend. For the former capacity he possesses a strong mind, well stored with thoughts on every subject, which a most retentive memory enables him to draw forth at pleasure . . . For the latter, unaffected good-nature, generosity, and every Christian virtue, stimulated and enlivened by a fervent piety and zeal for religion.[57]

Other associates were Thomas Sikes, Vicar of Guilsborough, childhood friend of John James Watson and son of a merchant banker, whose sister Mary became Joshua Watson's wife in 1797; and Baden Powell, a City merchant whose sister Henrietta became Norris' wife in 1805, and whose other two sisters were married to John James Watson and Thomas Sikes.

The strangest recruit to the group was William Cobbett, 'then better known by his first political name of "Peter Porcupine"', who arrived from America 'at the beginning of the . . . century, bringing a testimony from our ambassador that he had stayed the tide of republicanism across the Atlantic'.

Cobbett's prosecution in Philadelphia had given him the cachet of a 'martyr to loyalty', and his forcefulness fascinated Joshua Watson: 'We were then young, and his violence was rather a recommendation than otherwise: he was so hearty in hating what we hated.' The alliance was shortlived: Watson, repelled by Cobbett's 'unscrupulousness in seeking to repair his needy fortunes', gave him a courteous but firm brush-off.[58]

On Van Mildert's return to London, he and Watson rapidly became intimates. They may have met earlier: Watson was educated in Van Mildert's home parish of Newington. The house at Ely Place became a regular haunt for Watson and his friends.

Van Mildert was rapidly swept up into the circle's activities, joining the SPCK about 1797, and regularly enlisted on literary projects. He, Joshua Watson and Norris edited a two-volume anthology of reprinted tracts published in 1802 and 1803 under the title *The Churchman's Remembrancer*, and he also gave 'some literary assistance to the editor of the "Anti-Jacobin"'. It was probably at this time that he acquired the use-name 'Van'.

In 1800 fifteen of William Stevens' friends founded the exclusive dining society Nobody's Club (later Nobody's Friends), named from Stevens' *nom de plume* Nobody. Van Mildert's election to membership in 1802, on Stevens' own nomination, sealed his acceptance by the group who were to be his friends and fellow-workers for the rest of his life.

CHAPTER 2

'Van'

Van Mildert was now Chaplain to the Worshipful Company of Grocers and Rector of St Mary-le-Bow. Although situated in the London Diocese, Bow was a peculiar of Canterbury, making Van Mildert's diocesan not Beilby Porteus but again Archbishop Moore. The benefice was an influential one whose rich historical associations Van Mildert savoured.[1]

Bow was a popular venue for charity sermons and anniversary meetings: in 1802 the SPCK held its Annual Service at Bow instead of St Paul's Cathedral to protest against the replacement of 'the usual verses of the 113th Psalm' by an anthem.[2] It was also the traditional home of a number of memorial sermons and lectures, most notably the series endowed by Robert Boyle in 1692.

A long-standing wrangle over one of these lectureships gave Van Mildert the chance to establish himself with the Archbishop. The terms of this particular endowment required twelve respectable parishioners to appoint 'some honest Godly zealous & learned Preacher' to read 'a Lecture or Sermon' on one afternoon each week. This led to power-struggles between Rector and lay electors: the Rector had no control over the choice of preacher, but could ban anyone he disapproved from his pulpit. In 1774 the Rector, Dr Sclater, did just that when he lost the election to the Revd Thomas Clarke, and commenced delivering the lectures himself. The parishioners sued, filing an Information in Chancery in 1776. Sclater's death saved the immediate situation, but left the legal position unclear.[3]

Such parishioner-appointed lectureships were common in London at the time, and regularly led to friction. 'For various reasons, among them the fact that Dissenters voted, the successful candidates were often Evangelicals, and, if the more orthodox incumbents refused the use of their pulpits, disorder and riot might ensue.'[4] John Randolph's 1810 Primary Visitation Charge to the London clergy asserted that a conspiracy of covert Methodists, remaining members of the Church of England only to subvert it, 'were getting into their hands all the lectureships in the city churches.'[5]

In 1796 Van Mildert found the Bow lectureship held since 1784 by a Mr Abdy, whose sermons, delivered 'ad libitum, every Sunday Evening', were not what Van Mildert expected catechetical lectures to be. He researched the background and presented Archbishop Moore with detailed particulars. Moore was sympathetic, as was Horsley, now Bishop of Rochester. In January 1799 a vestry resolved to alter the investment basis of the endowment, necessitating an Act of Parliament. Horsley drew up regulations to include in the Act, requiring annual election of a preacher by twelve duly appointed trustees. The Rector was made an ex-officio trustee, besides 'the inherent & inalienable right, still reserved to him, with respect to granting or refusing his Pulpit'. A further safeguard stipulated that the lecturer be licensed by the Archbishop.[6]

This outcome was entirely to Van Mildert's liking. An infestation of ecclesiastical democracy had been controlled; and the new trustees appointed Van Mildert himself as lecturer.

Still more gratifying were 'the conversations with which Mr. V:M: was favoured by the Abp. of Canterbury and the Bp. of Rochester'. It was probably through this affair that Van Mildert became 'regularly known to his Grace, and . . . dined on public days at his table'.[7] Moore, who owed his own career to merit rather than birth, seems to have felt a tenderness for Van Mildert. This influential favour had decisive effects for Van Mildert the following year.

In 1800 a small group of lawyers noticed the provision for rewards to informers in Henry VIII's Acts suppressing clerical non-residence. Van Mildert was one of their first victims. None of his three parishes had a habitable parsonage,[8] and he was unable to find acceptable rented accommodation inside the benefice boundary. He settled at Ely Place, Holborn, 'within 10 minutes or a quarter of an hour's walk of every part of the United Parishes', but was technically non-resident. An 'unprincipled informer' earned the bounty by denouncing him.

The sheer scale of non-residence among clergy at that time[9] meant that the legal and ecclesiastical establishment faced an administrative nightmare unless the law could be changed. Unfortunately there was little political sympathy, particularly among the Commons, for the exigencies of absentee clergy. What was needed was a good sound *casus belli* – an incumbent of irreproachable professional character, conscientiously performing the spiritual duties of his benefice, whose parishioners and diocesan supported him to the full, yet who was defenceless before the law.

Van Mildert met the specification. Lord Chief Justice Eldon tried him in December 1800 at the Guildhall. As a further touch of pathos, he was too ill to appear in court, having suffered a physical breakdown after his father's death that April.[10] The Archbishop of Canterbury testified personally, writing afterwards to assure Van Mildert of 'the very high, and deservedly high character given of you by a very numerous and respectable part of your parishioners, as well as by your adversaries'.[11] Amidst this welter of public affirmation Eldon sentenced the sacrificial lamb to 'all the penalties' – fines totalling £110 – adding that he hoped this case would 'induce the legislature to intervene and take these matters out of the hands of a common informer'.[12] To complete the process of seeking redress in law, Van Mildert's counsel appealed vainly on a technicality.

In June 1801 relieving legislation came before Parliament. When it reached the Lords Eldon, who in April had become Lord Chancellor, piled on the agony: 'when he presided in the Common Pleas, he tried actions . . . in which, though the law went against the Clergymen, their case was the most severe and cruel that could be conceived'. He quoted the Rector of Bow as his paradigm. Eldon's sentiments, royally echoed by the Duke of Clarence, won Van Mildert his first mention in *The Times*.

While the injustice done Van Mildert was incontrovertible, remedying the situation posed major problems. Horsley gave the 1801 measure heavily qualified support, accepting the need to protect clergy who 'did the duty of their parishes, [but] could not reside in them on account of the glebe houses being in a state of decay', but urged a companion measure compelling culpably non-resident clergy to 'do their duty': 'the practice of Clergymen absenting themselves from their parishes had been carried to an extent the most shameful and scandalous that could be conceived, and which if not put a stop to, would overturn the established Church, and destroy the Christian religion in this country'.[13]

Clerical absenteeism was not seen as universally indefensible: Horsley in 1796 claimed that 'many non-residents are conscientiously engaged in various ways in promoting the general cause of Christianity; and are perhaps doing better service than if they confined themselves to the ordinary labours of the ministry in a country parish'. His proviso was that every non-resident incumbent should 'maintain a resident curate, with such a stipend . . . as may supply the curate with a decent maintenance, without his engaging in a second cure, and doing but half the duty of both parishes'.[14] Yet even this modest ideal was widely unmet. As Horsley remarked, non-residence affected poor benefices worse than rich ones, since poor incumbents could not afford acceptable curate-stipends. There were some '4,000 livings below the £150 p.a. which established itself as the clerical breadline, including about 1,000 below £50 p.a. Even the Bishop of Llandaff could hardly be expected to reside in London during sessions of Parliament and work a see which had no bishop's house, on an income of £900 p.a.'[15] Horsley, himself a pluralist whose see was among the poorest, and who died plagued by financial difficulties, well knew the poverty-trap that locked incumbents into pluralism and consequent non-residence.

Faced with this dilemma, Parliament twice ducked the issue by temporarily suspending the prosecutions. In 1803 government support enabled Sir William Scott, Eldon's brother and MP for Oxford University, to carry an Act widening the grounds for licensed non-residence, coupled with legislation to ease the financing of parsonage-house construction. None of these measures could realistically solve the non-residence problem. In reform-minded circles both outside and inside the church, the conviction remained that something would have to be done.

For Van Mildert the affair was personally costly. Despite Moore's bluff injunction 'not to let this matter affect your spirits in the smallest degree', but to 'be pleased, that such an opportunity had been given to purchase fame at so easy a rate', and practical kindness in paying half Van Mildert's fine, the expense of the trial was 'for some time so heavily felt, as to render expedient a contracted mode of living'.[16]

Despite his difficulties, Van Mildert continued establishing himself as a preacher and divine. In 1797 he preached at the annual Charity Schools service endowed by John Hutchins, a London goldsmith whose Trustees included the Lord Mayor of London. The sermon, customarily preached at Bow, was to consider 'the excellency and use of the Liturgy of the Church of England', and the advantages to 'poor Children' of being 'educated in the Doctrine and Principles of the said Church'. Van Mildert heartily approved:

The charity that provides for the body, but neglects the soul, is perishable, and, comparatively, of little moment. Lay the foundation of good Christian principles in the hearts of those whom you take under your protection, and you prepare the way for making every other gift you can bestow upon them, a real blessing. But without this, though you could give them all this world's goods, it would avail little to their true happiness.

Educating poor children benefited immeasurably when connected to 'the doctrines and liturgy of our Church'.[17]

Van Mildert's sermon eulogised the Anglican liturgy for holding a balance between the opposed errors of Enthusiasm and Lukewarmness, between the corruptions of Popery and the excesses of overzealous reformers. His text was 1 Cor. 14.15, 'I will pray with the Spirit, and I will pray with the Understanding also', used to similar effect in Daubeny's *Guide to the Church*.[18]

Van Mildert registered meticulous protest against the 'profane or idolatrous tenets' of the 'Romish church': adoration of the Host, 'the worshipping of images', invocation of saints 'and such like unscriptural devotions' (on revising the sermon in 1817 he added invocation of the Blessed Virgin to the blacklist). Roman liturgy, however, despite being in Latin and 'clogged with superstitious and exceptionable forms', was in many places 'truly scriptural, and well calculated for the comfort and edification of pious worshippers . . . some of the most admired parts of our Book of Common Prayer, were taken almost literally from the Romish Ritual'.[19]

Passion was reserved for Van Mildert's denunciation of those Reformed churches which

impressed, at first, with just indignation at the corruptions of the Church of Rome, . . . seem to have thought it impossible to separate from her too widely; and in their zeal to correct abuses, to have forgotten, that to *reform* is not to *destroy*. Hence, the primitive ordinances, and even the primitive faith, of the purest ages of Christianity, have by some of these Churches been . . . rudely shaken, or inconsiderately abandoned. In some, episcopacy has been totally abolished, and with it, many essential qualifications of the priesthood. Others have proscribed the use of any pre-composed liturgies. Almost all have, in some particulars, relinquished doctrines or ceremonies plainly deducible from primitive and even apostolical practice, as well as agreeable to the general tenor of the Scriptures.

Reform, while sometimes unavoidable, was always dangerous: potentially 'an opening for a vast inundation of licentiousness and disorder'.

Another sermon of this period, indicatively entitled 'Cautions against Innovation in Matters of Religion', lamented the contemporary disposition to dismiss many ordinances of devotion as 'obsolete, or superstitious; and more particularly to hold in contempt those which have apparently no other foundation than church-authority . . .' He quoted some examples: 'The devout observation of fasts and festivals, the attendance on weekly prayers in the church, the charitable office of visiting the sick, the appointment of sponsors in baptism, and many other customs . . .' Van Mildert thought church authority 'indecently contemned . . . Hastily to root up ancient customs, merely because they are ancient, is no proof of wisdom.'[20]

An unpublished confirmation sermon of the same period examined the place of the Sacraments in the scheme of salvation, tackling the controversial issue of baptismal regeneration. Van Mildert argued that baptism was a necessary but not a sufficient condition for salvation; the believer at baptism 'put on Christ', but also undertook a lifetime's commitment to 'conform his whole life & conversation to the precepts of his Lord & Master' through 'the practice of piety, righteousness & sobriety', the reverent study of God's 'holy will and pleasure in all things', and 'benevolence & justice towards Man'. Living the Christian life would be too demanding a task for human frailty without the 'assistance of the Holy Spirit', conveyed at baptism and confirmation, and replenished by 'that most comfortable & important duty of Prayer'.

Van Mildert struggled to define the part which receiving 'the Sacrament of the Lord's Supper' played in assuring the believer's salvation: he described the Sacrament as a 'high & important Ordinance', a 'duty positively enjoined by our Blessed Lord, . . . therefore of as great authority as Baptism itself'. The words 'and necessity', which originally followed 'authority', he struck out; but he was satisfied with the phrase 'Neither Baptism, nor Confirmation, can . . . be considered as sufficient without it'. The sermon also contained a strenuous defence of infant baptism.[21]

According to his biographer in the *Gentleman's Magazine*, he delivered Lady Moyer's Lecture at St Paul's Cathedral 'early in his city residence'; Van Mildert's research notes for his 1823 edition of Waterland state that Lady Moyer's Lecture was 'supposed to be' last delivered in 1774, and make no mention of his having served as Lecturer.[22]

Van Mildert's first major work, conclusively establishing his significance as a theologian, was his Boyle Lectures of 1802–5. The sermon series endowed by the Hon Robert Boyle 'for proving the Christian Religion against notorious Infidels, viz. Atheists, Theists, Pagans, Jews, and Mahometans, not descending lower to any Controversies that are among Christians themselves'[23] had by this time lost its first fame. It attracted the cream of the Latitudinarian ascendancy following the Revolution of 1688–9 and the consequent Non-Juring exodus: Kidder, the second lecturer, was Ken's 'intruded' successor in the see of Bath and Wells, and four of the next five 'Boyle preachers' became bishops.

The products of these early Boyle lecturers, if rather Rationalist for Van Mildert's taste, were far from being political ephemera. The first series, Richard Bentley's *A Confutation of Atheism* (1692), was recommended reading for divinity students more than a century later. Dr Samuel Clarke's 1704–5 *Demonstration of the Being and Attributes of God* and *A Discourse concerning Natural and Revealed Religion* acquired a lasting reputation, as did Gastrell's *The Certainty and Necessity of Religion in General* (1697) and Kidder's *A Demonstration of the Messias* (based on his series of 1693–4). Most popular of all, Dr William Derham's *Physico–Theology, or a Demonstration of the Being and Attributes of God from his Works of Creation* (1711–12) attained 'thirteen English editions by 1768, three new editions by the end of the century, and translations into Dutch, French, Swedish, and German'.[24]

As the eighteenth century advanced, the Boyle Lectures diminished in prestige. Van Mildert's text, committed to the press in 1806, was the first published in thirty-three years. One of his declared aims in applying for this most famous of Bow lectureships was 'to revive, or render profitable, an institution, which had ceased to attract the public notice'.[25]

Van Mildert was a curious successor for Bentley and Clarke. He found Boyle's injunction against 'descending lower' to interdenominational Christian controversy unattainable. The semiecumenical strand in eighteenth-century latitudinarian Christianity was as alien to Van Mildert as the willingness of his Evangelical contemporaries to collaborate with Dissenters. He could not keep from regular castigation of his twin bugbears, Popery and excessive Protestantism, attaching special odium to 'a tribe of [unnamed] Theologians' in Germany and Holland

and, perhaps, in other parts of Europe . . . who, professing a desire to make Christianity more acceptable to men of a philosophical and sceptical turn of mind, have manifested a disposition to abandon almost all it's distinguishing and essential doctrines, to explain away some of it's most important facts as merely allegorical representations, and to renounce it's claims to Divine authority, by throwing doubt upon it's miraculous testimonies, and treating it's sacred records as works of merely human composition.[26]

Van Mildert's theological position grew out of the 'High Church counterblast to the new philosophy and the natural theology based on it',[27] the Hutchinsonian school of Stevens, Jones and Horne.

John Hutchinson (1674–1737) was a self-taught Yorkshire layman who conducted a Procrustean reconciliation of natural philosophy with revealed religion.[28] Hutchinson's remarkable new system for translating the Hebrew Scriptures, entirely untrammelled by academic respectability, held no appeal for Van Mildert; neither did his extraordinary scientific speculations. Hutchinson's ideas nevertheless touched themes of abiding concern, making them far more resilient than their glaring deficiencies might suggest.

Hutchinson's thought was radically anti-Enlightenment. Few of the 'marks of enlightenment: an indifference to sectarian ecclesiology, a respect for secular learning and science, an increasing tolerance, an undogmatic moralism, a zeal for the practical good works of education and charity, a tendency to ignore all but the few essential doctrines of the faith'[29] characterise his system. Hutchinson's lack of tolerance was proverbial; ecclesiology was, to him and his followers, not a peripheral matter but central to the basis of redemption; and few indeed were the doctrines of the faith which he regarded as inessential.

As to secular learning, Hutchinsonians held that 'What commonly passes under the name of learning, is a knowledge of Heathen books: it should always be admitted with great precautions.'[30] Science they valued, but only on their own terms, parting from the accepted Newtonian model at a number of points. Secular metaphysics and moral philosophy, in particular, were 'held so detestable by the founder of This Sect, that in a book called the Religion of Satan or Antichrist delineated, he treats the duties taught by Nature and Reason as the Religion of the Devil'.[31]

The dominating characteristic of Hutchinson's thought was its God-centredness. Certainty came not from the perceptions of the individual, which give knowledge only of the merely material, but by gracious initiative of the Trinity. Fallen mankind could recognise spiritual truth only because God chose to reveal it.

Hutchinson articulated High Church anxieties about the anthropocentric individualism of much rationalist theology. No less concerned than the early Boyle Lecturers to combat Deism and Infidelity, Hutchinson adopted an entirely different battle-plan. Cruising with blindfold innocency among the ontological paradoxes, he eschewed all attempts to defend Christianity by reason alone: not only 'that simple and sublime argument *a priori*, which, by offering to us infallible demonstration, cuts off at once all doubt and difficulty',[32] but the Argument from Design as well.

Hutchinsonians always denied disputing the reasonableness of Christianity. Although the corrupt human reason was unable by itself to form a correct theological opinion, it was fully capable of recognising revealed truth; the human intellect was created to enable mankind to contemplate the self-revelation of God. Those who rejected the gospel did so not from sincere inability to recognise its truth, but from perverse and sinful reliance on their own intellectual self-sufficiency, for which they were justly damned. Their need was repentance. Well-meaning attempts to lead them to God by arguments from first principles would only reinforce their idolatrous trust in the primacy of their own judgement.[33] It was the reasonableness of rationalism that Hutchinsonians disputed.

They condemned Natural Religion from their conviction that salvation depended wholly on acceptance of God's revealed will. Hutchinsonians had no patience with the Enlightenment's Pelagianising concern for 'undogmatic moralism'. 'A system may be fabricated, and called natural; but a religion it cannot be', Jones wrote, in the apologia for Hutchinsonianism with which he prefaced the 1799 second edition of his *Life of Horne*. Accepting such systems 'produced the deistical substitution of naked morality, or Turkish honesty, for the doctrines of intercession, redemption, and divine grace'[34] – disastrous, for man was powerless to achieve his own salvation. Obedience to God was the one necessary virtue.

Van Mildert's relation to Hutchinsonianism at the time of writing his Boyle lectures was complex. He had abandoned – if he ever held them – the more spectacularly eccentric Hutchinsonian tenets: his explanation of the Tower of Babel, for example, differed markedly from the classic Hutchinsonian account.[35] His Appendices gave a few references to the works of Hutchinson; his copious use of Jones, Horne and Daubeny was not specifically for Hutchinsonianism. Although fully convinced of 'the inability of man to discover by the light of Nature the Attributes or even the Existence of God', and scornful of Natural Religion which 'makes no provision for our wants and infirmities, provides no remedy for our corruptions, offers no atonement for our offences, has no redeemer, no Sanctifier, no means of grace, no covenanted terms of acceptance', Van Mildert nevertheless valued Paley's version of the Argument from Design, and feared that attacking Natural Religion might 'furnish Atheism with the shadow of an apology'. His Lincoln's Inn sermons afterwards strictured 'the late Mr. Jones' "Trinitarian Analogy"' and similar attempts by 'other Hutchinsonian writers' for displaying 'the vain desire . . . to clear up points which it was of little importance to explain', and declared Hutchinsonianism, 'however blameless, or even edifying it may be, when kept within certain bounds . . . nevertheless exceedingly liable to mislead. In its very principle also, it savours somewhat of a prurient kind of inquisitiveness, unbefitting the reverence due to the sacred oracles.'[36]

The fourteenth lecture, 'The Inability of Man to frame a Religion for himself', offered a moderate and carefully reasoned exposition of the Hutchinsonian case. Van Mildert argued from history, from Scripture ('for the satisfaction of the Believer rather than of the Infidel') and from the nature of the human cognitive process, that only a Divine revelation could give reliable 'knowledge of the true God, and of His Will with respect to us', which was 'the foundation of all Religion'. *A priori* demonstration of the nature, attributes or existence of God was 'beyond the reach of man'; arguments from Nature, although their power as corroborative testimony to the revealed truth justified comparison with the rôle of the Baptist in relation to Christ, could not in themselves generate 'any firm and settled conviction'.[37]

Here is seen in Van Mildert's school, derived from Hutchinson, a continuous tradition of opposition to a natural theology and a religion of evidences based on reason alone, before Coleridge and Newman. Newman certainly must have known of this tradition, which writers on the nineteenth century have often overlooked in stressing the originality of Coleridge and other Romantic writers on this point.[38]

Jones of Nayland held

that if some man were to arise, with abilities for the purpose, well prepared
in his learning, and able to guide his words with discretion; and . . . were to
take up the principles called Hutchinsonian, and do them justice; the world
would find it much harder to stand against him than they are aware of. . . .
One man, as powerful in truth as Voltaire was in error, might produce very
unexpected alterations, and in less time than he did. Then might a new
aera of learning succeed; as friendly to the Christian cause, as the learning
which has been growing up amongst us for the last hundred years has been
hostile and destructive.[39]

Van Mildert was certainly 'well prepared in his learning'. His
exhaustive knowledge of divinity begot a parlour game: 'his familiar
friends would sometimes amuse themselves by bringing any rare
volume of theology which they had casually met with, open it in his
presence without shewing him the title, read a page or a paragraph,
and ask him whether he recognised the author; a question which he
seldom failed to answer'.[40] The Lectures drew on over three
hundred works in English, French, Latin and Greek: linguistic,
textual and interpretative studies of the Bible, history sacred and
secular, philosophy ancient and modern, Boyle, Bampton, Warburton and Lady Moyer's Lectures, writings of the Fathers and the
Reformers, sermons celebrated and obscure. Van Mildert accepted
'the painful task of wading through volumes of ribaldry, pro-
faneness, and impiety, no less disgusting to a well-principled mind,
than dangerous to those who are ignorant of the Adversary's
devices' but made few references to them, 'since they are such as
every true Christian and real Philanthropist must wish to be, if
possible, consigned for ever to oblivion'.[41]

From this rich mix Van Mildert set out to distil the comprehensive overview Jones prescribed. His twenty-four Lectures were
divided into two equal parts. The second volume examined the
proper rôle of Reason in defending Faith. The first offered a sys-
tematic treatment of 'Infidelity itself . . . in order to exhibit it in it's
true and proper light'. Incorrect religious notions of all shades
belonged within a massive anti-Christian programme devised and
directed by the Devil, a potent if ultimately doomed counter-
strategy to the Divine Plan.

Van Mildert distinguished this carefully from the Manichean
doctrine 'that there is an Evil Principle in the Universe coeval and
co-equal with God himself'. The Christian Devil was not self-

existent but a rebellious angel 'previously in favour with God' and therefore 'not originally of an evil nature'.

Acknowledging the risk that 'such a representation of the powerful influence of the Evil Spirit' might 'give encouragement to Unbelievers, to boast of the effect of their endeavours, and to despise the Faith', Van Mildert argued that 'the very existence of the Gospel at this advanced age of the world, after . . . such a combination of efforts to destroy it, affords a strong presumptive proof of it's Divine origin'.[42]

His analysis had two main objects. He wanted to establish his 'proof by survival': demonstrating the attacks which the Gospel had already weathered made 'even the perverseness and folly of it's opponents serve as attestations of it's truth'. He also hoped to 'convince the Unbeliever in how hopeless a cause he is engaged', and above all to wean well-meaning people away from contemporary radical currents of thought by alerting them to the true context.

On one side were partisans of 'the Gospel system' – Jews faithful to the Old Covenant; primitive Christians; Fathers of the Church; the Eastern Churches which, 'however sunk in idolatry and corruption, made a long and vigorous resistance to the unjust usurpations of the Roman Pontiffs'; the Reformers, with their precursors the Waldenses and Albigenses; Christian champions in every generation, some with 'distinguished names', many unsung. Against them stood Satan's teeming hordes of allies and dupes: pagans, backsliding Jews, Jews who perversely clung to the Old Covenant refusing to acknowledge the Messiah, heretics, Muslims, Schoolmen, Inquisitors, Papists, Protestant schismatics, Deists, philosophic infidels and heterodox theologians of every description. Men (and women[43]) were polarised into two types, Good and Bad. They might enlist under the banner of Redemption or Corruption, but they were not allowed a foot in each camp. Even unsatisfactory 'Sects of professing Christians', whose 'injury to the Gospel' Van Mildert was willing to presume unintentional, ought to have known better: 'it highly concerns them seriously to consider the mischiefs which have flowed from their erroneous principles'.

This classic conspiracy theory was, by the standards of 1805, judicious and moderate. Like Beilby Porteus, Horsley and Tomline, Van Mildert accepted the theory, independently documented by the emigré Abbé Barruel in 1797 and the Scottish mathematician Robison in 1798, that the French Revolution was spawned by a

grand international anti-Christian alliance of Freemasons, Encyclo-
pedists, Reading Societies and the mysterious Bavarian Illuminati.[44]
Van Mildert could quote sources of irreproachable orthodoxy for all
his arguments; his survey was novel only in its scope. Like many
contemporaries he thought 'the . . . close of the Christian Dispensation upon earth' might well be at hand, but he identified contemporary political issues with the Book of Revelation only spar-
ingly.[45]

While not inaugurating a new aera of irreproachably Hutchinsonian learning, the *Boyle Sermons* established Van Mildert, now forty,
as a theologian of note. A second edition, demanded in 1807,
appeared early in 1808, delayed by Van Mildert's determination to
expand the Appendices. 1820 saw a third edition, the fraught year
1831 a fourth, reprinted for the Memorial Edition of his complete
works in 1838. This was celebrity of a gratifyingly durable kind.
After Van Mildert's death, the official Durham Cathedral memorial
sermon paid particular tribute to this first and in many ways most
influential of his major writings.[46]

Archbishop Moore had died in 1805; it was his successor who
graciously accepted the dedication of the Lectures. Moore, a generous man of wide sympathies and a friend of Wilberforce, was a kind
patron to Van Mildert; but his death brought to Canterbury a man
so congenial to the High Church group as to be considered almost a
member of it.

Charles Manners-Sutton, George Horne's successor in the see of
Norwich and Dean of Windsor *in commendam*, was a grandson of the
Duke of Rutland. Open-handed, and with a large and expensive
family, he attracted censure during his Norwich episcopate 'as a
Churchman of profuse expenditure'. According to Churton he lived
this down at Canterbury without any 'revulsion from one vicious
habit to the opposite . . . his expenditure was liberal, his household
well provided for and well governed, his domestics orderly and
attached to their master, his public days marked by a degree of
chaste splendour, while his charitable donations continued to flow
abundantly, yet with careful discrimination'. Van Mildert's fortunes followed a similar pattern.

Manners-Sutton was a royal appointment to Canterbury in fact
as well as theory. Pitt wanted his own former tutor and confidant,
Tomline, Bishop of Lincoln. George III, who valued Manners-

Sutton's ministry at Windsor, executed a brilliantly simple coup by walking from Windsor Castle to the Deanery as soon as news of Archbishop Moore's death reached him and calling the Dean from dinner to congratulate him as Archbishop. The King faced Pitt down with the *fait accompli* next day.[47]

Not the least of Manners-Sutton's benisons to the Hackney Phalanx was his choice of domestic chaplains. The first, William Wordsworth's brother Christopher, was an able, ambitious and energetic man just past thirty who had tutored Manners-Sutton's sons. Van Mildert, making himself known to his new diocesan, also met Wordsworth; they were friends for the rest of their lives. At Van Mildert's house in Ely Place Wordsworth was introduced to Joshua Watson, who took to him at once, and by 1807 he was a core Phalanx activist.[48]

In March 1807 the nephew and successor of General Douglas' patron the Duke of Queensberry enrolled Van Mildert among his six chaplains. 'Old Q', progenitor of the Queensberry Rules and hanger-on to the Prince Regent, was an unlikely patron for an ascetic scholar;[49] but Van Mildert's new status as a nobleman's chaplain entitled him to hold two benefices in plurality.

In April Archbishop Manners-Sutton, graciously remarking that 'your claims on me, public and private, are better founded than your modesty will suffer you to state', presented Van Mildert to the vicarage of Farningham near Sevenoaks, which he had solicited 'as an agreeable retreat, within a convenient distance from town'.

This spacious eighteenth-century custom had not yet succumbed to the harsh winds of nineteenth-century anti-pluralism: as late as 1824 the Bishop of London could excuse a newly-appointed Marylebone incumbent from resigning his Northern parish on grounds of desirability 'that an Incumbent of a populous Parish in London should have a place of retirement in the hot weather'.[50]

Van Mildert's dispensation required him to preach thirteen sermons a year in each of his parishes and, in the parish from which he was most often absent, both to pay a competent substitute and to exercise two months' hospitality each year in person. The revenues of Farningham, about £170 p.a. less the curate's stipend, were added to the strictured family budget.

The Van Milderts, themselves childless, now had two foster-daughters: Mary, youngest daughter of Judge William Douglas,

came to live with her aunt in 1802 on her father's death, joined in
1806 by Robert's daughter Helen Margaret. Caring for their
orphaned nieces clearly gave them great joy; but it added to the
financial and domestic pressures.

The Farningham parsonage-house was in bad repair and 'insufficient'. Van Mildert put major rebuilding in hand. The work ran
dramatically over budget. In 1810, a bill which he was quite unable
to pay faced him with bankruptcy.

He was saved from ruin by Joshua Watson, acting with Thomas
Sikes and other friends, who paid the debt privately. Among the
contributors was John Bowles, a Phalanx associate whose own
career was destroyed in 1809 by a financial scandal.[51] 'Be so good as
to take charge of my contribution to Mother Church in the person of
one of her most faithful, able, and zealous ministers', Bowles wrote
to Watson.

The benefactors tried to keep Van Mildert ignorant of their
identities, but inevitably he found out. Although he was sincerely
and profoundly grateful, he confessed to Joshua Watson that

this feeling is in some respects a very painful one, and occasions a frequent
depression of spirits, which I am unable to overcome . . . It has been my
misfortune to be more or less embarrassed ever since I have been a
beneficed man; and every additional benefice has brought its additional
burdens, and made me poorer than before. So that, in spite of all the
friendly helps I have met with, I still am, and to all human appearance ever
shall be, a necessitous man. But it may be the will of Providence that these
trials should be sent to correct that pride which perhaps you will think
these sentiments discover. Be it so; and may I be enabled so to apply them!

Although it took him many years, Van Mildert repaid the gift in
full.[52]

As soon as the parsonage was ready, the family moved to Farningham. There could be no question now of maintaining two establishments: Ely Place was given up, and Van Mildert on his visits to
London stayed at Joshua Watson's house in Mincing Lane. His rural
isolation forced him to communicate with his friends chiefly by post,
a cause of considerable frustration.

'Where again is Van Mildert?' Christopher Wordsworth
demanded at Christmas 1810. 'I am at a loss that I hear nothing
from him. I wrote to him three weeks ago at least . . . I greatly regret
his absence from Town at the present important time.' The following June, hearing that Van Mildert was in London, Wordsworth

suggested a meeting at Norris' house in Hackney: 'There are many things which seem to me to need conferring about.'[53]

Even 'in his retirement at Farningham' Van Mildert remained a valued member of the Phalanx literary team. He helped Norris and Watson prepare the second part of the *Churchman's Remembrancer*, which appeared in three instalments between 1807 and 1810, writing the biographical notice to the third tract, John Norris' *A Discourse concerning Conventicles*.

In late 1810 or early 1811 Norris and Watson bought back the *British Critic*, which had changed its complexion since Jones and Stevens first launched it, siding against the Phalanx during the Bible Society controversies. The editor was Archdeacon Robert Nares, 'a respectable philologist and antiquary, who had done the public the service of pamphleteering against Tom Paine, and had published, among other sermons, one entitled "Thanksgiving for Plenty, and a Warning against Avarice", which was recommended to the orthodox by Sydney Smith's description of it as "trite imbecility"'.[54] Norris and Watson sacked him, and Van Mildert became editor for a short time before pressure of work forced him to withdraw. Archdeacon Nares bore no grudge, corresponding affably with Norris about book reviews.

In 1809 Van Mildert aroused controversy in Farningham by a privately circulated sermon on the necessity of attending public worship, which 'adverted to the unhappy prevalence of Schism and Fanaticism among us'. Early in 1810 a pamphlet entitled *Who is the Dissenter?*, attacking both sermon and preacher, was 'industriously circulated throughout the Parish'.[55]

Van Mildert's pamphlet response was addressed to his parishioners, not to the anonymous assailant: 'Opportunities (God willing) may often arise of explaining to you from the Pulpit what are the real doctrines of our church, on the points which its adversaries call in question, and to show how entirely those doctrines accord with the Holy Scriptures. This mode of "contending for the Faith" I much prefer to that of pamphlet controversy.'

The tract accused Van Mildert of uncharitableness, sophistry, buffoonery and scurrility, of being 'a deceiver, a blind leader of the blind, greedy of filthy lucre, addicted to pleasure, and negligent of pious duties'. The charge which stung was that of pleasure-seeking: 'The very few meetings of public amusement, in which I have appeared among you, were harmless festivities, on certain loyal occasions, and in which I was not witness to any thing that could give reasonable cause of offence.'

Van Mildert showed neither concession nor sensitivity to his opponent's outrage at the accusation of schism. To Van Mildert, calling Dissenters schismatic was a simple statement of fact; if a man feel pain at being so described, he should return to the Church.

In 1808 Van Mildert stood for election to the Preachership of Gray's Inn[56] but lost. In 1812 William Jackson, brother of the Dean of Christ Church, became Bishop of Oxford and resigned the Lincoln's Inn Preachership. Sponsored by his Hackney colleague James Allan Park, Van Mildert tried again.

The contest began with seven competitors. Fierce lobbying reduced this to four: Van Mildert, Archdeacon Nares, Peter Elmsley, and the Reverend Mr Gardner.

Elmsley, among the most distinguished of British Hellenists, was a formidable intellectual rival; he was also a Whig nominee – Van Mildert calls him 'the Grenvillite' – whom it was politically important to defeat. Nares, championed by the Solicitor General, refused to give way, defending his candidacy on the plea 'that he had been assistant preacher to Dr Jackson at Lincoln's Inn nearly sixteen years'.[57] Van Mildert accepted this cordially; but Gardner's persistence, which threatened to split the anti-Elmsley vote three ways, was, Van Mildert told Jane, 'generally reprobated; – not only as an act of hostility to me, but as disrespectful & offensive to a majority of the Benchers, who may, by his obstinacy, be prevented from returning the man of their choice . . . the Archbishop of York this morning mentioned it to me in the same way in talking it over with the Bishop of London'.[58] The hapless Gardner, although sure of at least three votes, caved in the day before the election.

Stress took its usual toll of Van Mildert's health and spirits. He was comforted by kind words from Spencer Perceval the Prime Minister, a Bencher of Lincoln's Inn, and by Park's assurance that should he fail, Perceval 'would show himself my friend in some other way'.

Elected, Van Mildert was jubilant, 'this being esteemed an eminent post, and an almost sure step to higher promotion'. Although he always insisted the emolument was comparatively small, he now had chambers at Lincoln's Inn, convenient for Bow and Hackney. He also nominated to the deputy preachership: Nares was replaced by Van Mildert's 'young friend Mr. Strong'.

The Lincoln's Inn Preachership inspired some of Van Mildert's best work; he enjoyed his duties so much that he sometimes preached out-of-Term, the Assistant's customary responsibility. Towards the end of his life he found time to publish a collection of fifty Lincoln's Inn sermons, on subjects ranging from 'God's moral government of the world' to 'The Gadarene Demoniacs' and 'Christian unity'.

Among the most important were a series of three on 'Cautions respecting theological discussion', in which Van Mildert set out to define the proper boundaries of theological inquiry. He condemned as a dangerous waste of time all endeavours to 'seek the reputation of being able to penetrate further than others can into the depths of mystery', citing the doctrines of the Trinity and the Incarnation as mysteries particularly unprofitable to probe. Of the Real Presence, he observed:

most of the Reformed Churches, while they declare the elements of bread and wine to remain unchanged, and deny the body and blood of Christ to be *corporally* present, acknowledge them nevertheless to be *mystically* and *sacramentally* present; that is, they acknowledge, that, by virtue of the spiritual grace which accompanies the elements, they convey to the penitent communicant the full and actual benefits of our Lord's death upon the cross. This, it might be supposed, would suffice to unite all parties in this great act of faith and worship.

Delving any further into whether the Communion might 'in any admissible sense be called a *sacrifice*' (a possibility Van Mildert did not wish to deny), or arguing about the appropriate title for this sacrament, would generate only sterile squabbles over differences of doctrine which Van Mildert suspected of being more verbal than substantial.[59]

Van Mildert's preaching style had by now matured considerably. His delivery attracted favourable comment, even if his 'deep, sonorous, and grave' tones were not always easily audible:

Though calling to aid little or no gesture, and often experiencing much physical infirmity, he always spake as fully convinced of the truth and importance of his doctrine, and as being much in earnest to convince others likewise. His accents, the expression of his countenance, and his whole bearing, became authoritative, argumentative, or persuasive, in agreement with the nature of his subject; at the same time, he generally appeared to be rather refraining, than urging himself, and under the influence of a judicious mind, to be exhibiting less emotion than he really felt.[60]

Shortly after the Lincoln's Inn election, Van Mildert was summoned to dine with the Prime Minister. 'The Preacher sat at the bottom of the Table, next to Mr. Perceval, – a seat which he naturally preferred to any other, for the benefit of so choice a companion, whom he found exceedingly pleasant & easy, though quite dignified, & with great vigour & energy of mind, tempered with the most perfect suavity & good breeding.'[61]

Van Mildert would have been less than human if the Premier's affability had not raised interesting possibilities in his mind. Less than a month later, however, Perceval was shot dead in the House of Commons lobby. His close friend Wilberforce grieved at the 'joy and exultation' Perceval's death aroused 'in Nottingham, Leicester, and I fear other places', coming 'at a moment when positive distress had stirred up a great disturbance in the country'. A few days after the assassination, Wilberforce found the 'state of the West Riding manufacturing districts . . . dreadful – next to rebellion, smouldering rebellion – great military force sent down, and now, but too late, vigorous measures taking. The aspect of affairs is very gloomy.'[62]

The government formed under these unpropitious circumstances, headed by Robert Banks Jenkinson, second Earl of Liverpool, was to continue in office for the best part of a decade. Perceval had been a good friend to the Established Church: in 1809 he secured a Parliamentary grant of £100,000 'to improve the condition of the poorer clergy',[63] and at the time of his assassination he was pondering how best to tackle the problem of insufficient church accommodation. Liverpool was to prove a greater benefactor still.

Van Mildert's memorial sermon for Spencer Perceval, preached at Lincoln's Inn on 31st May 1812 and published at the Benchers' request, further boosted his reputation. The sermon said all the right things with deft elegance: examined the possible intentions of Providence in the sudden death of a righteous statesman, praised the virtues of the departed with a warmth short of sycophancy, deplored the wickedness of the act and the 'savage complacency' with which 'some few of the refuse of our land' had received the news, and pressed home the lessons to be learnt – both collective, of 'a salutary alarm of danger, and a jealous solicitude for the national character'; and individual, of the need to live in perpetual readiness for the Divine summons.[64]

Soon after this, the Oxford Heads of Houses invited him to deliver the Bampton Lectures for 1814. He accepted with pleasure, choosing for his theme 'An Enquiry into the General Principles of Scripture-Interpretation'.

On 2nd September 1813, Van Mildert was at Farningham alone, Jane and 'the Girls' having gone to Cheltenham. Two friends, Strong and Ducane, were with him in the evening. They left at about seven, and Van Mildert walked out into his garden. There then arrived a private messenger from Lord Liverpool who, such was the stringency of the Van Milderts' domestic economies, 'could find only one servant – a female presiding at the churn. She was willing to seek her master . . . if the messenger would take her place, and keep the churn in motion.'[65]

The message requested Van Mildert to present himself at noon the next day. 'Of course, an affirmative answer was instantly returned, & by 5 minutes before Twelve appeared the humble Vicar (or, rather, the great Preacher of Lincoln's Inn) at Fife House.'[66]

Liverpool received Van Mildert 'with the utmost ease & courtesy' and offered him the Oxford Regius Professorship of Divinity, vacant by the elevation of William Howley to the see of London. The great Preacher, taken unawares, was inclined to panic:

> I told him instantly, that the matter came upon me so entirely by surprise, that I scarcely knew what to say or think, that I felt most deeply the weight of obligation to him for deeming me competent to fill so arduous & important a station, but that, for the moment, I felt quite overwhelmed with my fears that I might not be able to acquit myself in it, so as to do credit to such Patronage & to the University.

Liverpool was kind to him, assured him that 'the matter did not press for an immediate answer', and sent him off to confer with Howley, who proved to have left Town that morning.

Howley had himself initially been reluctant to take the Regius Professorship, partly because 'the difficulty of finding a Reg. Prof. may sometimes make it difficult for a person in possession to get out of it'. On this occasion too, at least one candidate had already declined the appointment.[67]

If Van Mildert shared Howley's anxiety, he never mentioned it. He feared that he was 'disused to Academical habits' and might fail to live up to expectation. The prospective workload daunted him: 'I have Bampton Lectures in hand, not half finished. The duties of the Professorship must, I suppose, be entered upon in about six weeks from the present time. I am in no state of preparation for *them* whatever.' Finally, he expected acceptance to mean resigning all his other preferment, and hated the thought of losing Lincoln's Inn. He said so to Lord Liverpool, who 'smiled & said, the Benchers would think it a good compliment to themselves that their Preacher was so soon promoted'.

Yet to be Regius Professor of Divinity at the University of Oxford was 'a dignity of the very first description, in point of reputation and importance. And *possibly* my acceptance may prevent it getting into worse hands.' Besides, Lord Liverpool 'very explicitly stated the *value* of the thing . . . at least, a clear £2000 per annum. This is a temptation, indeed, to poor *Van* & so it will be to his Wife.'

After careful consideration, Van Mildert accepted. His D.D., essential to the dignity of a Regius Professor, followed immediately. He was thenceforth known as Dr Van Mildert – Oxford tradition declining to use 'Professor' as a title.[68]

The Regius Professorships of Divinity and Hebrew both had annexed Christ Church canonries, a pattern Van Mildert remembered when founding his own University. His formal first appearance 'in the Chapter House between the Hours of Eleven and Twelve' was made on 3rd November 1813, and on 4th November Van Mildert again became a resident member of Oxford University.[69]

Van Mildert was a reasonably conscientious Canon. Chapter business meetings, held about once a week, dealt chiefly with college discipline and administration. Van Mildert usually contrived to be present when donations to High Church causes were agreed and absent from meetings for punitive purposes, such as that convened on 18th November 1816 to deal with 'Cleaver Student of this House' in whose rooms 'the Censors had Detected a Woman of the Town'.[70]

Van Mildert's major professorial duty was 'providing a Theological course for the young Academics' by reading lectures 'in such Terms & at such times' as he found most convenient. It seems clear that Van Mildert lectured: his Diary for 1816, during the four weeks he remembered to keep it, recorded the composition of the second, third and fourth Lectures in Divinity 'for the next course', and Ives, who was up at Exeter College from 1811 to 1815, 'listened to him, both in the pulpit of the University, and in his lecture room'. Writing more than twenty years later, Ives would not 'attempt from recollection a distinct account of his divinity lectures, lest he should be guilty of doing them discredit. In proof, however, that his admiration was not the result of a mere undiscerning predilection, he is able to state, that the attraction of them was more than ordinary, and that the hearers were always remarkably numerous and attentive . . .'[71]

Against this must be set Charles Lloyd's 1827 declaration to Peel that Van Mildert 'paid a Deputy to do the whole work of Professor, during the whole time he occupied the Professorship':[72] but Lloyd was in a rage, believing himself to have been passed over for the see of Oxford, and was in any case given to flamboyant statements. Van Mildert doubtless sometimes paid a deputy to deliver his lectures, especially during his recurrent bouts of ill-health and after his 1819 consecration to Llandaff. His lifelong commitment to the principle of residence makes it most unlikely that he delegated 'the whole work of Professor'.

Van Mildert also had the duty of 'presiding in the Divinity School at Exercises for Degrees in Divinity & presenting to those Degrees in Convocation'. Examination procedures in Oxford had been reformed by the New Examinations Statute of 1800 and subsequent further enactments to create a fair and searching final examination, with the possibility of Honours in two schools: Litterae Humaniores, and Mathematics and Physics. Examinations were still conducted orally, but pains were taken to make them genuinely public, and the results were classed.

Van Mildert further served as 'a delegate of the Clarendon Press', corresponding with Joshua Watson on 'subjects which engaged his attention'.[73]

The Regius Professor was expected to preach 'before the University'. Van Mildert's University sermons were delivered outside the Law Terms: he was still Preacher of Lincoln's Inn.

The announcement of his Oxford post brought him a number of gratifying letters from Benchers: 'Unless your duties of Regius Professor render your attendance at Lincoln's Inn impossible, I . . . entreat you not to resign, and three of your hearers, now in court, join in my request.'

Van Mildert yielded gracefully, although the need to compose a weekly sermon (during term time) for his 'learned audience in London' combined with his academic commitments, including 'the cares, and ceremonies, and hospitalities, inseparable from a new and eminent situation', to make heavy demands on his time and energy. 'Nevertheless, he persevered, and by tasking to the uttermost his powers of mind, was able to keep on until the termination of his Bampton Lectures, by which . . . he felt considerably relieved.'[74]

The decision strained his friendship with Christopher Wordsworth. The poet's brother had now finished his term as Archbishop's Chaplain, and chafed at his loss of influence. His letter of congratulation on Van Mildert's professorship enquired delicately about Lincoln's Inn. Van Mildert replied that he had promised at least to make 'a fair experiment' of the Preachership's compatibility with his Oxford duties.[75]

This was not what Wordsworth wished to hear. He had earlier thought he might make rather a good Regius Professor himself, soliciting Van Mildert to canvass the Bishop of Ely on his behalf.[76] In 1814, protesting to Norris that he was 'wretchedly poor' despite his deanery and rectory of Bocking, in Essex, and rectory of Monkseleigh in Suffolk, Wordsworth wrote to Van Mildert again. He mentioned hearing a rumour of Van Mildert's intending to resign the Preachership, hinting at the displeasure of mutual friends that he should have kept it so long. Wordsworth even went so far as to solicit the deputy preachership.

Van Mildert's reply was warmly intransigent. While 'nothing would go farther to reconcile me to giving up the situation, than the prospect of being succeeded in it by one who is personally so dear to me, & whom I know to be so eminently qualified for it's duties', he had no intention of resigning.

As to the deputy preachership, 'I should hardly think, if it were vacant, of paying you so poor a Compliment as to make you the offer of it. But it neither is vacant, nor likely to be so. My young friend Mr. Strong has, at present, no other occupation, & would be very reluctant to quit it under any circumstances.'[77]

Whatever annoyance this caused, the friendship survived. Wordsworth never became Preacher of Lincoln's Inn: in 1817 he was made Chaplain to the House of Commons when his erstwhile pupil Charles Manners-Sutton became Speaker.

Two of Van Mildert's new Oxford friendships were particularly close. Thomas Gaisford and Charles Lloyd were both Students of Christ Church, a generation younger than Van Mildert.

Gaisford, Regius Professor of Greek, was an outstanding scholar whose edition of Herodotus won the ultimate accolade, German academic esteem. The reforming Dean of Christ Church, Cyril

Jackson, discovered Gaisford as a freshman and secured him the
Regius Professorship in 1812. Absorbed in his studies, Gaisford
ignored Jackson's persuasions to an ecclesiastical career: 'I have
long wished & laboured to coax him into becoming a Divine,'
Jackson wrote to Howley in 1813, '– & have often tried to shew him
that with his abilities Greek was only a means to an end – But I think
he is too deeply bitten & smitten.' Howley thought of making
Gaisford his domestic chaplain when he became Bishop of London,
but accepted Jackson's verdict that Gaisford could not be
domesticated.[78]

The warm friendship which grew up between the two Regius
Professors, based on mutual respect and liking for each other's
company, was strengthened in 1815 by a family bond when Gaisford
married Van Mildert's elder foster-daughter Helen Margaret. The
Professor of Greek, whose laconic tactlessness was legendary, cut an
unlikely figure as a lover; a satirical verse to that effect circulated in
the University; but Jackson held 'the highest opinion of the goodness
of Gaisford's heart', and the marriage seems to have been a happy
one. Their six children were surrogate grandchildren to the Van
Milderts.

When Robert Peel the younger entered Christ Church in 1805,
Gaisford was initially his tutor. The relationship was not a success.
In a development with profound consequences for Van Mildert, the
rôle of Tomline to Peel's Pitt passed to Charles Lloyd.

'Honest Lloyd, blunt and bluff,' was a teacher of eccentric genius.
Unusually for Oxford in his day, he was a gifted mathematician.
Jackson rated him highly:

Next to G . . . I think that Lloyd has twenty times more sound materials in
him than any of those whom I left behind me at Ch. Ch. Besides his being
an excellent Classical Scholar, his Mathematicks have given him a hard-
ness of head, & a solidity of thinking wch. few possess. He is one of those
who always know whether his opinions are well founded or not, & when he
knows them to be so, nothing will ever move him from them . . . His heart is
capable of strong and devoted attachment – & he wd. undergo anything
for those to whom he is attached.[79]

Of Lloyd's former pupils, Churton remembered him 'for talents and
acquirements of all kinds, for his varied knowledge, and the ease and
skill with which he communicated his knowledge; and second to
none in the conscientious vigilance with which he watched over the
moral and religious training of his pupils. It was a penetrating

sagacity guided by affection, which was irresistible.' Newman, less hagiographical, is no less affectionate:

'He was free and easy in his ways, and a bluff talker, with a rough, lively, good-natured manner, and a pretended pomposity, relieving itself by sudden bursts of laughter, and an indulgence of what is now called chaffing at the expense of his auditors; and, as he moved up and down his room, large in person beyond his years, asking them questions, gathering their answers, and taking snuff as he went along, he would sometimes stop before Mr. Newman, on his speaking in his turn, fix his eyes upon him as if to look him through, with a satirical expression of countenance, and then make a feint to box his ears or kick his shins before he went on with his march to and fro.'[80]

Peel became, and remained, 'one of Mr. Lloyd's most intimate and attached friends'.[81] As his former pupil's career developed, Lloyd remained a loyal and confidential adviser.

Lloyd, nineteen years his junior, delighted Van Mildert, who told Norris: 'His principles are excellent, his judgment sound, his taste correct, his learning various and extensive, his manner engaging.' Through Van Mildert, Lloyd was introduced to Norris and Joshua Watson, drawn into Hackney Phalanx counsels, and elected to Nobody's Club membership. He it was who created for Norris the title Patriarch: '"for," said he, "your care for all the Churches is more than an archbishop's"'.[82]

Van Mildert's Bampton Lectures, delivered in 1814, were, like his Boyle Sermons, grounded in massive scholarship. The Appendix acknowledged well over a hundred works: Fathers, Reformers, Caroline Divines, trinitarian controversialists, continental exegetes and sympathetic contemporaries. His principal sources were Horsley, Waterland, Leslie and St Augustine.

While their tone was impeccably academic, their subject, *An Inquiry into the general principles of Scripture-Interpretation*, placed the Lectures squarely within the Bible Society controversy: the first and last included overt sideswipes at the BFBS. Van Mildert entered the arena opened by Herbert Marsh's 1812 *Inquiry into the Consequences of Neglecting to give the Prayer Book with the Bible*.

Marsh, Cambridge Lady Margaret Professor of Divinity, caused controversy by attacking Chillingworth, whose principle that 'the Bible, and the Bible only, is the religion of Protestants' was heavily relied on by Bible Society supporters. Marsh pointed out that

Bible-only Protestantism came in many varieties: 'Are not the Moravians, the Methodists, the Baptists, the Quakers, and even the Jumpers, the Dunkers, and Swedenborgians all Protestants?'[83] For Churchmen, the Prayer Book was the appointed 'clue' for guidance through the labyrinth of Biblical interpretation.

This was by Hackney standards a dangerously weak defence of the Anglican position, verging on pluralism. Daubeny's 1812 *Reasons for Supporting the S.P.C.K.*, while defending Marsh, regretted his failure to affirm the Church's apostolic authority.

Marsh was nevertheless attacked for putting the Church of England 'on a level' with the Roman Church by recognising '*some* authority . . . *in addition* to the authority of the Bible'.[84] Spurred by ironic plaudits from the Roman Catholic apologete Peter Gandolphy for conceding 'the vital principle of the Reformation', Marsh elaborated his views in his 1814 classic *Comparative View of the Churches of England and Rome*, a key text in the political battles over Catholic Emancipation. Van Mildert, who read it before completing his Bampton Lectures, described it as comprising 'within a short compass so much extensive research, forcible reasoning, and perspicuous illustration of the subject, as almost to supersede the necessity of further investigation'.[85]

The Bampton Lectures nevertheless exposed differences between Van Mildert's position and Marsh's. While their lines of argument were similar, Van Mildert showed far more warmth for catholic tradition. Marsh's *Inquiry* treated the Anglican formularies as literary documents rather than as expressions of a corporate faith; Van Mildert's, while insisting no less firmly on the paramount authority of Scripture, gave an honoured place to the historical faith community.

P. B. Nockles notes that Marsh's *Inquiry* 'ignored the principle provided by the Vincentian Rule and denied even the merely corroborative or testimentary value of catholic consent as an aid in scripture interpretation'.[86] The *Comparative View* reiterated this. Marsh declared the Church of England's single source of authority to be the Bible, disowning Tradition entirely. Any doctrine 'supported by Tradition *alone*, is rejected by our Church without further inquiry';[87] even in matters of ceremony the Church of England was free to discard traditional ceremonial where her duly appointed authorities found it unedifying, or to introduce new ceremonies unsupported by tradition. The 'rejection of Tradition, as a Rule of Faith, was the vital principle of the Reformation'.

In an oblique repudiation of Marsh, Van Mildert exchanged his twofold Boyle conception of Reason and Revelation as the principles governing enquiry into Divine truth for a trinity of Tradition, Reason and Inspiration, and with great delicacy set about analysing their interrelationship. Rejecting any of the three was dangerous; elevating any into an infallible guide was dangerous. At one extreme lurked theological anarchy, with each individual theologian free to promulgate any doctrine he pleased. At the other, 'sacerdotal, intellectual, and spiritual Pride . . . "taught for doctrines of God the commandments of men"'. Safety lay in holding the mean, avoiding the several errors of Romanism, Rationalism and excessive Reform.

Roman Catholics, Van Mildert claimed, made the Church their infallible arbiter in matters of faith, vesting this infallibility in the Pope. Like Marsh he declared the Church of England's repudiation not only of papal infallibility but of Church infallibility in any form. Since the Church's authority derived from Scripture, the Church could not have authority over Scripture. Infallibility belonged to God alone, and hence to the Bible as God's inspired Word. Van Mildert affirmed Scripture as 'the only Rule of Faith: and whatever benefit may be derived from other writings, reported to us, as apostolical traditions, additional matters, illustrative of our faith and worship; to them is to be assigned no more than a secondary rank, as being subsidiary, not essential to our Creed'.[88] Where Marsh under pressure jettisoned Tradition as an authority, Van Mildert however defended it: 'though the Word of God is itself a perfect rule of Faith, yet to the far greater portion of mankind it can only become so through some medium of human instruction. That medium the Scripture itself has pointed out to be the Christian ministry.' This differed noticeably from Marsh's emphasis on the Prayer Book as the churchman's only guide. For Van Mildert, the individual Christian must not 'wantonly or perversely' set aside the Church's real, though limited, authority over him. Van Mildert defined the Church as 'that, which has from age to age borne rule, upon the ground of its pretensions to Apostolical succession', with episcopacy as the mark of the Church's fidelity to her apostolic origins.[89]

Van Mildert was willing to claim a cautious and empirical indefectibility for the mind of the universal Church as 'exhibited, either in the decisions of General Councils convened for the purpose, or in the various Creeds and Confessionals framed by different

Churches', most purely in the creeds, Articles, liturgy and 'public Formularies' of the Church of England; although even these pure forms were subject to the right of appeal to Scripture, and must be defended as scriptural rather than as universally received.

Impartial examination of the Church Catholic's record would reveal no occasions when 'any *fundamental* or *essential* Truth of the Gospel' was '*authoritatively* disowned':

> Particular Churches may have added many superstitious observances and many erroneous tenets, to these essential truths; and in every Church, particular individuals, or congregations of individuals, may have tainted large portions of the Christian community with pestilential heresies. But as far as the Church Catholic can be deemed responsible, the substance of sound doctrine still remained undestroyed . . .

Van Mildert blamed the temporary triumph of Arianism, an acknowledged embarrassment to his argument, on 'the unwarrantable interference of secular power'.[90]

Newman quoted this passage at length in his eighth *Lecture on the Prophetical Office of the Church* (1837), 'The Indefectibility of the Church Catholic', while protesting Van Mildert's treatment of 'the main principle under discussion . . . more as a fact than as a doctrine'.[91] He also quoted Van Mildert's views on the Church before the East–West schism as support for his own argument that the Church Catholic's major loss of infallibility accompanied the loss of its unity.

Van Mildert's position differed from Newman's chiefly in emphasis. Van Mildert's 'belief that "until the great schism between the Eastern and Western Churches, and the full establishment of the Papal usurpation," the Fathers kept before them the duty of contending for the faith and guarding it against heretical innovations'[92] was very carefully qualified. The primitive Fathers, despite the respect due to them as hearers and successors of the Apostles, were 'not to be regarded as Divinely-inspired; since otherwise their writings would necessarily have formed a part of the Sacred Canon'. Orthodoxy did not 'claim for them any infallibility, any commission to make further revelations of the Divine will, or any absolute authority as Scripture-interpreters'. Van Mildert explicitly denied the infallibility of General Councils: 'The appeal still lies . . . from all religious instructors, to that Word itself, which was no less their Rule of Faith than it is ours.' Newman would not, perhaps, have dissented from any of these cautions; but he did not feel impelled to state them with the same vigour, nor was he as clear as Van Mildert against ecclesial infallibility.

Van Mildert's Bampton Lectures restated the 'traditional high church doctrine of "fundamentals"', aligning Van Mildert with Waterland's middle way between Latitudinarian and extreme Non-juring understandings of Tradition in the life of the Church. Despite the intensity of his attacks on Popery, Newman in *The Prophetical Office of the Church* was already showing discomfort with the place assigned to Catholic Tradition by 'the school of Waterland'.[93] He had begun the move away from a static High Church conception of indefectible truth as a completed deposit towards a dynamic conception of a breathed and evolving presence within the Church – a living Church with a living voice. Seeing the Church of England as a body unable to trust 'established truth' beyond this static sense took him inexorably beyond her communion.

Van Mildert's Oxford exploration, while grounded in the same basic convictions as his Boyle Sermons, showed a marked change of atmosphere. The Bampton Lectures were positive about 'the light of human reason, bearing some faint analogy to the light of inspiration'. Van Mildert thought the searching of Scripture the human intellect's highest and most appropriate task. He elaborated its possibilities in loving detail:

The Scriptures comprehend a vast extent of knowledge, human as well as divine; and, in the illustration of them, scarcely any acquisitions of human learning are useless or unimportant. The adept in ancient languages, in philology, rhetoric, logic, ethics, metaphysics, geography, chronology, history ancient and modern, will have a conspicuous advantage in the study of the Sacred Writings . . . the value of solid acquirements of this kind, soberly and discreetly applied, is fully proved by the signal benefits which the Christian Faith has actually derived from the various improvements and discoveries of modern times in literature and science, tending to corroborate many important truths in the Sacred Records . . .[94]

Van Mildert was even prepared to allow sufficiently well established scientific truths a rôle in detecting false interpretations of Scripture, claiming support from the French scholar J. A. Turretin's *de Sacrae Scripturae Interpretatione* (1776). This gave a novel twist to the Hutchinsonian insistence that no genuine contradiction was possible between empirical science and Revealed Religion. Using humanly-discovered facts to test Scriptural interpretation was, however, 'not the work of a rash or unskilful hand', and it would 'well become the man of science, rather to mistrust his own judgement . . . than hastily to infer that reason and revelation are irreconcileably at variance'.

The decision not to repeat his Boyle diatribe against German theologians is another indication of his respect for Marsh, whose 1793 annotated translation of Michaelis' *Introduction to the New Testament* and 1801 *Dissertation on the Origin and Composition of the Three First Canonical Gospels* had by now won modern German biblical criticism a degree of wary respect. While Van Mildert never espoused any radical German theory, Michaelis' *Introduction* appeared, under the subheading 'Canon of Scripture', on a booklist he gave his students in 1818.

With the Bampton Lectures Van Mildert took his place among the principal High Church statesmen of his generation. His critical appraisal of the Latitudinarian/Nonjuring ecclesiological debates in the light of his own day's needs led him to a reasoned and deep-rooted analysis of the complex interlocking issues confronting the Church of England. He laid no claim to the rôle of theological knight-errant, riding into the unknown forest to seek out, make trial of, and accept or overthrow new insights. He was content to see the age of primary inspiration as over, the work of the Holy Spirit in the Church as reviewing, interpreting and defending the living treasures inherited from the past.

Although his stand on contemporary issues such as Baptismal Regeneration, the Real Presence, the Bible Society or Christian Unity was uncompromising, the equability of his tone gave him a reputation for judicious moderation. He was never shrill or gladiatorial. An anonymous 'Onesimus' wrote in 1814:

Whenever he ascends the pulpit, it is evidently for the religious instruction of his hearers, and not to challenge their applause, or admiration . . . Nothing that savours of intemperance, nothing crude, nothing of flourish or of figure, is suffered to impair the substantial fabric of his compositions . . . His style is not homely, but studiously plain. He will doubtless fill the high office of Regius Professor of Divinity with credit to himself, and advantage to the students of Oxford; and may not unreasonably look to adorn that mitre, with which his professional exertions must eventually be recompensed.[95]

'Onesimus' was a true prophet. Before the end of the decade Van Mildert was a bishop.

CHAPTER 3

The prime of the Hackney Phalanx

The new century witnessed the deaths of a whole leadership generation: Jones of Nayland in 1800, Boucher in 1804, Horsley in 1806, William Stevens early in 1807.

Horsley was in fine form during the 1806 Parliamentary summer session, savaging the slave trade with characteristic vigour on 24th June. In September, arriving in Brighton to visit Lord Thurlow, he found his old friend and patron dead. Two weeks later Horsley himself became fatally ill. Although Trafalgar had inspired him to preach exultantly of victory, on his deathbed he despaired of the bloody and protracted struggle to break Napoleon's grip on continental Europe.[1]

Horsley's death was an irreparable loss to the group. No figure of comparable stature emerged among High Churchmen until the Oxford Movement; Van Mildert, later forced by pressure of events into something of the same rôle, could never match his master's breadth of intellectual sympathy and oratorical brilliance. Horsleyisms became part of the Lords' stock-in-trade, quoted in debate by all sides far into the new century; but Horsley himself was gone, depriving the High Church reform movement of its figurehead and statesman. Piloting schemes for the renewal of the Established Church past Radical hostility on one side and deeply suspicious High Tory peers on the other, when the political atmosphere tainted all reform measures with danger to the established order, was a task for a master. Horsley might have attempted it; without his leadership, the main current of High Church reforming activity was forced into extra-parliamentary channels.

The mantle of William Stevens fell naturally on Joshua Watson. Sharing Stevens' wealth, piety, efficiency, affectionate nature and preference for self-effacing action, he was ideally equipped to take Stevens' place at the focus of the group. He settled down to an

unostentatious life's ministry of nurturing a catholic range of ecclesiastical and civil contacts, encouraging and criticising the literary
activities of his more academically-minded colleagues, corresponding with large numbers of friends in various countries, and promoting the reform and renewal of the Church of England along
impeccable High Church lines. More than anyone else he held
together the group, sometimes referred to as the Clapton Sect (the
High Church answer to the Evangelical Clapham Sect), but most
commonly remembered as the Hackney Phalanx.[2]

The Phalanx is usually pigeon-holed as a pressure-group,[3] but the
description is too narrow. Webster's description, 'a compact group
with an agreed attitude to most of the religious and political
measures of the day', has some justice but risks circularity: in order
to make the Phalanx a compact group it is necessary to exclude the
fringe figures, men such as Herbert Marsh or Charles James Blomfield who allied strongly with some Phalanx activities but were
marginal to others.

Pressure the Phalanx certainly applied, with increasing effect as
their individual and collective influence grew: their heritage from
William Stevens also included a large concern with practical piety
and practical charity. Phalanx lobbying of the civil and ecclesiastical authorities was frequently in support of, or complemented,
their own initiatives. They always scrupulously enlisted support
from the proper powers before taking a hand in public ecclesiastical
affairs, envisaging their work as that of loyal servants to the Church
and her leaders.

Public affairs were not the Phalanx's only concerns. Their private
charities, often undertaken in concert, were extensive, unobtrusive
and important to them. No less important were their social activities, regular correspondence, mutual hospitality, and loving concern
for one another's families – many of them were related, by blood or
marriage. 'They remained to the end a body of friends, rather than
an ecclesiastical or a religious party.'[4]

The Hackney Phalanx programme of reform and renewal took
few independent initiatives. Its pattern was set in 1787, when the
Evangelicals' launch of a Society for the Reformation of Manners
was countered by Jones' and Stevens' abortive Society for the
Reformation of Principles, and by their founding of the *British Critic*.
While the main creative thrust usually came from Clapham rather
than Clapton, it was nonetheless true that the High Church

reformers, drawing on a different constituency from the Evangelicals and one less sympathetic in principle to ideas of reform, were able to extend considerably the acceptability, the perspective and the resources of the renewal movement within the Church of England, preparing the way for the greater resurgence under Victoria.

The work of the Phalanx proper began when Norris and Joshua Watson determined to breathe fresh life into the dry bones of the Society for Promoting Christian Knowledge. The Venerable Society celebrated its centenary in 1798. Its responsibilities included publishing and disseminating religious literature, oversight of the Charity Schools founded under its auspices in earlier years, and administering some missionary work.[5]

SPCK membership drew from both Clapham and Clapton Sects. Stevens had been a committed supporter, numbering the SPCK Secretary Dr Gaskin, Rector of Stoke Newington, among his close friends. Evangelical members included Wilberforce, Hannah More, Charles Grant, Zachary Macaulay and John Venn. By the end of the eighteenth century, however, the Society had lost most of its original impetus. Evangelical dissatisfaction with SPCK publishing policy, which favoured only material of irreproachable High Church orthodoxy, led in 1799 to the launch of the interdenominational Religious Tract Society which, under its Welsh Baptist secretary Joseph Hughes, commenced printing and selling vast numbers of tracts in many languages.

Even when a book appeared on SPCK's list, its ready availability was not guaranteed. Evangelical impatience reached boiling-point over the Welsh Bibles saga. In 1787 SPCK was asked for a printing of Welsh-language Bibles, principally for Welsh-speaking Methodists. The SPCK leadership had little stomach for encouraging Enthusiasm, and nursed sour memories of a 1768 edition of 20,000 Welsh Bibles which was blamed for cashflow problems including 'a Debt of above Two Thousand Pounds'. They took until 1799 to produce 10,000 Welsh Bibles with Welsh editions of the Prayer Book, the New Testament and the New Version of the Psalms, which were sold to inhabitants of Wales at a special discount price of 'half the prime cost'. The entire print run rapidly disposed of, SPCK began its excruciatingly slow preparations for a fresh impression.[6]

The Evangelicals' patience was exhausted. The new Religious Tract Society turned its attention to Bibles, its perspective coloured by Evangelical and Dissenting commitment to missionary work. Joseph Hughes 'asked the memorable question, "If Bibles were to be printed for Wales, why not for the British Empire and the world?"' The outcome was the founding of the British and Foreign Bible Society, in March 1804, while the SPCK Welsh Bible was still 'republishing'.

The Bible Society's membership basis guaranteed its hostile reception in High Church circles. Dissenters of all descriptions were welcomed; all ministers of the Gospel, Anglican or not, were accorded equal status; the executive committee's thirty-six members included fifteen Dissenters and six resident foreigners. High Church apologetes admitted no justification for a new society to compete with SPCK. The Bible Society's professed '*liberal basis* of admitting "Christians of all denominations"'[7] was particularly resented, as implying 'a charge of illiberality' against the Venerable Society's practice of requiring testimonials from would-be members certifying their attachment to 'the Church of England as by Law established'. SPCK testimonials also declared their subject 'well affected to His Majesty King GEORGE, . . . of a sober and religious Life and Conversation, and of an humble, peaceable, and charitable Disposition', guaranteeing the Society's trustworthiness to receive the money and support of orthodox Churchmen.

Beilby Porteus approved the BFBS scheme and recommended Lord Teignmouth, an Anglican former Governor-General of India and close Wilberforce associate, as Bible Society President.

The inevitable tract war broke out immediately. When Teignmouth's appointment became known, 'A Country Clergyman' sent him an indignant open letter. 'A Sub-Urban Clergyman' replied and was in turn attacked by 'A Member of the Society [for Promoting Christian Knowledge]', probably Van Mildert.[8]

The 'Member of the SPCK' warned every honest Churchman against associating with 'those who, he knows, can never be conciliated without a desertion of principle on his part, and who probably only court his alliance for the purpose of more successfully compassing his degradation and destruction'.

Evangelicals might see supplying Bibles as an uncontroversial logistical exercise peculiarly suited to interdenominational collaboration. The Phalanx saw this as naive:

Sub-Urban thinks that some good may be done both to Churchmen and Dissenters, by such an association; that it will take off asperities on both sides; that they will still retain their respective quantum of faith, hope, and charity, and get rid of many odious qualities which may very well be spared. This is plausible in theory: but is it justified by experience? If merely believing in the Scriptures, and promoting the circulation of them, could produce this effect, surely it might have been produced long ago: since on this point all descriptions of Protestants have long since been agreed. But when a different *interpretation* of the Scriptures is the alledged cause of the disagreement subsisting between them, and occasions all the asperities, bickerings, schisms, and divisions of which the Church complains, what reason is there to suppose that the proposed union would be attended with any such consequences; or that those breaches will ever be made up, except on the condition that the Church shall renounce both her doctrine and discipline?[9]

The Member of the SPCK sounded Van Mildert's characteristic note of qualified tolerance: he claimed no desire to 'interfere with the labours of any association among the Separatists from our Church, which has for its object nothing really mischievous: still farther, to molest them in the prosecution of so good and laudable a purpose as that of circulating the pure Word of God . . .' His fear was that the Bible Society would adulterate the Word. Its defenders' claim that BFBS only intended 'editing and distributing the versions, printed by authority' was not reflected in the 'first printed list of laws and regulations', and 'if Heretics and Schismatics of every description, are admissible into this Society, and even have a predominant interest in the management of its concerns, who will say that . . . some corrections in the versions of the Bible, adapted to the heterodox tenets of its members, will not in time creep in?' The Bible Society's intention to produce foreign language versions was alarming: only 'persons of tried and approved orthodoxy' could guarantee the 'fidelity and accuracy' of the translations. How could 'the purity of the Bible be safely lodged in the hands of Sectarists of all denominations, Papists, Socinians, Quakers, &c . . ?'

The Bishops declined to act against the BFBS, but High Church ire was thoroughly aroused, and the pamphlet bombardment continued for more than a decade. Despite the hostilities, BFBS flourished; under the imminent threat of Napoleonic invasion, the sending out of Bibles in all languages seemed a new Pentecost, a powerful stimulus to apocalyptic hopes.

In December 1811 a massively-supported inaugural meeting founded a Cambridge Bible Society auxiliary, bringing Herbert Marsh into the fray. Marsh's 1812 *Address to the Senate*, arguing that

SPCK 'was the appropriate authoritative Bible Society for Church-men', was applauded by Hackney and published at Joshua Watson's expense; his *Inquiry into the Consequences of Neglecting to give the Prayer Book with the Bible*, for reasons examined in the previous chapter, caused them unease.

Most of the Phalanx contributed to the war effort. Christopher Wordsworth wrote an 1810 open letter to the London clergy, *Reasons for Declining to become a Subscriber to the British and Foreign Bible Society*. Norris published *A Practical exposition of the tendency and proceedings of the British and Foreign Bible Society* in 1814. T. F. Middleton complimented him on being 'of all the writers on the subject, certainly the most amusing'.[10]

The Phalanx did more than attacking the Bible Society in print. As the BFBS grew, Watson and Norris determined to expand SPCK's membership and income. They joined the Society 'a little before the close of the . . . century', probably, like Van Mildert, in about 1797. Watson afterwards 'used to say that "they were both reformers," so much so, that a worthy dignitary of the London diocese predicted that their schemes would ruin the finances of the Society'.[11] The launch in about 1809 of the highly successful system of BFBS district committees soon led, despite the apprehensive reluctance of Gaskin's old guard, to SPCK's establishing a diocesan committee network. Watson gave the chief credit to Wordsworth, who excelled at quelling panic among the national leadership when the committees started supplying ideas as well as money.

The SPCK Board reached crisis in January 1811, when the Gaskin faction 'in a thin meeting' attempted summary disposal of some proposals from the Colchester District Meeting. Joshua Watson, who had 'never before been moved to speak in any public discussion', was provoked into proposing a counter-resolution, followed by a motion to appoint a special committee for handling suggestions from district level. Backed by Wordsworth, Norris and Bowles, Watson brought off his coup. The revised structure, with a strong central committee servicing the diocesan network, 'shortly trebled' the Society's income. It also gave subsequent Phalanx initiatives an administrative base.

Government of the diocesan committees was vested firmly in the bishops. Episcopal government became the Hackney reform movement's shibboleth for two reasons: firstly, it sheltered the reformers from accusations of working against the Established Church. Among the Church of England's more rigid defenders, Reform was a transparent synonym for Destruction. The Phalanx demonstrated its devotion to the Church's best interests by giving the episcopate direct supervisory control over its initiatives.

Secondly, it prevented the Societies' becoming marginal 'holy clubs', associations of individual enthusiasts pushing pet causes, or worthy bodies simply raising money for good works. For the Hackney reformers, who regarded the office of bishop as God's appointed means for ensuring the Church's fidelity to her apostolic origins, this special relationship with the episcopate was uniquely appropriate to stamp their Societies as aspects of the Church's corporate action.

The deplorable readiness of bishops to join the Bible Society embarrassed this understanding. In 1812 *A Vindication of Churchmen who become members of the British and Foreign Bible Society* by William Otter, a moderate High Churchman who was the first Principal of King's College, London, reckoned that twenty English and Irish bishops were members.[12]

Eighteen hundred and eleven was a key year. Beginning with the SPCK boardroom triumph, it also saw launched the first, and in many ways most significant, major Phalanx public initiative, the educational venture known as the National Society.

The education of the poor was one of Horsley's cherished causes. He dreaded the consequences of the increased circulation of radical literature among the lower orders, denouncing in his 1800 Charge 'schools of Jacobinical religion and Jacobinical politics . . . in the shape and disguise of charity-schools and Sunday-schools, in which the minds of the children of the very lowest orders are enlightened – that is to say, taught to despise religion and the laws and all subordination'. He responded to this, not by demanding an end to the schools, but by challenging the Church to act: 'the proper antidote for the Jacobinical schools, will be schools for the children of the same class under the management of the parochial clergy'.[13] This defensive stance, characteristic of Phalanx educational thinking, provided useful apologetic for steering educational proposals past suspicious High Tories inclined to prefer repression.

Horsley was chiefly concerned with Sunday schools. In the new century, attention rapidly focused on elementary weekday education. Existing provision for teaching poor children – dame schools,

'schools of industry' for pauper children, and charity schools, many founded by SPCK – reached pitifully few.

Given the tensions responsible for the Religious Tract and Bible Societies, the Evangelicals would hardly choose to work through the SPCK. As early as 1802, Wilberforce and Bernard were 'busy together about education plan for children of lower orders'.[14] The Clapham Sect took no direct action; Hackney anxieties targeted the work of Joseph Lancaster.

Lancaster, like Van Mildert a Southwark man, joined the Society of Friends in his teens and, after an early impulse towards the mission field, began a small venture teaching poor children to read. The work grew. 1801 saw his first school opened in 'a large room in the Borough Road': 'All who will may send their children and have them educated freely, and those who do not wish to have education for nothing may pay for it if they please.'[15]

The school proving highly successful, there were soon more pupils than Lancaster could himself teach. He developed a pyramidal system whereby more advanced pupils instructed the less advanced. This to some extent paralleled earlier work by the Anglican clergyman Andrew Bell in the Madras Asylum, based on traditional Hindu teaching patterns.

The exact relationship between Bell's scheme and Lancaster's was controversial: Bell had undeniably published first.[16] The originality dispute was part of a still hotter controversy over the relative value of the two schemes, notably in their respective approaches to religious instruction.

The 1805 *Letter to the S.P.C.K.* attacked Lancaster in an enormous footnote:

If Mr. L. be a sincere Quaker, he must hold in contempt, as superstitious and absurd, many things which we regard as of the most sacred obligation. Can, then, any sound member of the church consent that the opinions of such a teacher should be inculcated on the rising generation? Or, supposing that Mr. L. should adopt no plan of religious instruction, but leave his pupils, in this respect, to themselves; is it desirable, that the infant poor should be brought up in a sort of indifference towards religion, and an ignorance of its truths? . . How the patronage of such an institution, so conducted, is likely to promote the real interests of the community, either religious or political, I am at a loss to understand. But . . . if the plan itself be really of such importance as to merit public support, it ought to be put immediately into the hands of persons on whose fidelity to our Establishment in Church and State we can safely depend; that it may be made an instrument of 'training up children in the way wherein they should go', and not an engine of heresy, schism, or disaffection.[17]

Other 1805 High Church attacks came from John Bowles and from Mrs Trimmer, who accused Lancaster of usurping the Established Clergy's proper responsibility as educators of the nation's children and 'applying to the pupils the stimulus of selfish motives, dread of ridicule, and love of praise, the fear of man not the fear of God'.[18]

The Society of Friends provided Lancaster's main moral and financial backing; his System was also promoted by the group of Radical politicians associated with the *Edinburgh Review*, notably Whitbread, Brougham and later Bentham. Sydney Smith gleefully dissected Mrs Trimmer's opus in the *Edinburgh* of October 1807.

Most significant was Lancaster's cordial reception by George III in 1805. The King, Queen and Princesses subscribed to what were renamed the Royal Free Schools in the Borough Road. Apologetes for the rights of the Established Church were forced to recognise that there was now no question whether the poor should be educated, only how and by whom.

In 1807 Whitbread's private member's Bill requiring every parish to set up a school, governed by the incumbent, the churchwardens and the parish overseers, in which every child of the parish aged between seven and fourteen would be entitled to two years' free education, was passed formally by the Commons and killed by the Lords: the Home Secretary, Lord Hawkesbury, declared its religious clauses insufficient.

In 1808, the Quakers Fox and Allen founded the Royal Lancasterian Society to disentangle Lancaster's chaotic finances and take over the administration of his schools. The Hackney public response, Daubeny's 1809 Charity Schools sermon, denounced the Lancaster System as aiming to amalgamate 'the great body of the people into one great deistical compound'.[19]

As usual, however, polemic was only part of the Hackney armament. Behind the scenes, Joshua Watson and his friends were plotting action.

Phalanx strategy centred on the work of Andrew Bell, a far more respectable figurehead than Lancaster. Scots by birth, Bell was a priest of the Church of England, an able administrator, and regarded 'unsectarian religious teaching' as a contradiction in terms. The public record proved that his experiments and writings came first: a select few English schools had been using the 'Madras system' for some years when Lancaster began his work.

A committee of Watson, Norris and Bowles drafted plans. Despite SPCK's existing foothold in education, through its charity schools, they decided to found a separate society – the years of wrestling with Gaskin had left scars. Lancasterians vaunted the Establishment adjective 'Royal'; in a simple but brilliant countercoup, Watson's committee stole the Radical adjective 'National', naming their new association the National Society for Promoting the Education of the Poor in the Principles of the Established Church. This caused anxiety among conservative supporters, who 'objected to the name . . . as if it had been borrowed from late Gallican precedents: but its meaning was explained by the principle set forth in its first report, "that the national religion should be made the groundwork of national education"'.[20]

This argument was aired in the 1811 Charity Schools Sermon by Marsh, who, indignant at the popularity of the Lancasterian charity school founded at Cambridge in 1808, had allied himself with the Hackney committee. Talk of a 'Church Education Society' was now general, and the Phalanx was in a ferment of activity enlisting support. Marsh canvassed bishops on the one hand and Cambridge divines on the other; the Evangelical Dean Milner helped, subscribing fifteen guineas. John Richardson was actively involved. Park, while expressing willingness to 'do anything', favoured a new SPCK department rather than a separate society, and deplored the name: 'amazingly misunderstood, and gives much offence to excellent people'.[21]

Founding the National Society was the Phalanx's most controversial achievement. It opposed them to not only their more radical rivals, but also the not inconsiderable number of their natural political allies for whom teaching anything to the lower orders was anathema. 'Many Tories believed, to use Mark Twain's words, that "soap and education are not as sudden as a massacre, but they are far more deadly in the long run", and it was openly said in the House of Commons that education would make the workers insolent.'[22]

The general response was favourable. Manners-Sutton accepted the National Society Presidency and chaired the inaugural meeting on 16th October. Marsh dined with the triumvirate of Bowles,

Norris and Watson on the 15th, to give one last polish to their plans. All went smoothly: Watson was elected treasurer, Norris 'temporary acting secretary', and a further meeting arranged for 21st October to agree the Society's regulations. Poor Bowles, still untouchable, was kept firmly in the background, although 'none took a more lively interest in the establishment of the National Society, even when, to his severe mortification, it was not thought expedient that his name should appear upon the committee, or accompany any public notice of the proceedings'.[23]

The second meeting, held at St Mary-le-Bow, established indubitably that 'this was not a mere private society run by a group of self-appointed zealots, but the Church acting in its corporate capacity'.[24] The Prince Regent's offer of patronage, secured by Bowles, was formally communicated and accepted; all the Bishops became Vice-Presidents and ex-officio committee members. Vice-Presidents representative of the State Establishment included Eldon, his brother Sir William Scott (now Speaker of the House of Commons), Lords Grenville, Kenyon and Redesdale, and the Earl of Liverpool, who as Lord Hawkesbury had demolished Whitbread's Education Bill. Richard Richards, a friend of William Stevens who afterwards became Chief Baron of the Exchequer, and Sir Thomas Plumer the Attorney-General were appointed auditors.

The National Society adopted as policy firstly, to collect subscriptions and build schools, to be run on the Bell System; secondly, to 'encourage parishes to open their own schools, so that the schools "should be under the immediate inspection and government of those whose local knowledge would be likely to make better provision for each case, and who will naturally take a livelier interest in that which they have instituted and conducted themselves"'.[25] Paying homage to SPCK proved divisive: Shute Barrington, Lord Grenville, Sir William Scott and others 'strongly opposed' the regulation requiring National Society schools to use books only from the SPCK Catalogue. It was carried by a narrow majority, and Barrington's amendment adding books 'approved by the bishop of the diocese' negatived.[26]

The National Society was immediately and spectacularly successful:

The nation in 1811 was struggling on to support the long-exhausting war with France. There was a dawn of hope from Sir Arthur Wellesley's brave and skilful defence of Portugal: but the field of Salamanca had not yet been fought, and Napoleon was arming for his gigantic contest with Russia, his spell of success as yet unbroken. At such a time it was something if a sum of £15,000 was at once contributed, in the course of about a month from the first advertisement of the Society's formation. The two Universities contributed shortly afterwards a sum of £500 each from their public chests, and several of the colleges voted sums of £100 or £50 from their separate bodies.[27]

Van Mildert's only recorded contribution to the National Society launch was providing a venue for the second public meeting, although he remained a constant supporter of its activities for the rest of his life. He was not in a position to contribute much money, and his time was heavily committed to other concerns. He did, however, set up a parochial Sunday School at Farningham to supplement the two existing commercial Day Schools. In October 1811 a Vestry agreed 'That a sufficient number of Forms & Seats be provided for the use of the Sunday School Children, to be placed in the Chancel.' In 1812 a house was rented for Sunday School use. Van Mildert seems to have paid the £10 per annum rent from his own pocket; the master of the larger Day School also ran the Sunday School, and in return was allowed use of the house.[28]

When Lord Liverpool's administration took office in 1812, the influence of the Hackney Phalanx reached its zenith. Liverpool had been at Charterhouse and University College, Oxford, with John James Watson. Convinced of both the necessity and the dangers of Church reform, he was the Phalanx's ideal Prime Minister. His exercise of ecclesiastical patronage was particularly praised. Although the venerable practice of nepotism did not entirely disappear – Liverpool's cousin John Banks Jenkinson became Bishop of St David's in 1825 and Dean of Durham *in commendam* two years later – it came to be understood that no unsuitable man would be preferred, whatever his connections, and that no sound and able man would be passed over simply for lack of influence. Liverpool went 'out of his way, so far as George IV let him'[29] to appoint men of blameless character and irreproachable orthodoxy; his bishops were conscientious (by the standards of the day) in performing their episcopal duties and uncontentious in their public utterance. By 1828 Wellington could plausibly write to a fellow-peer that 'dignities of the Church and benefices of the higher value' in the Crown's patronage were open only to 'those who have distinguished themselves by their professional merits'.[30]

SPCK remained a constant backdrop, its Bartlett's Buildings head-quarters the Phalanx administrative focus and meeting-place. The National Society's expanding work provided a second focus; it also led the Phalanx for a time into closer co-operation with the Evangelicals.

William Wilberforce was particularly attracted by the National Society, giving generously to its funds and attending a number of its public meetings. After a July 1814 meeting at the Central National School, Wilberforce noted in his diary '. . . children admirably taught, and general spirit delightful and animating – the difference between them and the Lancastrians very striking – exemplifying the distinction between church of England and Dissenterism – the intelligence, and fixed but not apparently nervous or feverish atten-tion pleased me much'.[31]

In 1815, when after the final break with Lancaster the Royal Lancasterian Institution had become the British and Foreign Schools Society, Wilberforce was persuaded to accept a vice-presidency, but he continued his public and financial support for the rival institution. His preference was generally shared: by 1833 the National Society had 690 schools, the British and Foreign Schools Society 190.[32]

This educational collaboration inspired Wilberforce to seek Phalanx support for another cherished cause. The evangelisation of India was a politically contentious issue: despite notable work by the great Baptist missionary William Carey and the Evangelical chap-lains to the East India Company, Thomason, Claudius Buchanan and Henry Martyn, the colonial administration remained generally hostile to missionary activity. Indian fears of forcible conversion were widely blamed for the Vellore Sepoy Mutiny of 1806 – although Carey and his fellow missionaries equally firmly blamed 'the hatlike turban then ordered'.[33]

When Parliament agreed the East India Company's Charter in 1873, Wilberforce tried strenuously but unsuccessfully to have 'pious clauses' incorporated giving Christian missionaries and school-teachers free rein in India. The Charter came before Parliament for renewal in 1813. Wilberforce was determined not to waste this second opportunity.

Early in March 1812, Wilberforce talked to Archdeacon Pott of London, a longstanding Phalanx associate and outgoing SPCK Treasurer, about possible SPCK support for the Indian missionary cause. Pott's attempt to organise representations to Parliament was blocked by John Randolph, Bishop of London, a hardliner whose 1811 primary visitation charge denounced the Evangelicals in violent terms as traitors more dangerous to the Church than avowed Dissenters.[34]

Randolph's view proved unrepresentative: 'the spiritual wants of India' fired High Church as well as Evangelical imaginations. On 5th May 1812, Bartlett's Buildings hosted a 'very full' public meeting on 'East India Christianising', with Archbishop Manners-Sutton presiding and Wilberforce present 'by special summons'. A committee was appointed to draft a report and resolutions for presentation to Spencer Perceval and Lord Buckinghamshire – 'meaning in Church of England way', Wilberforce noted.[35]

The committee based its resolutions on a scheme Wilberforce supplied via Pott, drawn up in Serampore by Claudius Buchanan from a suggestion of Beilby Porteus. Presented to the Evangelical sympathiser Spencer Perceval as originally intended, it might have served well enough. Less than a week after the Bartlett's Buildings meeting, however, Perceval was dead, and Liverpool's administration took over the India establishment question.

In July 1813, after an Evangelical-led campaign including some 900 petitions to Lords and Commons, Parliament authorised the admission of missionaries to India and created a small establishment of one bishop and three archdeacons. The change of government meant the bishop would be a High Churchman. In the Indian context this could hardly but be unfortunate.

Recruiting to the See of Calcutta, with authority over 'three Provinces in India' and an annual stipend of £5,000, proved time-consuming. In January 1814 Archbishop Manners-Sutton con-fidentially offered it to Christopher Wordsworth,[36] who declined. By the end of January T. F. Middleton, Archdeacon of Huntingdon, had accepted the impossible challenge.

Middleton, one of the Phalanx's ablest and most energetic members, achieved some important results before his new ministry killed him. A letter to Norris illustrates both Middleton's courage and the inevitability of his failure to relate to the North Indian mission situation:

I shall carry with me sentiments of affection & veneration for the Church of my native country, and happy shall I be under every difficulty & trial, to which the Almighty may reserve me, if I can only thro his blessing, establish some degree of reverence for its ordinance, and impart to a careless & licentious people some portion of its Spirit.[37]

Wilberforce accepted the inevitable gracefully, inviting the Bishop-elect to dine with himself, Teignmouth and Charles Grant; Lord Gambier and Henry Thornton of the Church Missionary Society also waited upon Middleton 'in deputation'.

Wilberforce's diary noted: 'Long and highly interesting talk with Bishop Middleton. He seems very earnest and pondering to do good – hopes for churches in different parts of India – favourable to schools and a public library – a college with discipline. His powers greater than we conceived.'[38]

Middleton horrified his Phalanx colleagues by proposing to co-operate with the Bible Society's widely respected Calcutta branch. Wordsworth wrote to Norris in early February:

If he associates himself with the Bible Society, what will he do thereby for Education – what for Truth – what for the Liturgy – what for Missions – all of which are severally and distinctly of hardly less importance (perhaps I might justly say, in the present circumstances of that country are of more) than the Bible – and of all which he is now about to be the constituted Patron & Guardian?

Wordsworth urged confrontation: establishing 'a grand Oriental Auxiliary Society for Promoting Christian Knowledge – built as nearly as might be on the model of ours, in the method of education adopting the Madras System . . . In the meantime, all respectable Persons, lay-men or Clergymen (Archdeacons &c.) going out to India should be interested as much, but as quietly as possible, in favour of our Society.'[39]

Middleton refused to be hustled: as late as 13th May, Joshua Watson felt his 'open and decided patronage' for SPCK was still in doubt, suggesting that a timely grant of money, or rather credit, for Middleton to do some prestigious work of charity in his diocese might help settle the issue.[40]

Middleton was consecrated at Lambeth on 8th May. The new India establishment inspired such 'jealousy and alarm . . . that it was thought advisable to perform the Consecration Service in private and to suppress the sermon preached on the occasion'.[41]

He left for his immense diocese at the end of June, furnished by the SPCK with £1,000, 'the most splendid inkstand, that ever doubled the Cape', and parting instructions from Manners-Sutton 'to put down enthusiasm and to preach the Gospel'.[42]

In Calcutta he kept faith with his Phalanx colleagues: although 'almost every body' belonged to the Bible Society, he staunchly declined invitations to join and set up an SPCK diocesan committee in competition. He wrote rather sadly to Norris: 'this could not be a popular step, but it was necessary'.[43]

Staying with the Van Milderts at Oxford shortly before his departure, Middleton made 'a promise of writing to you, if Providence should conduct me safely to the banks of the Ganges'. The following February he sent them a lively account of his arrival in his new see, to a reception so low-key that when he entered Calcutta, without ceremony of any kind, he found himself homeless and spent his first two months as the guest of a Council member.[44]

The main achievement of Middleton's brief episcopal reign – he died in 1822 aged 53 – was the founding of Bishop's College, Calcutta, whose plan he had discussed with Wilberforce.

Middleton, convinced of the need for an indigenous clergy, intended the College to provide Christian instruction for 'native and other Christian youth', to undertake translation of 'the scriptures, the liturgy and moral and religious tracts', and to serve as a missionary base. His fourth objective showed the breadth of the Hackney educational vision at its best: Bishop's College was also 'for teaching the elements of useful knowledge and the English language to Mussulmans and Hindus, having no object in such attainment beyond secular advantage'.[45]

Middleton's plan had both the flaws and the strengths of all that the Phalanx undertook. Convinced of the simple identity between God's will for humankind and High Church Anglicanism, he imposed limitations on the work's Christian basis that were damaging in the ecumenical tradition of the Indian Church. The Bishop's College proposals cut straight across the massive work of scriptural translation on which Carey had been engaged since 1793,[46] excluded the entire Baptist and CMS missionary heritage, and were interpreted by many as high-handed Anglican colonisation.[47] Yet there was also an element of genuinely disinterested love of learning both Christian and secular, affording a basis for work of lasting value. Middleton, like too many of his compatriots, thought 'useful knowledge' was a one-way traffic from European Christians to 'Mussulmans and Hindus' – particularly ironic given the Hindu origins of the Bell System; but his insistence that the educational needs of the unconverted had a legitimate claim on the resources of a

Christian college looked beyond the confines of an introspective sectarianism.

The successful co-operation between Saints and Phalanx over India led Christopher Wordsworth to investigate the possibility of merging the Church Missionary Society with the Society for the Propagation of the Gospel in Foreign Parts, at this time little more than 'a board for holding various trust funds' with a total annual income around £8,000.[48] Reginald Heber of CMS, later the second Bishop of Calcutta, drew up a detailed union scheme, but the negotiations foundered over the High Churchmen's adherence to episcopal government.

Hackney missionary fervour was not so easily quenched. Wordsworth and Joshua Watson, who had recently, like William Stevens before him, retired from business to devote himself full time to his church work, set about converting the SPG into a full-fledged missionary society.

Van Mildert succeeded Archdeacon Pott as SPCK Treasurer in February 1812. Given Van Mildert's disastrous financial record, this can only have been a delicate piece of Hackney tact, designed to repair his self-confidence and prove that no-one questioned his integrity. He now resigned, pleading pressure of work, and was replaced by Watson.[49] Becoming Treasurer facilitated Watson's next step of rationalising the allocation of missionary responsibilities between SPCK and SPG.

In 1817 Watson sent Archbishop Manners-Sutton, and through him the Prime Minister, a substantial memorandum on the future of mission in the Indian subcontinent. Watson's covering letter openly acknowledged his intent of providing a loyal Anglican alternative to compete with the existing missionary societies: 'By thus putting forward the Society for Propagating the Gospel, your Grace cannot fail to direct into a proper channel much of that well-intended bounty which is now, I fear, running worse than to waste . . .'[50] The criticism was directed more at the Dissenting missionary societies than at CMS; the Saints and the Phalanx maintained a measure of co-operation despite the failed union plans. In 1819 the CMS Secretary, Rev Josiah Pratt, produced a volume of Bishop's College fundraising resource material for clergy, concealing his authorship 'for fear it might hinder the circulation of the book'.[51]

The grand rationalisation plan brought out the poet in Watson (also poet's licence regarding the National Society's antiquity):

And then, my Lord, the Church of England, strong in her three chartered and ancient Societies, each with undivided energy pursuing its own single and simple object, and having a common centre of union in your Grace's presidency, might, in her Education Society, her Bible and Religious Tract Society, and her Missionary Society, boldly offer to her members all that the most zealous of her communion need desire in the great concern of religious and moral instruction at home and abroad.[52]

The ability to discern the sweep of great pinions in a mundane juggling of responsibilities between committees marked Watson's particular genius. Combined with his formidable administrative skills, it gave this unassuming layman a crucially important rôle in revitalising his beloved Church of England.

It is easy to criticise Watson's vision as narrowly High Church, parasitic on the creative energies of the Evangelical and Dissenting pioneers, unable to recognise a Christian of Carey's calibre as an equal servant of the same Master as himself. His views were however powerfully shaped by political circumstances.

The end of the Napoleonic Wars demanded massive social and economic reconstruction; Watson put much time and energy into administering German relief funds.[53] In England peace brought not prosperity but hardship and public unrest. The agitations and disturbances surrounding the passage of the Corn Law in 1815, the Luddite troubles, the rick-burnings and riotings in the spring and summer of 1816 when a sudden rise in the price of corn brought agricultural labourers' grievances to the boil, the Spa Fields Riots of December 1816 leading directly to Lord Sidmouth's repressive measures of 1817, all refurbished memories of the French Terror as awful warnings of present danger.[54] In 1812 Southey's *Quarterly Review* article on a biography of distinguished French Revolutionaries made explicit connections:

the example of France must be our security at home: it has been lost upon our Heberts and Marats, and Chaumettes, who go on inflaming the passions of the ignorant and ferocious part of the community, as if they themselves were not sure to be the victims in their turn, of the revolution which they are labouring to produce.[55]

Although Southey's predicted rebellion never materialised, the fear of rebellion was real, widespread and sufficiently plausible given the course of events. In this atmosphere any attempt to whip up working-class enthusiasm, whether by political radicals or 'tub-preachers', seemed fraught with danger. Dissenting street evangelists were widely and sometimes warrantably credited with populist political opinions; Watson's 1817 memorial, denouncing 'those exertions of irregular zeal in making proselytes which compromise at once the character of our Religion and the quiet of the State' expressed a broad strand of Establishment opinion.[56]

What distinguished Joshua Watson and his associates is that, holding these views, they went far beyond merely negative criticism. Having decided that the initiatives taken by the Dissenting and Evangelical missionary societies, the Bible Society and the Lancasterians were incompatible with their own understanding of Anglican social responsibility, they developed, and marshalled the resources to implement, proposals for more acceptable styles of working. In so doing, they separated the principle of the work decisively from the taint of Enthusiasm, placing the responsibility for its continuance on the whole Church of England, irrespective of political allegiance either secular or ecclesiastical. Besides widening the spectrum of Anglican involvement in their Societies' specific interests, the Hackney Phalanx placed social and mission issues on the agenda of every bishop – and also every aspiring would-be bishop. While, naturally, some bishops took these concerns more seriously than others, the long-term effect was a sharpening of awareness and greatly enhanced possibilities for future action.

Although Van Mildert was not a prime mover in any of this work, he kept in close touch with it. The Christ Church Chapter made substantial benefactions to the National Society and the 'German Sufferers'. Van Mildert also watched over Phalanx publishing activities, advising on the distribution of the SPCK Family Bible, and counselling during the 1816 SPCK panic over a Bible Society order for Arabic bibles.[57]

The next Phalanx enterprise involved Van Mildert directly. The effects of rapid industrial urban expansion on parish structure had for some time concerned both friends and opponents of the Established Church.

In June 1809, Archbishop Manners-Sutton told the Lords, 'the fact was, that our population had, particularly in some large towns, far exceeded the machinery by which the beneficial effects of our church establishment could be universally communicated'.[58] The anonymous *State of the Established Church, in a series of letters to Spencer Perceval*, published in 1809 with an expanded second edition in 1810, highlighted the shortage of church space particularly in London parishes. The *Quarterly Review* excoriated the writer for attacking the Established clergy, but entirely agreed about the church-room shortage: 'Unquestionably, if we wish the people to remain attached to the church establishment, we must give them the means of attending the church service.'[59]

The problem had a long history. In 1710 Parliament provided for the building of fifty new London churches, although only eleven were actually built. In 1800 Wilberforce introduced a Bill to encourage church-building by private individuals; he proposed giving the subscribers the advowson, opposed by the Bishops 'on the ground that it would multiply unlicensed chapels of an Evangelical flavour', and the Bill fell.

Church-building involved four of Establishment's most intractable aspects: patronage, a facet of the property right so central among High Tory freedoms; the rights of the incumbent; the dual nature of the parish as an entity both in civil and in canon law; and the increasingly vexed issue of church rates and church finance. To divide a parish, build a new parish church and establish a new cure of souls required the support of the patron, incumbent and, for impropriated tithes, the tithe-owner; it required a special Act of Parliament; it raised difficult questions as to how the new parish should be endowed and who should hold the advowson. Even under ideal circumstances this was a time-consuming and enormously expensive business. It might also involve unpleasantness of another kind: anti-clerical radical politicians frequently used debates on Church business as platforms for attacking non-residency, pluralism and the fabulous wealth of the Established Church.

In the early nineteenth century it was simpler to build Dissenting chapels than Anglican churches, an anomaly infuriating to apologetes for the rights of the Established Church. Church-building posed problems even without parish division. Chapels-of-ease or parochial chapels required the incumbent's consent, and their financing was a bed of nails. Where incumbent and chapel minister were wealthy men, on friendly terms with each other and committed to the principle of church-extension, the arrangement worked well – but few parishes were as lucky as Hackney, where John James Watson and Norris met all these conditions.

In 1810 Lord Sidmouth 'moved for returns by dioceses of the number and capacity of churches, the number of dissenting places of worship, and the population, in parishes of one thousand or over'. The results created widespread shock. The *Quarterly Review* reprinted some of the worst examples: the diocese of Lichfield, with church room for 122,756 of its 420,231 population; the archdiocese of York, with 149,277 places for 591,972 people; London, with church-room for 162,962 and a population conservatively estimated at 661,394. 'Even where chapels have been opened, they have almost invariably been appropriated to those who can afford to rent a pew . . . The bulk of the common people are disregarded.' The *Quarterly* urged immediate remedial action: 'Till this is done, we abandon that most numerous class, who have no other means of religious instruction, to the practices of every ignorant and ranting enthusiast, or to the condition of a heathen to whom the gospel is not preached.'[60]

For the Phalanx, the National Society's success provided a further spur to action. The point of educating the poor in the principles of the Established Church was to make them loyal church-members: 'it matters comparatively little how much, or even how well, we teach our children in the week-day, if we do not carry them to church on the Sunday', wrote Joshua Watson.[61] It was more than embarrassing for the National Society's promoters if 'their' children could find no church to attend. In 1813 the banker and Phalanx ally William Cotton wrote to John Bowdler suggesting the foundation of a Church Building Society.[62]

Phalanx members were already involved in church-building. Daubeny was 'perhaps the first Churchman who had made a public step to provide free accommodation in a new Church for the poorer classes'.[63] The Hackney chapel-of-ease was built in 1806. Middleton promoted a special act of Parliament for building a new church in his parish of St Pancras, shortly before becoming Bishop of Calcutta:

I am labouring incessantly, certainly (writing included) not less than nine or ten hours in the day, in the business of the new Church, and I am sorry to observe that nearly the whole of the burthen rests upon my shoulders . . . If the Legislature shall determine, in deference to bad Politics & false Theology, that this Parish, already enormous & rapidly increasing, shall remain without Religion or Order, I shall at least have the consolation of having thought differently.[64]

Individual action, however, was incommensurable with the scale of the need.

The Phalanx's first collective move was a letter to Howley, new Bishop of London. The letter, signed by Bowdler, Park, Charles Davis and Cotton's friend Charles Hampden Turner, drew Howley's attention to the shortage of church-room in his diocese and requested his sanction for 'calling a private meeting, chiefly clergy, nobles, and other excellent laymen, well-affected to such a measure, to digest some plan, and for carrying it into immediate execution, for the erection of churches and chapels, in districts where they are most wanted'. The plan proposed inviting the nation to provide free church places (rather than rented pews) as a thank-offering for victory in the Napoleonic Wars.[65]

Howley declined lending his name to this scheme. Churton attributes this to scholarly reserve, 'which ever attended him in public speaking'.[66] Howley was a lamentable public speaker, and no doubt knew it:[67] he was also intelligent and well-informed enough to realise what a web of conflicting interests he was being invited to involve himself in. He adopted a low profile, as did Lord Liverpool on receiving a memorial from Watson and Bowdler, signed by 120 leading High Church and Evangelical laymen, early in 1816.

The authorities refused to be hurried. In the autumn of 1815, Lord Sidmouth corresponded with Christopher Wordsworth on ways to raise public awareness. In November 1815, Sidmouth informed Kenyon confidentially that Liverpool intended to 'submit a proposition to parliament, in the ensuing session, for an augmentation, to be progressively made, of the number of places of worship under the established church'.[68] Nothing happened until June 1816, when Vansittart, Chancellor of the Exchequer, torpedoed a Commons motion 'for free churches to be erected in London as the promised national monument to the victories of Trafalgar and Waterloo'.

The signatories to the 1816 memorial were growing impatient. Despite Christopher Wordsworth's protest that 'if government would not act, the friends of the Church should rest silent, because many cries and nothing done begat despair in even the best-disposed', a public meeting held at the City of London Tavern in May 1817 appointed a committee to consider the next step. It recommended a 'Society for promoting public worship by obtaining additional Church Room for the middle and lower classes'.[69]

A deputation headed by Sir Thomas Dyke Acland waited on Lord Liverpool to ascertain government reactions to the proposal, particularly to avoid threatening 'any more comprehensive plans which the Government might have in contemplation'. The deputation went on to Manners-Sutton, who was gracious and welcoming. Howley, who Liverpool suggested should also be consulted, 'was away from home, but wrote to the acting-secretary, William Davis, giving his approval'.[70]

A committee formed on 4th July 1817 prepared a constitution and draft prospectus for the new Society. In October Lord Chancellor Eldon questioned the Society's legality on grounds of possible infringement to the rights of patrons and incumbents. In November the committee met with a formidable ally, Richard Yates, chaplain of Chelsea Hospital, whose 1815 pamphlet *The Church in Danger* decisively convinced parliamentary opinion of the need for church building measures.[71]

The Church Building Society was launched on 6th February 1818 at a public meeting in the Freemasons' Hall. Archbishop Manners-Sutton took the chair, the Duke of Northumberland moved the resolutions, and the Duke of York consented to be a patron. Ninety people attended, 'more than half of them laymen' including William Wilberforce and Robert Peel, also a bevy of bishops. Wilberforce was 'chosen Vice President with a multitude of high-churchmen, and great men – said a few words'.[72]

The thirty-six member committee included Yates, Archdeacons Pott and Cambridge, Sir John Nicholl, Joshua Watson and Christopher Wordsworth, since 1816 Rector of the 'swole, & swelling Parish' of Lambeth; also Van Mildert, now reconciled to the pressure of his Oxford work and ready to resume active Phalanx involvement. Writing to inform Joshua Watson of the Christ Church Chapter's substantial donation, 'the Sum of One thousand Pounds', Van Mildert shrewdly noticed the scheme's major defect: 'there seemed to be wanting some security for the endowment as well as for the erection of new churches'.[73]

The Government's plans matured soon after. In March Vansittart presented a 'Money Bill' allocating one million pounds of public money to build new churches, administered by a specially created Church Building Commission.

The Bill included a kindred clause to Wilberforce's episcopal hackle-raiser, 'granting to persons building a Chapel by *private Subscription*, without the aid of Parochial Assessments or of the Parliamentary Grant, the nomination of Life Trustees, in whom the

Patronage of the Chapel shall be vested for the first Three Turns'. High Church protests gained particular edge from the circumstance that a Money Bill could not be amended in the House of Lords but must be either accepted or rejected in total as passed by the Commons. At the end of March, Lord Harrowby warned Liverpool that the Archbishop was unhappy about 'some of the concessions' he had made; Harrowby attributed this to pressure from 'some of his most strait-laced brethren'.[74]

At the end of April Van Mildert lobbied Peel, now Secretary of State for Ireland, who in June 1817 had become MP for Oxford University. He tried for a private conversation, but failing to find Peel at either Stanhope Street or the Irish Office attacked the obnoxious patronage clause by letter.

Accepting that 'any single Individual building a Church or Chapel entirely at his own Expence' should enjoy its patronage, 'subject to the approval of the Diocesan Bishop', Van Mildert protested strenuously against extending 'such a privilege' to

a body of Subscribers even of so moderate a Sum as Fifty Pounds each . . . I very much fear that it will operate as a great encouragement to a certain party in the Church, who are known to be exceedingly desirous of getting into their hands the patronage of large & populous Districts, & who have a considerable Fund appropriated to that object. Among the opulent of that description, nothing will be easier than to raise Subscriptions of Fifty Pounds each for the promotion of this object; & the Bill, by giving them the Patronage for *three* Incumbencies . . . will enable them most effectually to accomplish their views; views, which, I conscientiously think, cannot be realised without great hazard to our Church Establishment. I am well aware, however, that this is too tender a point to be mooted in the H. of Commons.[75]

To a person with Van Mildert's absolute confidence in High Church principles, the Evangelical fund for the purchase of advowsons could not but appear in a sinister light, whatever his personal esteem for men such as Wilberforce and Harrowby, and his insinuations are mild by comparisons with the crudities of much contemporary polemic. The argument that only those rich enough wholly to finance the building of a new church should expect right of presentation was an orthodox piece of quasi-feudal paternalism, rooted in the premise that government is the proper responsibility of those whom Providence has placed in positions of wealth and power. Van Mildert objected to the patronage clause because it was democratic in tendency, and democracy was a dirty word with mob rule connotations and echoes of the Reign of Terror.

Lurking behind the clause Van Mildert discerned the appalling principle of 'popular Election to the Cure of Souls'. 'Wherever this system already prevails, it is found to be productive of great evils, & ought therefore, as much as possible, to be discouraged.' The turbulence of contemporary politics, and the disorderly scenes regularly featured in those few parishes with elective incumbencies, lent colour to this view.[76]

The Commons removed the offending clause: 'the excrescence', Van Mildert told Watson, 'was separated from the main body of the tree',[77] and the million pound grant was agreed on 15th May. The selection of Church Building Commissioners began at once, but not until 24th June, when the process was well advanced, did Manners-Sutton request Liverpool to include all the bishops. Liverpool was not pleased, and sent a sharp reply: the Archbishop had already approved the composition of the Commission, which had been repeatedly discussed, and it was too late to make changes. He also pointed out that adding 'the whole bench of Bishops' to 'all the other Ecclesiastics included in the Commission, would give such a decided and large preponderance in point of numbers to the Clerical part of the Commission as I should think by no means expedient'.[78]

The Commission first met on 31st July 1818 at Lambeth. It included both Archbishops, the Bishops of London, Winchester, Chester, Lichfield/Coventry and Lincoln, six Archdeacons including Pott and Cambridge, Dean Ireland of Westminster, Lords Kenyon, Sidmouth and Harrowby, Vansittart, Sir William Scott, Sir John Nicholl and the younger Charles Manners-Sutton, Speaker of the House of Commons. Hackney representation further included Christopher Wordsworth, Joshua Watson and Richard Mant, another able young priest drawn into Phalanx service through becoming Archbishop Manners-Sutton's chaplain.

In 1825 Van Mildert became a Commissioner, serving from 1826–7 on a standing committee appointed to look into pew-rent schedules and appropriation.[79]

The Church Building Commission, which continued in being until absorbed into the Ecclesiastical Commission in 1857, was an example of quiet but solid achievement. It was responsible for building 612 churches, handling a total of more than three million pounds, while the Church Building Society concentrated on the complementary work of church repair and extension. But if it provided, in G. F. A. Best's words, 'a classical illustration of the workings of the church–state relationship in the early nineteenth century',[80] so it also marked the end of an era. Although a further grant of £500,000 was secured for the Commission in 1824, the debate was a stormy one. Increasingly, the church–state relationship was to follow the path prefigured by Lord Holland during the Lords debate on the 1818 Church Building Bill, when he suggested 'the suspension of a few deans and canons'[81] as the appropriate way to find finance for building new churches.

CHAPTER 4

Toil and tribulation

In March 1819 John Parsons, the reforming Master of Balliol, personal friend of Van Mildert and Bishop of Peterborough, died. Marsh, who had become Bishop of Llandaff in 1816, was translated to Peterborough. Liverpool offered Van Mildert Llandaff.[1]

Van Mildert hesitated over the financial implications:

> Until, by your Lordship's unexpected patronage & recommendation, I was brought to my present station, my preferments had been very inconsiderable in point of emolument, & my private means scarcely sufficient to my station. Consequently, I am now but just beginning to reap the fruits of my improved condition: & I feel it incumbent upon me to weigh well the possibility of involving myself in any pecuniary difficulties by accepting a higher station.[2]

This was entirely reasonable; it was the poorest diocese, with net revenues averaging £924 per annum. Herbert Marsh, congratulated by a friend on his elevation to Llandaff in 1816, replied, 'You had better call me the Bishop of 'Aff, for the land is gone.'[3]

As a temporary measure, Liverpool agreed to Van Mildert's keeping Bow, Ewelme and the Regius Professorship *in commendam*. In January 1820 Liverpool offered him the Archbishopric of Dublin, assuring him he 'need make no scruple about accepting it upon the ground that not being an Irishman your appointment might be unpopular in Ireland'. Van Mildert had no intention of becoming embroiled in the Irish Question: he declined by return of post, protesting his 'attachment to England, and to the many ties and connections which must in a great degree be sacrificed by a residence in the sister country'.[4] He correctly judged this unlikely to damage him with Liverpool, who in July offered him the Deanery of St Paul's instead.

There were two conditions to the *commendam*: Van Mildert must reside at the Deanery for six months each year, and do something about the scandalous state of the Cathedral:

It has been long felt by the Public, that the Church of St. Paul's has been greatly neglected: and I understand that the Service is performed there in a much less creditable manner than in any other Cathedral in the Kingdom . . . I know I speak the sentiments both of the Archbp. of Canterbury & of the Bp. of London that this is an occasion on which a thorough Reform ought to take place as to all these Particulars.[5]

Liverpool also requested '5 minutes Conversation' about Van Mildert's other preferment. Van Mildert agreed to resign Bow and the Regius Professorship as soon as practicable after his institution to St Paul's.

On 24th May 1819, with 'unfeigned regret', Van Mildert resigned the Lincoln's Inn Preachership, offering to 'continue the duty of the pulpit, either by himself or his assistant, until his successor be appointed'.[6] Charles Lloyd and Reginald Heber contested the vacancy. Van Mildert felt 'espousing the interest of either of the candidates' would be improper, but defended his 'excellent friend Mr. Lloyd' against accusations of 'relying upon undue Government interest', pointing out that while Peel was naturally doing his best for Lloyd, Vansittart supported Heber, and 'some other Benchers connected with the Administration' had not yet revealed their intentions.[7] To Van Mildert's delight, Lloyd won.

Consecrated on 31st May by Manners-Sutton, Howley, Marsh and John Luxmoore of St Asaph, Van Mildert made no immediate plans to reside in his diocese. One of Llandaff's ancient palaces was in ruins, the other had long ago been alienated. Oxford and Ewelme remained his 'usual places of abode, except when an attendance in Parliament will require me to be in London'.[8]

His chief Llandaff contact was Marsh's examining chaplain W. Bruce Knight. Marsh valued Bruce Knight, preferring him to the Chancellorship of the Church and comparatively rich Howell prebend. Van Mildert found him 'a friend . . . in all respects worthy of his entire confidence and affection', appointing him Chancellor of the Diocese. They corresponded for the rest of Van Mildert's life.[9]

Llandaff's cathedral had its west roof missing, and the cathedral establishment was rudimentary. A 1795 account noted 'twelve pre-bendaries, of which the bishop is one . . . There are neither choris-ters, singing-men, nor organist. There are two vicars-choral, who are obliged to reside, but have no houses appropriate to their office . . . The dignitaries are not resident. There are now no prebendal houses; the ruins of the last remaining one were taken down some few years since.' The bishop served as dean and diocesan treasurer. There was one archdeacon. The only other diocesan officers were the two Chancellors and the Precentor.[10]

While Bishop of the neighbouring St David's diocese, Horsley re-established the office of rural dean. Thomas Burgess, succeeding him in 1803, found a thriving network of 'twenty Rural Deans, who make very minute reports of the state of the churches in their respective districts. Their assistance to the Bishop is, I think, capable of being turned to a very good account.'[11] Marsh followed suit. Van Mildert's 1821 Primary Visitation Charge mentions returns made by the Llandaff Rural Deans to Marsh in 1817 and to Van Mildert himself in 1819 and 1820. C. R. Sumner, Van Mildert's successor, reintroduced the office in his next diocese of Winchester.

Van Mildert found his rural deans' reports on 'the state of the parishes placed under their respective surveillance' useful but stark reading. Even after Marsh's attempts to stimulate church repair, fewer than one in five churches was 'in decent and respectable condition'. Less than a third of the livings had glebe houses at all, Van Mildert found, 'and of those which have any, a large portion are so mean, and so unimprovable, as to afford but too good a plea for non-residence . . .'[12]

Shortage of church room was 'less extensively felt in this Diocese than in most others', with exceptions: Merthyr Tydfil parish church, even after the addition of galleries, accommodated only about 900 people from a population over 18,000. In 1827, Van Mildert's membership of the Church Building Commission standing committee enabled him to secure Merthyr Tydfil a share of the Commissioners' remaining monies.[13]

Van Mildert served with Pelham of Exeter, Ryder of Lichfield and Law of Chester on a committee Queen Anne's Bounty set up in 1822 to list livings of annual value less than £50 and 'make recommendations for at last getting rid of them'. The committee discovered nearly 400, enabling the Bounty Board in 1824 'to bring them all summarily up to £50, and put them on the road to £60', but the problem of livings under £50 was not finally solved for another forty years.[14]

In 1821 Van Mildert created a stir by going to live in his diocese, renting Coldbrook House near Abergavenny. Marsh had never resided, nor in thirty-four years had his predecessor Richard

Watson, a Whig stranded by the long Tory ascendancy and by his own imprudence in voting for the 1788 Regency Bill.

Van Mildert held his Primary Visitation in August 1821: his Charge apologised for this 'much later period than I had at first intended', blaming the delay on 'the course of public events'. He had probably not previously set foot in the diocese, the journey into Wales being a major undertaking. His Charge derived its information from correspondence with 'several of the Parochial Clergy' and up-to-date official returns from the rural deans. History does not relate whether Norris, presented to a Llandaff prebend by Marsh, was in Wales to greet his new diocesan.

The Visitation, if delayed, was thorough. Van Mildert travelled round his diocese conducting local visitations and confirmations, 'hospitably welcomed and entertained by the principal inhabitants' at each stop. Ives claims his 'Christian urbanity and conversation . . . won the hearts of all who met him', but a later passage suggests, chiefly by omission, that Van Mildert was not much loved by 'the Presbyterians and others, within his Diocese'. This is hardly surprising: his Charge declared the increase in numbers of Dissenting chapels 'a growing evil', reminded his clergy of their ordination vow to 'banish all erroneous and strange doctrines', and expressed the 'hope . . . to bring back them who have already strayed from the fold'.

Van Mildert saw these as innocent commonplaces:

We concede toleration freely and fully: we claim only to be equally unmolested in our own privileges, and thus to preserve the relations of peace and amity. What more does Christian Charity require? Or what further advances can be made towards an interchange of good offices, without a compromise on one side or the other, or perhaps on both, of sincerity and truth?[15]

He seems to have had a genuine blind spot where the sensitivities of Nonconformists were concerned. Because he could sincerely say that he never intended to insult them, Van Mildert was always honestly surprised when people unchurched by his views showed a disposition to resent it.

Dissent was strong in the diocese. 1812 official figures showed twenty-one Anglican churches and chapels, forty-two Dissenting chapels.[16] Welsh Nonconformity, the driving force that launched the Bible Society, flourished in profusion: Van Mildert discovered 'with regret . . . that in this Diocese, besides numerous congregations of Calvinists, Wesleyans, Independents, and other sects of frequent occurrence, there are found, in the remoter parts of it, some few Socinian or Unitarian places of worship', which he regarded as tantamount to open Infidelity.

Van Mildert cautioned his clergy against naked bigotry: 'Towards our Dissenting brethren, intent as many of them undoubtedly are upon promoting in common with ourselves the great purpose for which the Gospel was imparted to mankind, it behoves us to demean ourselves with charity, with good-will, with respect.' They were not, however, to be treated as equals.

For Van Mildert Dissent presented continual threats of liturgical and ministerial anarchy. He attacked the 1823 Dissenters' Marriages Bill, allowing Dissenting places of worship to be licensed for weddings, because it established neither means to identify Dissenting ministers entitled to conduct marriages, nor a duly approved form of service.[17]

Determination not to compromise with Dissent fuelled Van Mildert's struggle to secure ordinands with respectable academic qualifications. Like Marsh before him, he insisted on those who were not Oxbridge graduates studying at one of the two divinity schools in the diocese, at Cowbridge and Usk. Van Mildert kept himself informed of these two schools' activities, doing what he could to regulate their proceedings and improve standards.

During Van Mildert's episcopate, Bishop Burgess was busy with founding St David's College at Lampeter to serve the St David's diocese. The College opened on 1st March 1827, by which time Burgess had been translated to Salisbury and Van Mildert to Durham. Van Mildert's 1827 Charge commended Lampeter: 'an establishment which offers to the students many of the peculiar advantages of academical discipline'.[18] Sumner agreed to accept Lampeter graduates as qualified for Orders.

Working with Bruce Knight as examining chaplain, Van Mildert gradually but steadily increased the stringency with which his ordinands' 'religious, moral, and literary fitness for the sacred office' was assessed. He required Bruce Knight to examine every candidate's Welsh language ability: 'I should not think of licensing any person to a Curacy, or of instituting any person to a Benefice, where that language was necessary to the pastor, without being assured of his competency . . . and every candidate should understand, that without a proficiency in Welsh, his sphere of utility, and consequently of admissibility in my Diocese, must be very circumscribed.'

Even his nephew Harry Douglas was warned: 'I fear this promotion will enable me to be of little service to those who are not skilled in the *Cambrian* tongue, which you may take as a hint to begin studying that harmonious language at your leisure hours.'[19]

Although Van Mildert seems not to have gone so far as to learn Welsh himself – Burgess tried, with mixed success – he organised Welsh versions of several SPCK tracts.

Van Mildert actively promoted the SPG, 'the Society for the enlargement and rebuilding of Churches and Chapels', and the Diocesan and District Committees of the National Society and the SPCK, warning loyal members of 'our ancient and venerable Church' against 'popular and captivating associations . . . formed, on the acknowledged principle of obliterating every mark of religious distinction'. His Charge hoped 'the time is at hand, when none among us need complain that Evangelical light and truth must be sought elsewhere than within the pale of the Church of England'. Although his personal finances were still parlous, he was a generous supporter of diocesan charities 'in accordance with Church principles', particularly the 'Charity for the Relief of the Widows and Orphans of necessitous Clergymen'.[20]

Besides commending the National Society, Van Mildert's Charge exhorted his clergy to set up 'those humbler Village Schools, by which some portion of instruction may be imparted to every individual of your flock'. His 1820 Charity Schools Sermon was an emphatic if qualified defence of mass education, arguing that intellectual advancement was good both for the individual and for society 'when associated with that RELIGIOUS PRINCIPLE, which stamps its real value'. Those who wished 'to leave the Poor in a state almost destitute of mental cultivation' were guilty not merely of wishful thinking – the educational machine was already in motion and could not be halted – but of 'odious selfishness'.[21]

R. A. Soloway seems to have overlooked these passages in forming his judgement that

Van Mildert, as one of the prelates least able to come to grips with post-war England, in contrast to most Church leaders of the 1820's and 1830's rarely mentioned the question of lower-class education. As far as he was concerned, it had proceeded far enough, and he could not abide the receptivity of his colleagues to plans for still greater expansion . . . Not even the security of the National Society and its dedication to Church principles reconciled Van Mildert, and his coolness towards the schools was only exceeded by his bitter hostility to reform of any kind.[22]

As a bishop, Van Mildert had an automatic seat in the House of Lords. He made his maiden speech on 10th December 1819, the sole episcopal contribution to the third reading debate on the Blasphemous Libel Bill: his Boyle lectures, still much esteemed – a third edition appeared in 1820 – made him clearly the episcopate's leading expert on blasphemous libel.

Blasphemy, though an age-old offence, now wore an 'entirely new aspect':

It was formerly limited to books of infidelity and free-thinking, which fell into the hands only of persons of education, who could resist their influence or refute their errors. In the present times, blasphemous and infidel productions were brought down to the level of the meanest capacity – learning and argument and reason were discarded, and the meanest understanding joined to the grossest ignorance assumed the privilege of abusing what the most cultivated and sublimest minds had defended and venerated. There was no reason in that called the 'Age of Reason'.[23]

The character of these publications made it 'vain to suppose that they could be put down by legitimate reasoning or fair argument', and 'the distribution of moral and religious tracts' and the 'efforts [of] . . . ministers of religion' while valuable as counter-measures, were 'not alone sufficient'. It was time to try 'the terrors of the law'.

In May 1820 Van Mildert joined the Lords defence of Bishop Pelham of Exeter, under Whig attack for refusing testimonials to a Devon curate who in supporting 'Roman Catholic claims' had publicly declared that ninety per cent of Anglicans signing the Thirty-nine Articles disbelieved the Athanasian Creed's damnatory clauses. Van Mildert protested the lack of consideration for Pelham's feelings, who had acted 'only in the strict discharge of his duty'. A rancorous debate climaxed with the Earl of Carnarvon's assertion that 'they who did believe' the damnatory clauses 'could not be Christians'; a procedural motion forestalled Pelham's reply.[24]

In January 1820 George III's death at last made the Prince Regent George IV, and the disastrous condition of his marriage became a State matter. Liverpool's government offered Caroline a pension in exchange for permanent exile; her champion Henry Brougham kept

this information from her, and she returned to England on 5th June
to claim her rights as Queen. A Bill of Pains and Penalties was
drawn up degrading and divorcing her for adultery with her Italian
chamberlain Pergami. The 'wronged Queen' gave popular discontent with King and government a rallying-point: Parliament was
lavishly petitioned on her behalf, and the Bill's passage through the
Lords proved expensive in window-glass. Testimony as to the state
of bedsheets was gravely debated amid widest publicity: Archbishop
Vernon Harcourt of York lamented 'how deeply the interests of
religion and morality must have been injured by the introduction
into every family, of such odious and disgusting details'.[25]

The Bishops were faced with declaring an opinion on a case where
nobody was unambiguously in the right. Ecclesiastical disagreements proliferate around divorce, and the debates exposed deep
differences within the episcopate. On the facts they were virtually
unanimous: even Vernon Harcourt, the Bill's staunchest episcopal
opponent, agreed that the Queen had committed adultery, and the
King's marital shortcomings were undisputed: he had abandoned
his wife a scant year after their wedding, and his subsequent liaisons,
some doubly adulterous, were common knowledge. The bishops
chiefly differed over the propriety of the divorce clause.

Vernon Harcourt declared the whole proceeding repugnant to
both 'impartial justice' and Scripture, dishonouring 'not merely a
civil contract, but a solemn ordinance of religion'. The evangelical
Bishop Ryder of Gloucester opposed divorce because the Queen had
been refused proper means of defence. The Archbishop of Tuam
revived an argument of Horsley, who had assisted Caroline at the
time of the original separation:[26] that the King could not expect
relief because he had put his wife away. Marsh proposed a compromise solution annulling the Queen's civil matrimonial rights while
retaining her religious ones; whatever this may have been intended
to mean in practice, nobody took it up. These four, and six other
bishops, voted against the divorce clause at the committee stage. It
was retained by 129 votes to 62. York, Tuam and Gloucester then
voted against the third reading.[27]

Manners-Sutton, Howley and Van Mildert voted consistently for
the Bill, with all clauses. Caroline's conduct was not at all such as to
command their sympathy. The Attorney General revealed that she
had been attending Roman Catholic Mass with Pergami, 'such was
her abandonment of those religious feelings and rites, which ought

to be observed by all persons under all circumstances'.[28] She had made common cause with the Radicals: her principal Commons supporters were Hume, Brougham and Tierney, and from mid-July 1820 Cobbett wrote her speeches.[29] Her view of royal dignity and decorum was incomprehensible to High Church bishops.

All three thought the divorce issue simple. Van Mildert put the argument most concisely: 'according to the law of the country, he knew of no other cause of divorce than adultery, and no other punishment for adultery than divorce; and, as to the Christian law, it certainly provided that dissolution of marriage might take place in any case of adultery'.

Manners-Sutton was more emphatic: divorces 'were expressly declared to be lawful by our Saviour himself'.

Uneasy at the Queen's even stronger case against her husband, Howley tortuously explored the constitutional maxim 'that the king could do no wrong', which 'would seem to remove all ground for recrimination, all inquiry into the conduct of his majesty in his conjugal relations', before denying that he meant to argue from this principle. He added the scarcely diplomatic reminder that 'there were many instances of bills of divorce having passed that House, though the conduct of the husband was notoriously reprehensible'.[30]

Howley's luckless excursus on 'the king can do no wrong' was 'calculated to act as a conductor to direct the electric fluid of public wrath upon the heads of the bishops'.[31] The nine bishops who voted for the Bill's third reading attracted greater fury than the ninety and nine Lords Temporal who did likewise. Had the Church not bowed to the King's order omitting the persecuted Queen from prayers for the Royal Family?

Van Mildert spoke and voted against the Queen. When, after the Government abandoned the Bill, he returned to Ewelme, 'a tumultuous crowd of country-people' attacked the parsonage, 'hurled stones at the windows, and were with difficulty deterred from further acts of violence'.[32] Since Van Mildert had 'within the last two years entirely renewed a very stout & high Wattle Fence along one Side of the Premises, & built a substantial high Brick Wall on one Side of the Garden',[33] there may have been previous incidents.

Van Mildert and Jane decamped to Christ Church leaving the curate, their nephew Henry Douglas, in charge of the Rectory with a warning 'not unnecessarily' to 'incur the enmity of such malignant spirits as haunt the parish of Ewelme'. Van Mildert published a handbill defending his actions. An 'abusive paper' was pasted up in reply.

The Oxfordshire authorities treated the mini-riot casually. By 23rd November Van Mildert had little 'expectation of any disclosures respecting the perpetrators of the late outrage. It is more for public justice than for private redress that I wish the offenders to be found out. For their own sakes too it is, in one respect desirable, since impunity too often hardens the offenders, & tempts them to similar or even worse conduct.'[34]

On 17th November the Queen's personal representative, Hon. Keppel Craven, announced to the Lord Mayor of London that Her Majesty proposed attending public worship at St Paul's on Sunday 26th November, to give thanks for her deliverance from prosecution.[35] This was never intended as an act of devotion; it was a demonstration of popular triumph.

The news reached Van Mildert at Christ Church on 19th November. 'Fully resolved that he would in no way sanction what he could only regard as "a mockery of religion & an insult to the Church", he was yet somewhat perplexed how to act without danger of exciting a riot, and acts which might desecrate the sacred building.'[36]

He wrote at once to Liverpool and Home Secretary Sidmouth urging 'some Interference on the part of His Majesty's Government' to avert 'incalculable mischief'.[37] While these letters awaited posting, Van Mildert received the Queen's official notification: 'two letters from Mr Keppel Craven'.

The letters have not survived, but Keppel Craven's style is sufficiently clear from his letter of 18th November to Liverpool on the forthcoming prorogation of Parliament: 'Defeated in their first attempt, disgraced in the Eyes of the People, consigned to the contempt of all Europe, deserted by the most rational & respected of their adherents, they [Liverpool's government] meditate a new attack on the Honor of the Queen . . .'[38]

Liverpool also heard from Keppel Craven but sent no reply. Van Mildert, less wary, sent a note which 'informed the Queen's officer of the ordinary times of Divine Service'.[39] Keppel Craven handed it straight to *The Times*:

We have been informed, from a quarter which leaves no room to doubt the authenticity of a statement otherwise hardly credible, that the answer which the Bishop of Llandaff returned to the Queen's communication, made by the Hon. K. Craven, was carefully worded so as to exclude all those expressions of courtesy which the ordinary forms of civilised life prescribe in the correspondence between gentlemen. Who or what Bishop Van Mildert may originally have been, it is unnecessary to conjecture, and might possibly be fruitless at this late period to inquire. But rudeness of the nature described to us it is difficult to suppose could be the effect of habit merely, since men who are raised to high station in the Church, without any claims either from birth or merit, transgress, for the most part, on the side of indiscriminate servility, instead of failing in the observance of decent respect to their superiors, especially such as are superior to them in the former of those two qualifications.[40]

'Bishop Van Mildert's letter' made him briefly a household name. Readers of *The Times* learned that 'his father was formerly an eminent distiller in Blackman-street, Southwark, a man eminent likewise for piety and charity' from a letter which added 'I would that the son were as much distinguished for the latter virtue.' On 29th November the paper printed a satirical verse.[41]

Liverpool replied to Van Mildert by reporting the content of his own letter to Dr Hughes, the St Paul's Canon in residence for 26th November, making Hughes, not the Dean, responsible for all arrangements. It was 'quite impossible for the Govt. to prevent the Queen going to any Public Church to which she may think proper to resort during the regular time of Divine Service, nor would a remonstrance be likely to have any other effect than to confirm her in her Determination'. Hughes was instructed to conduct the service 'in the usual manner, without alteration or addition, or without any deviation from the accustomed course'.[42]

Liverpool also gave Van Mildert permission, on the double grounds of ill-health and work pressure, to miss the prorogation of Parliament on 23rd November. Van Mildert was busy preparing his departure from Oxford to come into residence at St Paul's on 1st December, and his function at the prorogation would have been purely ceremonial.

Soloway renders this exchange: 'During the tense coronation of George IV in 1820 Van Mildert was so frightened that the Queen would cause a riot at St Paul's that Liverpool told him to stay at Llandaff till it was all over. He did.'[43]

George IV was not crowned until 19th July 1821 (and Van Mildert was present),[44] the original date, 1st August 1820, having been abandoned on the Queen's return. While Van Mildert may have foreseen the disorderly scenes at the prorogation, the two reasons he gave Liverpool for staying away are more plausible than fear. Van Mildert was no coward. As to Liverpool's telling him to stay at Llandaff, he was, as his letter makes plain, in Oxford.

Van Mildert naturally absented himself from the controversial service. Liverpool's bluff 'hope that you will remain where you now are until the beginning of next month' maybe underlined this. Although Joshua Watson advised that 'since the Queen's rank was now recognised, and the prosecution abandoned, she should be received with all the outward respect due to her title',[45] it was a charming and eirenical nonsense. The Bill of Pains and Penalties might be abandoned, but since no reconciliation between King and Queen was even faintly probable, graceful public gestures by the Church would be merely inept. Moreover, the charges found proven against Caroline could not casually be forgotten, whatever political expediency might dictate about Pains and Penalties. Van Mildert would hardly assist a notorious adulteress to give thanks for escaping the punishment he had declared she merited, nor lend decanal and episcopal countenance to the triumph of a political faction he saw as dedicated to overthrowing the Church.

In the event, Caroline attended Mattins on Wednesday 29th November 'accompanied by the Common Council of the City of London and a guard of honour composed of 1,000 gentlemen on horseback'. The hapless Hughes had a trying day, but Van Mildert's fears of riot or sacrilege proved unfounded. *The Times* noted sourly: 'The Bishop's throne and the Dean's seat were not occupied at all, both these reverend dignitaries having written to the Lord Mayor, prohibiting them from being used.'[46]

At St Paul's, Van Mildert launched into an ambitious programme of repairs and improvements to both Cathedral and Deanery. When it came to plumbing he was a radical reformer, installing a 'new water closet' in the Deanery and extorting the Chapter's consent to a bold 'experiment' of heating the choir, where cathedral services were conducted. Here he faced problems familiar to twentieth-century colleagues: disastrous convection currents and unheatable roof spaces, contractors always busy with other projects, and vexed decisions whether 'entirely inclosing the Choir' would 'very much disfigure the edifice'.

There was also finance. Van Mildert promised the Chapter his experiment would involve them in no expense. Liverpool offered government assistance, but by 1823 Van Mildert felt the project's success was so modest as scarcely to justify it. The heating machines poured warm air up into the Dome, 'the cold air . . . consequently descending with such force as to be almost intolerable to those who officiated in the Choir'. At best, running the machines constantly 'outside the hours of service' might raise the ambient temperature and reduce damp.[47]

While the builders were in the Deanery, Van Mildert and Joshua Watson undertook joint tenancy of a house in Great George Street. The arrangement suited all concerned, lasting until the Van Milderts moved into the Deanery early in 1823.[48]

Watson was awarded an honorary Oxford LL.D. in 1819 as recognition of his work for 'the community at large, and . . . the Church in particular', and his 'munificent support of all those institutions which give stability both to Church and State'.[49] Watson, whose veneration for scholarship accompanied a sharp sense of his own educational inadequacies, was more shocked than pleased and tried hard to decline 'a distinction to which services of a very different order from mine can rarely aspire'. Bullied into submission by representations 'that the refusal would be so unprecedented a thing, that it would really painfully embarrass his friends, and be liable to misconstructions which all would regret', he never used his new title.

The Great George Street house, Churton notes, 'was soon made famous by the choice society which it assembled together, some of the best and ablest and most distinguished characters in the sacred and learned professions . . .' The Hackney Phalanx was prospering: John James Watson was Archdeacon of St Alban's, Cambridge Archdeacon of Middlesex. Thomas Rennell the younger became Christian Advocate at Cambridge in 1816. Park was Justice of the Common Pleas in 1816 and knighted the same year; Richardson, Justice of the Common Pleas in 1818 and knighted the following year. In 1820 Christopher Wordsworth became Master of Trinity College, Cambridge, D'Oyly succeeded him as Rector of Lambeth, and Mant was consecrated Bishop of Killaloe.

There were recruits as well: the elder Thomas Rennell, Dean of Winchester, an intimate of Norris; Charles James Blomfield, Rector of St Botolph's, Bishopsgate, who became Archdeacon of Colchester in 1822 and Bishop of Chester in 1824; John Lonsdale, another Manners-Sutton chaplain.

In June 1823 the Phalanx gathered at Bartlett's Buildings for Reginald Heber's official send-off as second Bishop of Calcutta. The choice of Heber for Middleton's successor 'rather than . . . a zealous parish priest or studious divine' raised Hackney eyebrows; besides being Evangelical, he was thought too young and insufficiently earnest; but the farewell meeting was a success.

Manners-Sutton spoke. Churton, evidently an eye-witness, noted 'the grave and dignified address of the aged primate, and the eloquent and expressive answer of the newly-appointed missionary bishop'.[50] Van Mildert wrote afterwards 'The impression of yesterday's delightful business still glows upon my mind . . . It was everything that the purest taste and the most unaffected piety could desire.'[51] Heber died less than three years after reaching his diocese.

This was one of the last Phalanx assemblies at Bartlett's Buildings. Gaskin's thirty-eight year secretarial reign ended in 1823; in 1824, arguing insufficient 'accommodation for the General Meetings, and indeed for the daily transaction of the Society's increasing business', SPCK moved to Lincoln's Inn Fields.

The loss of Bartlett's Buildings, place of so many good memories, prefigured other losses. During the Twenties the critical solidarity between Phalanx and Saints which had marked joint ventures in the great years gradually disintegrated.

In 1819, year of the Blasphemous Libel Bill, SPCK struck its own blow against cheap Radical literature by forming an Anti-Infidel Committee. This Committee, financed by a public appeal which raised £7,000, published and distributed 'Books and Tracts against Infidelity and Blasphemy'. In less than a year, 'nearly a million copies' were circulated.[52]

A second Anti-Infidel Committee was set up in 1830, but this time the magic failed to work. Its virtual failure led, in 1831, to the founding of a Committee of General Literature and Education, charged with publishing 'all kinds of useful and interesting works' to counteract cheap periodicals from other sources, notably the provocatively-named Society for the Diffusion of Useful Knowledge founded by Radical educationalists in 1825. Its recommendations were to prove contentious.[53]

1831 saw a first trial of strength when Joshua Watson, backed by the Phalanx, successfully blocked a 'well-known manual of the pious Dissenter, Dr Isaac Watts' from being placed on SPCK's list of approved literature. Van Mildert and Watson saw 'admitting a separatist to a place among the Church's teachers' as a breach of principle, whatever the personal merits of the separatist concerned. They carried the point, although H. T. Powell complained privately to Norris that the alleged principle had not stopped inclusion of Watts' hymns 'upon the Society Catalogue', nor 'many extracts from the works of dissenters' in the annotations of the SPCK Family Bible.[54]

Watson and Norris next succeeded in defeating the General Literature Committee's proposal to produce 'cheap Commentaries on the Bible in penny numbers' and 'a poetical version of the Epistles and Gospels', but control was slipping from their grasp. Watson, whose much loved wife Mary died in June 1831, began to find the Society's internal conflicts intolerable.

Blomfield, translated to London in 1828, tried to take a mediating position between High Churchmen and Evangelicals; some years earlier his personal intervention had won reversal of a decision to reject Charles Simeon's application for SPCK membership. In the early part of 1833 he wrote to Watson, pleading

that you will not forsake us; for I am perfectly sincere when I assure you that, in the present unsettled state of men's feelings and opinions, I do not think our two great Societies can go on well without the balance which is supplied by your experience and judgment. I am quite sure, that even those individuals who have been most opposed to your views on some important questions would be among the first to deprecate your retirement . . .

In vain: Watson resigned as Treasurer on 2nd July, officially for health reasons.

A florid official farewell followed, Howley and Blomfield eulogising Watson's services, Van Mildert's tribute 'appealing to the experience of forty years of his own uninterrupted friendship with him'. Watson 'could not prevail upon himself to encounter such a scene by being present'.[55]

In August, H. J. Rose wrote to Christopher Wordsworth: 'Lyall and I are very anxious that when the Society has paid its public mark of respect to Mr. Watson, his *friends* [twice underlined] in the Society shd. (quietly) pay him an exclusive mark of their respect to wch. no one shd. be asked to contribute but those who agree about him, & about the usage he has met with. We thought that if £1000 cd. be raised to found a Divinity Scholarship in his name, it wd. be acceptable to him.' Rose asked Wordsworth to discuss the suggestion with Norris, but otherwise to keep it a 'profound secret'.[56] What came of this is not known.

In October 1833, Newman cited 'the present state of [the] Christian Knowledge Society' as part cause for 'a growing feeling that Societies are bad things'.[57] The following March, A. P. Perceval wrote to Newman that the SPCK, 'which is virtually getting to be the Council and mouthpiece of the Church', was 'exercising the functions of a Synod by putting Bishops and clergy on their trial for heterodoxy and heresy . . . They are now actually sitting in judgment upon Bishop Gray of Bristol and the late Bishop Heber . . .'[58]

On 1st April, Newman gave a more detailed account of the Society's 'melancholy plight': 'The Evangelicals, taking advantage of the distracted state of the Church, are making a push to get their way in it – and the Bishop of London . . . temporizing, conceding ½ way, and so making matters clear for their ultimate triumph.'[59]

A tense meeting was held at Lincoln's Inn Fields on 8th April. Newman, protesting that the 'organs of the innovators profess they account the doctrine of baptismal regeneration *heretical*', was heavily involved in rounding up High Church attendance, but afterwards reported the meeting 'very sad . . . To the old stagers like Joshua Watson, it must be very painful indeed.' The triumph of the Evangelicals was marked by the setting-up of an SPCK Tract Committee.[60]

Van Mildert was probably at the meeting: he later reported to Bruce Knight 'I opened my mouth . . . at Lincoln's Inn Fields, to deprecate an unhappy spirit, which is getting the ascendancy there in our venerable Society.'[61]

Van Mildert kept up his scholarly interests after leaving Oxford. He prepared thoroughly for his parliamentary duties: notes on an 1822 Bill 'for the better preventing of Clandestine Marriage' included lengthy abstracts from Warburton on the nature of the marriage vow, Stebbing on the proper limits of state control over the validity of marriages, Gibson's Codex on laws respecting marriage, Ibbetson on the Marriage Act of 1754, and parliamentary debates of 1753 and 1689 concerning marriage legislation.

In 1823 he published his most durable piece of scholarship, a ten-volume edition of the works of Daniel Waterland (1683–1740). Churton described it lavishly as 'one of the most masterly and perfect pieces of ecclesiastical biography which the Church of

England has yet produced'. For some decades 'Van Mildert's Waterland' held the position of a classic.[62]

G. F. A. Best sees Van Mildert's massive scholarly labours of love as exercises in soft-centred antiquarianism: 'Controversies had to be dead – stone-dead – before they gripped Van Mildert; and then he dug them up like a ghoul, reconstructing with delicate and loving skill the historic triumphs of orthodoxy.'[63] Certainly Van Mildert devoted the bulk of his 'Review of the Author's Life and Writings' to charting the different controversies which engaged Waterland, explaining the positions taken by Waterland and his opponents, and relating the different arguments briefly to their historical context. He became fascinated by Waterland's 'Arian' opponent Dr Samuel Clarke, observing that Clarke 'disclaimed the character of an Anti-Trinitarian; and appears to have been firmly persuaded, that the doctrine of the Trinity was a true Scripture-doctrine'.[64]

Van Mildert's intentions were however not antiquarian. He hoped by 'facilitating to less-informed students . . . a readier insight into the ecclesiastical history of a brilliant period in our Church annals' to 'promote the interests of pure and sound religion' in his own day. Trinitarian doctrine was a highly strategic contemporary battleground, and Van Mildert thought it

scarcely possible, that any reader of solid understanding, not warped by prejudice, or attached to error by some more unworthy motive, should rise from a careful and attentive perusal of Dr. Waterland's writings, without feeling himself more strongly rooted in the faith, better able to vindicate its truth, and more internally satisfied in adhering to it as the guide of life.[65]

P. B. Nockles interprets Van Mildert's decision to identify himself publicly with Waterland's writings as a statement of alignment with a Waterlandian view of Church–State relations rather than the 'stream of high churchmanship . . . represented by the later Non-jurors'; Nockles links this with Hurrell Froude's increasingly hostile characterisation of Van Mildert as the last of the 'school of Water-land'.[66] J. C. D. Clark makes Van Mildert's choice of 'the greatest theologian of Gibson's Church–Whig alliance' exemplify the efforts of 'traditional, pre-Tractarian High Churchmen . . . merely to preserve as much as could be preserved of previous theology and practice', by contrast with Tractarian strivings 'to distance the Church from the State'.[67]

In 1823, living under a government for which he felt deep respect, Van Mildert still accepted a powerful doctrine of State–Church engagement: he was to give this its strongest expression in his 1825 Lords speech against Catholic Relief. It was not until the Hookerian concept central to Van Mildert's ecclesiology had been irretrievably overturned by the legislative changes which ended the decade that he found himself driven to doubt Waterland's middle way.

Van Mildert's respect for Waterland was no sudden conversion. Churton credits Van Mildert with the 'short literary notices' prefaced to the two Waterland tracts in the first volume of *The Churchman's Remembrancer* (1802);[68] citations and quotations of Waterland writings pepper the Appendices to Van Mildert's Boyle and Bampton lectures. Although not slavishly in agreement with him, Van Mildert valued Waterland's 'ardent zeal for the truth, under the discipline of a sober and well-regulated judgment, and of feelings equally remote from lukewarmness and extravagance'.[69] It seems probable that, by claiming this redoubtable Whig as a theological and political ally, Van Mildert hoped to alert a broader Church constituency to the dangers of Radical free thought and anti-Trinitarian Dissent, and mobilise them in defence of the embattled Church–State Alliance.

Van Mildert clearly felt strong affinity for Waterland, like himself a vigorous, but not a venomous, controversialist. His defence of Waterland anticipated the arguments of his own biographers: 'Whatever imputations of bigotry or uncharitableness may . . . have been cast upon him by those who felt themselves unable to cope with him, the general good-humour and even suavity of his disposition are attested in the strongest terms by those who most intimately knew him.'[70]

The Waterland memoir was finished on 19th September. By October, Van Mildert was critically ill.[71] He underwent 'a severe surgical Operation' in January 1824, a serious matter in the days before modern anaesthesia and antisepsis; Waterland had died a lingering death from an operation for an ingrowing toenail. Van Mildert's pain after the operation inspired him to write a devotional poem discounting his sufferings against those of his Redeemer.[72]

He convalesced slowly, missing the Lords' April debates on the Unitarian Marriages Relief Bill and the important May and June debate on the affairs of Ireland and the Irish Church. May found him at Fulham, 'enjoying the sweets of this delicious retreat with the highest possible gratification. Yet I cannot boast of any material amendment.' He was not well enough for the journey to Coldbrook House that year. Llandaff had no 1824 ordination, and the planned second Visitation was deferred to 1825 due to the Bishop's 'painful and distressing malady'.[73]

Van Mildert returned to his duties at St Paul's before the end of the year, only to find himself deaf. He wrote to Joshua Watson:

If this should continue, my taking the chair at the meeting you speak of will be quite out of the question. Yesterday morning I could neither hear the responses of the Litany, nor of the Commandments, and was obliged to blunder on by guess as to the proper time of interposing my part of the service. Should this continue, there is an end of me as a public man, or even as a member of society.[74]

The deafness persisted with varying severity for the rest of his life.

In the spring of 1826 Shute Barrington, thirty-five years Bishop of Durham, was on his deathbed. Liverpool cleared the choice of Van Mildert as successor with George IV in early March; a vacancy in the Palatine See had serious civil consequences and must be kept as short as possible.[75]

Barrington died on 25th March. By evening Liverpool had made the offer and Van Mildert had accepted. Howley wrote to Liverpool 'I . . . entirely approve of the translation of the Bishop of Llandaff to Durham . . . I know no man who possesses in a higher degree all the qualities essential to the character of a Christian Bishop.'[76]

Van Mildert's appointment offered irrefutable proof that under Liverpool's administration, 'merit and morals were now at least as weighty qualifications for the highest preferments as birth and connexion'.[77]

As Bishop of Durham he was also Earl Palatine of Durham and Earl of Sadberge. His humble origins were noted in the diocese. The prominent Newcastle barrister James Losh, meeting Van Mildert for the first time in 1828, thought him 'an amiable man. His manners are good which is not often the case with men who have been raised to high situations from low beginnings.'[78]

The formalities surrounding Van Mildert's translation from the poorest see to the richest after Canterbury were completed by 24th April. The ceremony of Installation and Inthronization was performed in Durham Cathedral on 30th May 1826, the Prebendary of the First Prebend, Thomas Gisborne, acting as Van Mildert's proxy.[79]

Legal business halted by Barrington's death could now be resumed. During the vacancy 'no juries could be summoned (the Sheriff being only in office during the life of the Bishop) and therefore the Sessions were necessarily adj[ourne]d for the trial of prisoners'.[80] C. J. Clavering was reappointed High Sheriff. His resignation in 1833 gave Van Mildert the responsibility to appoint a successor, and much grief with it.

Pomp and ceremonial were the hallmarks of Van Mildert's new palatine rank, and he coped with them to general admiration. His triumphal entry into the diocese on 14th July 1826 was a masterpiece of traditional pageantry from the crossing over Croft-on-Tees bridge into County Durham, greeted by 'about forty other carriages besides a large cavalcade of horsemen, and some hundreds of people on foot', to the final arrival at Auckland Castle escorted by an honour guard of 'about 30 or 40 horsemen' who 'preceded us to the Castle Gate and there drew up on each side in rank and file while we passed through them into the Castle Court . . .'[81]

It was a long way from Llandaff, a sudden and substantial dislocation, and Van Mildert's letters to Bruce Knight suggest a certain wistfulness. Writing to give Bruce Knight the news of his translation, Van Mildert expressed 'regret . . . on quitting a Diocese, where I have received such invariable kindness and attention, and have derived so much real satisfaction. More especially do I feel this with regard to yourself, and continually am I wishing that I may be fortunate enough to meet with such an one in Durham, to be my constant friend and coadjutor . . .'[82]

Van Mildert found his coadjutor in Charles Thorp, a former Fellow and Tutor of University College, Oxford. Made Rector of Ryton in 1817 when his father Robert, Archdeacon of Northumberland and Rector of Gateshead, vacated it in his favour, Thorp acted as 'official' to Archdeacon Prosser of Durham. Although they had a common friend in Charles Lloyd, Van Mildert never met Thorp until his own arrival in Durham; Thorp was then forty-three.[83]

Much of their correspondence survives, characterised on Van Mildert's side by warm affection. When in December 1831 Archdeacon Prosser's resignation finally gave Thorp the office as well as the work, Van Mildert gleefully wrote to him 'My dear *Archdeacon* . . .', adding in his next day's letter the hope that Mrs. Thorp 'bears "meekly" the honour of being an Archdeacon's Lady . . .' While Thorp's terms of address are always correct and respectful, his letters frequently include friendly enquiries about personal matters. By 1831 Thorp was well established as Van Mildert's confidential 'adviser and prime minister'.

At Durham Van Mildert had two domestic chaplains: his long-standing friend and protégé T. L. Strong, and C. J. Plumer, a fellow of Oriel. Henry Douglas' brother Robert Archibald Douglas-Gresley became his personal secretary and in due course succeeded T. H. Faber as diocesan secretary. Douglas-Gresley, educated at Rugby, was 'admitted a Solicitor, and practised in the Temple' before accepting the position with his uncle. He was clearly able, being retained by Van Mildert's successor Maltby, a Whig nominee very unpopular with High Tories, and by Maltby's successor.[84]

Although by the standards of his own day Van Mildert was certainly no nepotist, his use of patronage shows a few instances of classical nepotism, and rather more of 'extended nepotism': preferment of friends and their families. As Bishop of Durham Van Mildert exercised enormously valuable patronage, even if he protested that it by no means afforded 'such frequent opportunities as seems to be imagined, of satisfying the many claims upon me for Preferment'.[85]

Virgin, examining the extent of nepotism in the Georgian church, observes disapprovingly 'the tenets of conventional morality' which dictated 'that it was a clerical parent's duty to provide for his offspring'.[86] Van Mildert's own career owed its first impetus to family loyalty: Cornelius Ives gave him his first benefice, his uncle William Hill secured his first major promotion. It would have been the act of an ingrate to repudiate a similar family responsibility when Van Mildert acquired influence of his own.

Here as in other branches of his life, however, Van Mildert put the needs of the Church above all else. He never gave preferment to anyone, family or not, whom he thought unsuited to it; and in general, none of his protégés let him down. The chief exception was his nephew William Ives, whom Van Mildert priested himself in a private St Paul's ceremony in 1825, and of whom he once remarked to Thorp 'I have sometimes said, the only person I regretted having brought into the Diocese was the Vicar of *Haltwhistle*.'[87]

Van Mildert preferred Gaisford, his foster son-in-law by marriage to Helen Margaret, to the full extent his patronage allowed; but the kin-tie was the least of his reasons for doing so. Van Mildert thought Gaisford combined 'being among the first scholars (perhaps, the very first) in Europe' with 'the most estimable qualities in private & social life, & would fill any station whatever in the Church with real credit and respectability'.[88] Since Van Mildert saw cathedral dignities principally as 'objects of fair & laudable ambition, to persons of . . . learning & talents', awarding Gaisford the best prebend in his gift was only logical.

Of his five other nephews in Holy Orders, Van Mildert gave preferment to only one. William Ives' brother Cornelius had the family living at Bradden. Van Mildert took a cordial interest in the volume of sermons Cornelius published in 1832, wrote him affectionate letters, sent Christmas gifts of money for distribution among 'your flock, (some of them formerly of my flock also)', and left him at Bradden.[89]

Four of Van Mildert's Douglas nephews were ordained. The only one to receive preferment was Helen Margaret's brother Henry.[90] Having proved himself as Van Mildert's domestic chaplain and Ewelme curate, Henry was given the Gloucester living of Newland, and in 1825 made Rural Dean, Prebendary and Precentor of Llandaff. Van Mildert brought him into the Durham Diocese in 1832 to be Rector of Whickham. Henry's private merits were maybe not so powerful as the fact of his being the Bishop's nephew, but he was able and diligent, performing his duties to the satisfaction of all concerned. In 1833 Bishop Ryder of Lichfield, who knew him from his own days as Bishop of Gloucester, asked to be remembered to Henry 'as one for whom he entertains sincere regard'.[91]

Politically, Van Mildert arrived into a situation governed by a powerful conviction that the Durham clergy were lined up along the stockade confronting the local Radical establishment.

A series of trials of strength over first Peterloo, then the Queen Caroline affair, climaxed in a celebrated libel action brought against the newly founded Radical-financed *Durham Chronicle*, and in a 'controversial and unsuccessful' attempt to unseat the MP for Durham County, 'Radical Jack' Lambton (afterwards Lord Durham). The 1820 controversies transferred the conflict to a national canvas. The protagonist on the Church side was Henry Phillpotts, Bishop's Chaplain and Rector of Gateshead, whom Barrington rewarded in 1820 with the 'plum' Rectory of Stanhope. Lambton was backed by his friend Henry (later Lord) Brougham and his father-in-law Earl Grey, whose seat at Howick was also in the Durham Diocese. Phillpotts was nephew-by-marriage to another powerful national figure: the ultra-Tory Lord Eldon, a native of Newcastle, who until 1827 was Lord Chancellor. The duels stirred deep political passions both locally and nationally, attracting wide publicity, which the politicians handled more skilfully than the priest.

The Durham clergy won their libel action but were generally admitted to have lost the propaganda war.[92] Assisted by the continuing attentions of the *Durham Chronicle*, the Durham clergy, and in particular the Durham Chapter, acquired a reputation of mythical proportions for pluralism, non-residence and unseemly opulence. The myth, indeed, reflected its share of truth. Durham had the best-paid Dean and Chapter in the country, and a substantial number of the diocesan clergy, including Phillpotts, were rich non-resident pluralists. It did nothing to sweeten the atmosphere when, in an 1827 tangle of ecclesiastical chess-moves, which Van Mildert tried unsuccessfully to resist, Gerald Valerian Wellesley, the Duke of Wellington's 'image in a surplice' and younger brother, added a Durham prebend and the rich rectory of Wearmouth Episcopi to his already ample preferment.[93]

Wellesley was instituted to Wearmouth on 1st June and collated to the prebend on 18th July. At the end of September Wellington himself visited the Marquis and Marchioness of Londonderry at their seat Wynyard, near Stockton. The visit became a triumphal progress through the North-East, a Wearside and Tory equivalent to the immense 1822 celebration on Tyneside when the Duke of Sussex, 'the Most Worshipful Grand Master of the Ancient Freemasons of England', laid the first stone of the Newcastle Literary and Philosophical Society's new building.[94] Van Mildert and Jane made a special journey from Harrogate to attend the magnificent initial banquet at Wynyard. Before returning to Harrogate they secured Wellington's promise to be the guest of honour at Durham Castle on Wednesday 3rd October.

Of all Van Mildert's episcopal acts of hospitality, the Wellington banquet was the most renowned. The civic authorities joined in the razzamatazz. Wellington was met at Framwellgate Moor by 'a number of men with pink ribbons round their hats, lettered "Wellington for ever!"', appointed to draw the celebrated warrior into Durham'. 'See the conquering Hero comes' was played to salute his arrival, 'the people loudly cheering, cannon roaring, and bells ringing'. In front of the Town Hall stood a 'commodious' platform approached by an arch of laurels and flowers and a display of laudatory banners, the largest of which was six yards long. Wellington received addresses from the Mayor and Corporation and from the Citizens of Durham on the platform, then an address from the Magistrates and Gentlemen of the County was delivered by the Hon. W. K. Barrington on the steps in front of the County Courts. Ladies watched from temporary seating erected inside the Town Hall, whose windows had been removed to give a better view. Wellington then

re-entered, with the Marquis and Marchioness of Londonderry, the open carriage, amid the cheering of an admiring multitude, and was drawn by the populace to the Bishop's Castle, where the Duke was received by his lordship and his Chaplains, and almost immediately took a hasty view of the Cathedral and College, whilst the company were assembling at the Castle.[95]

The banquet was all that the occasion demanded. The *Durham County Advertiser* said it 'united all the sumptuousness of a noble banquet, with the comfort of a private entertainment'. The Van Mildert Papers preserve sheafs of bills for everything from hire of twenty-one dozen wine glasses to fluting of doors with crimson moreen and 'covering door way with crimson Drugget', from $27\frac{1}{2}$ pounds of Cheshire Cheese to an intolerable deal of alcohol. Besides Canon Wellesley, the guest list included a galaxy of nobility, Bishop Bethell of Gloucester, the Archdeacons of Northumberland and Richmond (but not Durham), and 'nearly 100 of the principal Gentry and Clergy of the County'. The feast was held in the Great Hall; Jane Van Mildert, although the *Advertiser* deemed it not worth a mention, entertained 'the ladies' elsewhere in the castle.[96]

After the removal of the cloth and the rendition of 'Non Nobis Domine' by the Cathedral choir, the serious drinking began. Toasts were drunk to the King and the Royal Family; the choir sang the National Anthem; and Van Mildert proposed the toast to Wellington in a speech carefully worded to be generous in its praise of 'the Illustrious Guest' while 'avoiding every topic which could have excited a jarring sentiment'.[97] The most inflammatory phrase Van Mildert permitted himself was to offer the Great Captain 'that humble tribute of veneration and gratitude, which is due from every one who knows how to value the blessings of our admirable Constitution in Church and State'.

Some among his hearers must have been disappointed by this moderation. The pink ribbons and banners, pink being the local Tory electoral colour, make quite clear the party nature of the civic celebrations, and the Duke's progress through the North-East had blatant political overtones. Waterloo was twelve years past: the 1827 lionising owed less to past vainglory than to present anticipation. The mixed administration of Canningites and Whigs which had taken office after Lord Liverpool's stroke in April, fatally weakened in August by Canning's death, staggered towards dissolution; Tories saw Wellington as the prime minister in waiting. Van Mildert, whatever his personal political preferences, was however no party man: 'had Van Mildert been indisposed, and . . . Prebendary Henry Phillpotts done the honours instead, the rafters would have rung to louder loyal cheers, and Whiggery perhaps been given some notable snub'.[98]

Van Mildert further blunted the party edge by taking the opportunity to honour another of his guests, 'a native of our Sister Country . . . with whom I have this day, for the first time, become personally acquainted; but for whose incomparable writings I have long entertained . . . the highest possible admiration', not least because 'his unrivalled talents . . . have invariably been employed in upholding what is good and excellent, and have never . . . been perverted to a sinister purpose'.[99] The Bishop kept his listeners waiting until the end of the speech for the mystery guest's name: Sir Walter Scott, also visiting in the neighbourhood. Scott 'expressed his thanks with evident emotion, . . . saying, that he must ever consider it one of the proudest moments of his life, that he was praised by the Bishop of Durham, in his own hall, when he was entertaining the Duke of Wellington'.

Howley wrote to Van Mildert's chaplain T. L. Strong: 'The Bishop's manner of receiving his illustrious guests has been much spoken of, – and I have heard disappointment expressed that no detail of the Speeches has appeared in the London Papers: – Perfect as was the entertainment with all its accompaniments, the Bishops [sic] admirable demeanour, & eloquence, are said to have outshone every other part of the celebrity . . .'[100]

Van Mildert was an instinctive Tory; he once wrote a rhyming fable 'The Mastiff, the Fox, & the Wolf', which described how the Whig fox leagued with the Radical wolf had taken advantage of the master's gullibility to drive the faithful Tory mastiff from his rightful post as guardian of the State castle, and declared that matters would never go well again until the restoration of 'old Trusty to the Castle Gate'. Despite his conscientious efforts at moderation – or at least not to be caught taking sides: he was willing to help fund a 'Conservative paper', the *Newcastle Journal* founded in 1832 to counter the *Durham Chronicle*, provided his involvement could be kept secret[101] – Van Mildert failed to escape the overall pattern of confronting Whigdom. In April 1831 he clashed sharply and publicly with the new Grey government on a matter of his secular jurisdiction.

The spring of 1831 was a time of high tension in the North-East coalfields. The 1830 founding of the Colliers' 'United Association of Durham and Northumberland' led on to preparations for mass industrial action aimed at securing specific improvements in the pitmen's working conditions: an end of the colliery-viewers' right to lay the pits idle for up to three days at a time without compensating the men, a shorter working day for boys to give them some hope of education, relief from the notorious 'tommy-shops' system. The great miners' strikes of 1831–2 at their peak saw some 17,000 men idle.

Because local Radical Whig gentry, no less than their Tory counterparts, made their money from coal, they were not keen to see this democratic manifestation succeed. The *Durham Chronicle* carried references to 'the infatuated pitmen, dupes as they are of a set of artful and designing rogues'.[102] When the 1831 Commission of the Peace was prepared, local Whigs pressed for suitably respectable senior colliery officials to be made magistrates.

Van Mildert, who served *ex officio* as Custos Rotulorum for the County, considered this and found it inadvisable. The Bench objected strongly to the intrusion of 'Coal-Owners' Agents', protesting that 'it is well calculated to induce an apprehension among the Pitmen that they are not likely to obtain an impartial hearing & unbiassed Decision, from the Magistracy in any differences which may arise between them, & their employers'.[103]

This touching concern for the pitmen's confidence, which cynics might doubt whether the Durham magistrates enjoyed to quite the degree they claimed, was a prime example of the paternalist apologetic whereby high Tories – including, on occasion, Van Mildert himself – saw themselves as the poor's truest defenders.[104]

Defeated locally, those determined to stiffen the Durham and Northumberland magistracy behind the coal-owning interest appealed to Lord Chancellor Brougham.

On 2nd February 1831, Brougham wrote to Van Mildert 'as one of your former flock & brother benchers – & as joining with all others in the sense of Your Lordships learning, talents & worth', to query one of the names proposed for inclusion in the roll of County Magistrates. He also 'suggested' the insertion of a further 'three (or four)' – in fact six – names recommended by his own (unnamed) contacts in the County.[105]

Four of the names had colliery connections. Brougham acknowledged this in only one case: John Buddle of Penshaw, Lord Londonderry's agent and one of the best-known figures in the North-East.[106] 'Mr. Buddle is the celebrated viewer & surveyor & has an influence with certain Classes – very likely to prove beneficial in these times.' Henry Moreton, described as 'an excellent agriculturist & a literary man, whom I have long known', was Lord Durham's colliery agent; Henry Stobart of Pelaw and William Bell of Sunderland, mentioned without comment, were both colliery officials. The other two names were uncontroversial, 'if numbers be thought desirable'.[107]

Van Mildert's reply was the very flower of courteous intransigence, acknowledging Brougham's 'obliging expressions' and begging permission to present him with a copy of the *Lincoln's Inn Sermons*. The original list had been drawn up in careful consultation with the Chairman of the Quarter Sessions, the High Sheriff and 'other Magistrates of high respectability'; it provided a more than sufficient number of names; might not the six be kept for 'some future Commission'? If Brougham forced the issue, Van Mildert was 'perfectly ready to acquiesce'; only, he would feel bound to make the government interference public.[108]

Brougham never replied. The Bishop of Bristol, a Durham prebendary, had a related discussion with Lord Durham, who 'intimated some urgent Necessity for the Insertion of the Names of some Gentlemen connected with the Collieries'.[109]

On 9th April, as coalfield tensions built towards explosion point, Brougham's Secretary of Commissions wrote directly to the Durham Clerk of the Peace, demanding assurance that the six names had been inserted.

John Dunn, Deputy Clerk of the Peace, replied simply that they had not, and sent a full report to the diocesan secretary T. H. Faber, who sent it immediately to Van Mildert in London. Dunn also consulted J. R. Fenwick, a senior magistrate. Fenwick appealed to Losh, who 'had not heard the subject mentioned before', and wrote to Brougham urging that 'Colliery Viewers' were not 'proper men for Justices of the Peace'.[110]

Indignation ran high at Brougham's underhandedness: Thorp, also a magistrate, was briefed by Fenwick; he thought the 'unusual, & I believe unprecedented proceeding' conveyed 'a most undeserved censure upon the Custos', a view generally shared. A meeting of magistrates at Gateshead on 16th April passed resolutions expressing entire confidence in Van Mildert as Custos Rotulorum, opposing the colliery agents' appointment, and urging the Lord Chancellor to act only in co-operation with Van Mildert. Rowland Burdon, a senior magistrate, wrote to inform Lord Londonderry that if the colliery agents were appointed to serve as magistrates 'in the Coal district, where they are interested', he would not serve as their assessor. The High Sheriff, C. J. Clavering, wrote to Van Mildert, 'Should the Lord Chancellor please to put their names into the Commission without your Lordship's approbation, I shall intreat your Lordship to request the Lord Chancellor to strike mine out of it and I believe that others will follow my example.'[111]

The postal time lag between London and Durham meant it was 15th April before Van Mildert learned of the 9th April letter. He immediately requested a meeting with Brougham and Lord Durham to discuss the matter, but received no reply until 18th April.

A second letter, demanding the Commission of the Peace by return of post for insertion of the names on Brougham's authority, reached Dunn on 17th April. It caused uproar in Durham. Brougham's action was extraordinarily high-handed; Dunn told Van Mildert he had 'never before received Directions from the Chancellor, or any of His Lordship's Officers, regarding the Commission of the Peace'.[112] Thorp enlisted Gaisford, made a Durham Prebendary two years earlier. They agreed Brougham should be challenged in Parliament. Gaisford sent Peel a 'succinct narrative of the facts', writing by the same post to Van Mildert:

The Ld. Chancellor works so rapidly that a day's post was not to be lost if any good were to be expected to accrue from the communication . . . This business alone is enough to shew what we are to expect from the Whigs, but here I think they have overstrained themselves – for their own party has now taken alarm, and is enraged I am told beyond measure at the step.[113]

Rowland Burdon wrote to Van Mildert on 18th April:

The State of the Collieries begins to be awkward, and it is made more so by the circumstance of their original complaints being in several instances too well founded. The total neglect of Education, & a want of feeling, in some Collieries, for the necessities of the Pitmen, have laid the foundation of much Mischief. I hope still to be able to avoid making use of the Military.

The same day, with details of the Gateshead magistrates' meeting and personal letters from several magistrates to hand, Van Mildert sent Brougham a careful summary of the objections and an unambiguous refusal to insert the names. This at last brought a hastily scrawled reply: Brougham, regretting that he had received Van Mildert's earlier 'kind note too late to avail myself of it', acknowledged 'new letters from Durham & Newcastle throwing much doubt on the expediency of coal agents being in the Comn.'

On 19th April Van Mildert received news of the second letter to Dunn. He immediately wrote warning Brougham that forcing the issue would mean 'many respectable Magistrates now in the Commission will cease to act'. He also took an unprecedented step on his own account, notifying Dunn's London agents that 'those names were sent up to them without the Bishop's knowledge or concurrence'.[114]

Brougham capitulated, pleading a misunderstanding: he had never directed any name to be inserted in any Commission of the Peace without the recommendation of the Custos Rotulorum, if the fiat for the insertions had been issued without Van Mildert's recommendation 'it was through a manifest mistake', and he had directed the fiat to be withdrawn. The correspondence closed with written confirmation from the Secretary of Commissions on 20th April.

This fiasco came just as the first Reform Bill reached its tumultuous climax in the House of Commons: the Bill was withdrawn on 21st April following a government defeat on an amendment, and on 22nd April Parliament was prorogued, with extraordinary scenes in both Houses. Losing this fringe skirmish to his foes of the Durham ecclesiastical establishment rankled with Brougham. From now on Van Mildert was indelibly a Radical bugbear.

During the 1832 General Election which followed the Reform Act, the *Durham Chronicle* accused him of using 'the whole weight of his secular influence' against John Bowes, candidate for the new electoral division of South Durham.

Bowes, acknowledged illegitimate son to the Earl of Strathmore, was a prominent local land-owner who outraged Tory opinion in April 1832, four months after appointment as a deputy-lieutenant for Durham county, by declaring in favour of Parliamentary Reform. The *Durham Chronicle* gloated: 'The Tories have long calculated upon making this young gentleman their rallying point in the county; but the spirit of the times is too powerful . . . Their disappointment will be excessive.'[115]

Bowes' second electoral address was appalling to Van Mildert. Besides demanding 'wide and searching reform' of disparities in clerical income, 'non-residence, pluralities and sinecures, the mode in which tithes are collected, and the prostitution of clerical preferment to political purposes', Bowes declared 'disabilities in religious faith' indefensible; 'one man should not be made accountable to another for his belief'.

In a poll with no Tory candidate, Van Mildert's views could have influenced Tory voters; but South Durham was a notorious den of Liberals. The Darlington Quaker Joseph Pease topped the poll; Bowes was elected in second place; Van Mildert's supposed protégé, Robert Duncombe Shafto, came last.

In 1833, High Sheriff Clavering resigned after an accident. Van Mildert initially favoured Robert Surtees of Mainsforth as successor, but ruled him out on discovering he had 'presided or made himself conspicuous' at Bowes' election dinner. Another possibility was W. L. Wharton of Dryburn: 'my only fear is that I shall be vehemently assailed for honouring an *ultra-Tory*. But I think I could bear this reproach, better than the *credit* I might get for setting up a Whig-Radical . . .' Despite government pressure for a quick appointment, Van Mildert spent nearly three months on fruitless overtures to more moderate local dignitaries before plumping for Wharton.[116]

Van Mildert's Primary Visitation, in the summer of 1827, took a full month. He kept the Sundays free of official business, spending the first at Ryton Rectory with Thorp.[117]

Van Mildert began his Primary Visitation Charge with a generous eulogy of his predecessor, whom he had earlier described to Bruce Knight as 'my late venerable friend'. The Honourable Shute Barrington, thirty-five years Bishop of Durham, has been called 'a fine example of the harmless and even meritorious clergyman who owed great preferment entirely to family interest'.[118] A conscientious and energetic bishop, imaginative in his personal charities and an indefatigable supporter of religious and philanthropic societies, regardless of ecclesiastical hue, he liked to sign letters to his clergy 'Your affectionate Brother, S. Dunelm'.[119] Within the Diocese of Durham he contributed generously to educational causes, endowing the Barrington School at Bishop Auckland. He also created the Barrington Fund to augment small benefices and help needy widows and orphans of Diocesan clergy.

Despite personal esteem for Barrington, Van Mildert deplored aspects of his diocesan administration: 'many things require to be scrutinized and rectified', he wrote in October 1826.[120] Like Barrington, Van Mildert committed himself to meeting the spiritual needs of such expanding urban centres as Sunderland, Gateshead and Stockton. He made it clear at the outset, however, that he was prepared to allow much less latitude than his predecessor in the means employed. All was to be done in decent Hackney order, as near as could be managed. Van Mildert added a characteristic commitment to countering the spread of Primitive Methodism in the mining communities; Barrington's approach had been less abrasive.

The 1827 Charge indicated Van Mildert's most urgent specific anxieties. Barrington had encouraged the building of schools, but had shown little concern for their affiliations. Van Mildert took this rapidly in hand. In 1831 his second published Charge reported not only twenty-seven new schools founded, but also eighty-five previously existing schools 'united to the National Society'.

Van Mildert set about tightening up standards of learning and doctrinal soundness in his clergy. He urged the importance of ensuring proper licensing for curates. A bishop needed to 'know with certainty who are the actually officiating Clergy of his Diocese', in order to be able to 'exercise that effectual superintendence over them, which is one of the most important functions of his office', and protect curates suffering 'real' grievances. Using unlicensed curates risked introducing 'exceptionable persons into the Diocese, of whose character and qualifications sufficient evidence may be wanting'. Van Mildert announced his intention to accept as ordinands, 'with as few exceptions as possible', only graduates of Oxbridge or of the theological college founded at St Bees in 1816 by Bishop Law of Chester.

Accommodation for public worship was another major concern. Barrington took action after a 'Report of Church Accommodation in the Archdeaconry of Durham' Thorp compiled for him in 1824 revealed that the archdeaconry's parishes averaged church-room for only one in five of the population. Barrington attempted to provide new plant – eight churches were built during his episcopate – but also, in the particularly hard-pressed parishes of Stanhope, Darlington and St Andrew's, Auckland, licensed schoolrooms for Sunday afternoon worship.[121]

Van Mildert abhorred the practice of licensing unconsecrated buildings:

In some special cases this may perhaps be, at present, the only practicable expedient for supplying the spiritual wants of the people. But that it is, in some respects, an evil, can hardly be denied. Places of religious resort so little consonant with the solemnity of the purpose tend, if not to create irreverence for religion itself, yet to diminish . . . respect for the Established Church.

He was also anxious lest widespread use of secular buildings for worship undermine support for the Church Building Society, a diocesan branch of which was founded by the Anniversary Meeting of the Sons of the Clergy in September 1827 after the Visitation was completed. Van Mildert's Charge appealed for 'increased efforts to erect and endow a sufficient number of regular Chapels of Ease', promising his own 'best endeavours' in support.

Van Mildert's ten-year episcopate saw fourteen new churches built, opening the way for the still larger church-building programmes of Victoria's reign. He contributed generously from the episcopal revenues, and would also have had a hand in the Church Building Commission's grants to projects at Winlaton, Bishopwearmouth, Hetton-le-Hole, South Shields and Deptford. His enthusiasm helped to stimulate a surge of building activities. By 1831, in addition to the fourteen new places of worship built or in process of construction, thirteen were 'rebuilt, or greatly altered and enlarged' and eight more in the pipeline.

He also gave attention to the perennial problem of clergy accommodation, subscribing to a number of parsonage-building projects. Progress to 1831 included four new glebe-houses built, four 'rebuilt or considerably enlarged, and three more . . . proposed to be built'.

In addition to the work on bricks and mortar, plans had been made to divide seven parishes, producing new parishes of more manageable size; ecclesiastical districts were being established in three more. Van Mildert took a particular interest in the twin ecclesiastical districts of Shildon and Etherley, carved out of the enormous parish of St Andrew's, Auckland: he built and endowed Etherley's church, subscribed £200 towards building Etherley's parsonage, contributed to the Shildon church, and undertook to provide a Shildon parsonage, but died before he could keep this promise.

The 1827 Charge outlined the priorities which Van Mildert wished his clergy to make their own:

If Schools, if Glebe-houses, if Churches, be still wanting or defective; if any portion of your flocks still betray ignorance or error, in doctrine, in discipline, or in practice; if any thing be still requisite to relieve the wants, spiritual or temporal, of those who are committed to your charge, no past labours, however meritorious or successful, can supersede the obligation of additional efforts to complete the work of your ministry.

He recommended assiduity in the discharge of pastoral duties: 'not only such as relate to the public ritual of the Church, and your discourses from the pulpit; but also the visiting of the sick, the instruction of the ignorant, the consolation of the afflicted, the relief of the necessitous, and the education of the poor in the principles of our Established Church'. Joining the Anglican Societies, he suggested, would be a sure guide to carrying out this programme effectively.

The Durham clergy, hit by the Phalanx vision of the Church in its most ideal form, must have wondered just what was happening. Van Mildert was in a hurry. He had money at last, for as long as he could keep breath in his decrepit body; he saw the possibilities and the need for action with terrible clarity. In his ten years at Durham, most of them spent in constant pain, he poured the episcopal revenues into church-building, parsonage-building, stipend augmentation, public education. His correspondence shows many unostentatious gifts to people he considered deserving, even some he considered undeserving. Thorp estimated his private giving at £1,400 per annum, with 'subscriptions and other known charities' accounting for a further £2,600.[122]

This urgency had an explicit political context. Van Mildert saw his clergy in 1827 as engaged, whether self-consciously or not, in a struggle to defend the Church of England's political ascendancy. This understanding was 'sometimes almost forced upon us by our opponents themselves: who, however at variance with each other on

many essential points, declare their readiness to suspend, for a time,
their mutual disagreements, that they may more successfully cooper-
ate in one common purpose, that of . . . raising every religious sect
and party to a level with the Established Church'.

The Church's position would be saved or lost, Van Mildert
realised, by the place she held, or failed to hold, in the affections of
'the Laity'. 'Public esteem . . . is not to be extorted by arbitrary
mandates. It results from opinion, from observation, from comparison, from those mixed feelings and sentiments which, however
they may occasionally err, afford, upon the whole, a pretty accurate
criterion of real desert.'[123]

Van Mildert's diagnosis was a constructive one, and his prescription well worth trying. Unfortunately he was out of time. By the
time he delivered his second Visitation Charge in 1831, the battle for
Anglican political ascendancy had been decisively lost.

CHAPTER 5

And tumult of her war

In theory, Parliament in 1825 contained only practising members of the Church of England, the Church of Scotland or the established Church of Ireland. Protestant Dissenters were debarred by the Test and Corporation Acts, Roman Catholics by a patchwork of anti-Catholic legislation, from any active part in government. By 1825 the Test and Corporation Acts had been allowed to fall into abeyance. Roman Catholics, however, while no longer liable to penalties simply for professing their faith, were proscribed from serving as MPs, Crown ministers, judges or county sheriffs, and enjoyed no relief.

In England, Scotland and Wales this state of affairs was not particularly contentious. In Ireland it was a serious political grievance. An emancipation measure was widely expected to follow Pitt's Act of Union (1800), but the 1801 Catholic Relief Bill was abandoned in face of George III's opposition.

Throughout the first quarter of the nineteenth century, unsuccessful Bills and petitions for Roman Catholic relief punctuated the parliamentary calendar – Beilby Porteus debated one in May 1805.[1] By 1821, the principle of Catholic Emancipation commanded a majority in the House of Commons, 'despite the dominance of a Tory government committed to the union of church and state'.[2] The Lords still stood firm. The Roman Catholic Disability Removal Bill of 1821 fell by 120 votes to 159, the Roman Catholic Peers Bill of 1822 by 129 votes to 171, the English Catholics Elective Franchise Bill of 1823 by 73 votes to 80, the English Catholics Relief Bill of 1824 by 101 votes to 139.

On each occasion Bishop Bathurst of Norwich, now approaching eighty, rose to harrow the massed opposition of his fellow bishops. 'Christianity itself was a glorious innovation', he reminded them in 1823, warning 'the christian high churchmen of the present day, who were alarmed at the bare mention of any innovation in church or state . . . that a blind, doting, obstinate adherence to old establishments, resolutely opposed to all reform, was as weak and dangerous as a wild and irrational desire of change.'[3]

The only other bishop to break ranks was the Evangelical Henry Ryder, who supported the 1824 Bill on the ground that it conceded only the electoral franchise denied to English (but not Irish) Roman Catholics.[4]

Political exclusion was not the only Irish Roman Catholic grievance against the Protestant Establishment. The fact that the established but numerically small Church of Ireland enjoyed all the financial benefits of Church–State alliance, including tithe, caused deep anger. It was not paranoia that led opponents to interpret Roman Catholic emancipation as creating a substantial new Commons interest bloc dedicated to plunder the Irish Established Church.

In June 1824, the Irish Tithes Composition Amendment Bill gave both sides a platform. Bishop Jebb of Limerick strenuously defended the Church of Ireland clergy, claiming them an important role in repairing the damage done to the Irish social fabric by absentee landlords. Lord King responded with a scorching attack on the Church of Ireland, its wealth, its irrelevance to the Irish peasantry. Lord Liverpool 'said, that the remarks of the noble Lord withdrew the veil. The friends of the establishment would know now what they had to expect. It was no longer the granting a few more political situations; nothing would satisfy but the total destruction of the church establishment in Ireland.'[5]

Van Mildert voted against the Bills of 1821 and 1822 but did not speak in debate. In 1824 he was asked for advice by a member of the commission set up to look at the state of educational institutions in Ireland and report on measures for mass education. Van Mildert was pessimistic about 'bringing up Papists and Protestants together in the same schools'; he thought a joint syllabus for religious education not merely unattainable but undesirable:

having long been of opinion, that an honest avowal of diversity of sentiment in matters of religion, (provided it be not maintained by absolute intolerance and persecution on either side,) is preferable to . . . insincere professions of unanimity, which can only serve to throw one or the other of the parties off their guard, and probably make the better and unsuspecting among them ultimately victims of the crafty and insidious.[6]

Co-operation posed practical difficulties: Roman Catholics used a different translation of the Bible, regarding the Protestant versions as heretical; catechisms and formulae of interpretation likewise differed, while to use the Bible 'without note or comment' would be as unacceptable to the Roman Catholic authorities as to Van Mildert himself. Van Mildert felt that any arrangement would necessarily be precarious, more likely to foster confusion than community.

The 1825 Bill, besides Catholic Relief, offered sops to Protestant anxieties by providing for State payment of Roman Catholic clergy, thus giving the State a degree of control and removing one main motive for asset-stripping the Church of Ireland, and by abolishing the Irish forty-shilling-freehold franchise. This Bill passed its third reading in the Commons by the unusually large majority of 284 to 227, and the 'Protestant party' viewed it as a serious threat. Petitions against the Catholic claims were organised. On 13th April Van Mildert presented the Lords with the petition of the archdeacon and clergy of the Oxford diocese. Bishop Carey of Exeter had one from Totnes. Blomfield, now Bishop of Chester, brought one from the Manchester clergy, also an 8,000-signature petition from the magistrates, clergy and inhabitants of Bolton-le-Moors containing 'some stigmas . . . on the Catholics, of which he did not approve'. Further petitions were presented on 18th April by the Archbishop of Canterbury, Blomfield and, with his own expressed dissent, Bathurst of Norwich.

On 25th April, presenting the petition of the dean and canons of Windsor, the Duke of York went so far as to blame George III's illness on the agitation for Catholic Emancipation.[7]

On 17th May the Roman Catholic Relief Bill was presented to the Lords for its second reading. Van Mildert was the first bishop to speak in the debate, and his speech achieved instant celebrity. Published by Rivingtons, it was widely circulated and was, Ives says, 'generally . . . esteemed his principal speech' in the House of Lords.

Van Mildert opposed the Bill on the principle set out in Marsh's 1814 *Comparative View of the Churches of England and Rome*, that Roman Catholics, owing allegiance to a human and earthly ruler outside the jurisdiction of the British State, could not be admitted to participation in the British political process without destroying the relationship between Church and State on which the whole constitution was founded. The same argument had enabled his Hutchinsonian spiritual forebears to accept the Act of Settlement.

Van Mildert elaborated this by a distinction of Horsley's between two component parts of spiritual authority, Order and Jurisdiction. Order, which the State neither did, should nor could exercise, was 'that power which confers the capability of exercising spiritual functions': the power to preach, to baptise, to administer the Eucharist, to ordain, to confirm, to consecrate. Jurisdiction, the power to appoint 'particular persons to exercise spiritual functions throughout the State', to regulate their conduct, determine their remuneration and settle other details of ecclesiastical polity, 'belongs to the State, as allied to the Church, and although exercised by the Church, is derived from the State'. Since the Pope exercised spiritual jurisdiction over Roman Catholics, their loyalty to the State rested on intrinsically less secure foundations than that of Protestants.[8]

Having drawn up this basic thesis at length, Van Mildert proceeded to bury his audience under a landslide of scholarship. He claimed support for his view from Laud, Stillingfleet, Jeremy Taylor, 'Leslie the non-juror', Hickes, Atterbury, the two Sherlocks, Horsley and Marsh 'among those who are commonly reputed to have been what are called High-Churchmen'. He then painstakingly demonstrated that opposition to Papal Supremacy was not confined to High Church circles, citing Archbishop Wake and the Anglican–Gallican conversations of 1718–19; 'Tillotson, Burnet, and Gibson, all strenuous opponents to Popery, yet sincere advocates of Toleration'; Locke, Hoadly and Sykes. He added Milner's strictures against Locke and Hoadly, with the comment 'So much . . . for the good-will which Papists bear towards writers whom . . . their Protestant friends are continually holding up as models of liberality of sentiment.' On Roman Catholic views of Papal Supremacy he, like Marsh, took Bellarmine as his authority, observing that 'Bellarmine was not in the best odour with the See of Rome, his notions of the Papal prerogatives not being sufficiently high'.

Van Mildert explained his own attitude to Roman Catholics: tolerant, as he himself understood the word. He claimed to respect, even esteem Roman Catholics individually and as a body, refused to question their personal integrity, carefully eschewed 'any hostile or unchristian feelings' towards them. However, he opposed all attempts to blur what he saw as very real differences between Roman Catholic and Anglican doctrine. Transubstantiation, the invocation of saints, 'image worship' were simply 'errors and corruptions of Christianity'.

To those who argued that Roman Catholicism had changed its nature and the days of sweeping Papal claims were long past, he retorted that 'there can hardly . . . be a greater cause of offence to a Roman Catholic, than to question the immutability of his faith'.

Having devoted thirty pages to theological reasons for opposing the Bill, Van Mildert gave one paragraph to the merely pragmatic. The Bill was intended to 'conciliate the Roman Catholics'. He seriously doubted that it would have any such effect on 'the lower orders, at least', and thought its likeliest outcome a renewal of acrimonious controversy between Anglicans and Catholics. 'I am too conversant with polemics, (perhaps have been too much of a polemic myself,) not to know that these contests unavoidably engender strife, and enmity, and bitterness, of which no one can foresee the termination.'

This was a political speech not an ecclesiological treatise, and Van Mildert made no attempt to elaborate the practical consequences of assigning 'the entire government of the Ecclesiastical Body' to 'the Legislative and Executive Government of the Country'. Like Horsley before him, he refused with abhorrence the doctrine that priests were 'the mere hired servants of the laity', and priesthood 'a part to be gravely played in the drama of human politics'.[9] Van Mildert's Bampton Lectures indicated the centrality he assigned to the priesthood within the Divine economy: 'if the Sacraments be not only signs or emblems of spiritual benefits, but the instituted means of conveying those benefits, – and if the ministration of the Priesthood, as a Divine ordinance, be necessary to give the Sacraments their validity and effect; then are these interwoven into the very substance of Christianity and inseparable from its general design'.[10] Without the power of Order, which for Van Mildert no less than for Horsley it was simply impossible for the State to exercise, there could be no Church. Bishop Bathurst, speaking next in the debate, was less than just to imply that Van Mildert was in danger of making establishment an essential part of the Christian Faith, a position which the Hackney Phalanx had always explicitly rejected.[11]

Van Mildert stood in a tradition that valued establishment, not as sustaining the Faith (whose security was eternal not temporal) but as sustaining the political constitution of 'almost every well-constituted government', and pre-eminently of Britain. He refused any pietistic principle that the Church should or even could hold herself aloof from secular politics, rather accepting Bellarmine's conception of the temporal and the spiritual as interconnected with the same intimacy as body and soul. Concerned to establish that Papal Supremacy was as dangerous to the British Constitution in the spiritual as in the temporal realm, Van Mildert was willing to say that the Church could not act independently of the State without directly infringing 'the temporal authority of the Sovereign'. He had already made it clear, however, that this depended critically on the permanent and inviolable establishment of a Protestant and Episcopal Church in England and Ireland. Establishment once breached, the whole 'alliance between Church and State' would be imperilled.[12]

The Lords refused the Bill a second reading by 130 votes to 178. Of the twenty-nine bishops voting, only King of Rochester sided (by proxy) with Bathurst in support of the Bill.

Catholic Relief's next direct appearance in the Lords was not until 1829. In 1826, a short parliamentary session followed by a general election meant that no Catholic Relief Bill was introduced, although in Ireland the election saw significant gains for the emancipationists (and blatant electioneering by Catholic clergy).[13]

Events in 1827 decisively altered the political map. In February, Lord Liverpool suffered a stroke which ended his career. Van Mildert felt 'a gloom and sadness . . . which I cannot dispel. God only knows what may be the result. In my estimation, no loss could have been so irreparable to the country, especially at this awful crisis, when matters of the highest importance, both to Church and State, seem to be hanging by a thread.'[14]

Lord Eldon saw the Duke of York's death on 5th January as yet more damaging to the 'Protestant party'.[15] The way was now open for Canning to head a coalition ministry committed to Catholic Emancipation. Nevertheless the position was far from clear: in March, shortly before Canning's ministry took office, Burdett's motions for Catholic relief were unexpectedly defeated in the Commons by a margin of four votes, and the Lords motions were dropped.

In August the situation somersaulted again. Out of the blue, aged only fifty-six, Canning died. His coalition promptly collapsed, to be replaced by a ministry with Wellington as Prime Minister and Peel as Home Secretary. There was one significant difference from the Liverpool administration: Eldon was dropped.

Astonished and alarmed, Eldon drew the obvious conclusion: Wellington and Peel were preparing to concede Catholic Relief.[16]

Wellington took office in January 1828, replying to a parliamentary question that the government had no intention of bringing forward a measure for Catholic relief. That same month, Howley gave a dinner in honour of the latest Hackney recruit to the episcopal bench: Charles Lloyd had become Bishop of Oxford.

January also brought Wellington the beginning of an unexpected correspondence. Henry Phillpotts, Rector of Stanhope, Dean of Chester and doyen of Durham anti-Radicals, 'had made his reputation as an anti-Catholic polemicist; now he wrote privately to the Duke with suggestions for ways of arranging a compromise'. His letters 'accepted that sufficient securities could be exacted to safeguard the Church', thus satisfying the arguments of his own 1828 pamphlet on the Coronation Oath. Phillpotts' change of direction was pure expediency: he told his uncle-by-marriage, Eldon, cynically that '"the true principles of the British constitution require that concessions should not be made", but circumstances "make it certain that, ere it is very long, concessions will be made"'.[17]

In February the Catholic Question took a novel twist. Lord John Russell announced his intention of moving for repeal of the Test and Corporation Acts, a proposal which he had made the previous May but postponed due to Government changes.

The Acts, which submitted members of corporations and Crown officers to the 'sacramental test' that they should, within the twelve months previous to their appointment, have received the Anglican Sacrament of Holy Communion, were, by 1828, in a decidedly frail condition, propped up by annual Acts of Indemnity to excuse the numerous breaches of their provisions. There was thus a clear common-sense argument for repeal. Moreover, there had always been theological objections that the Test incited Dissenters and Infidels to profane the Sacrament for the sake of gaining office.

Proposed at that juncture, and from that quarter, the Repeal Bill could not but be seen as a manoeuvre towards Catholic Emancipation. A number of speakers, in both Houses, explicitly made the connection; Eldon, indeed, had urged against the 1821 Catholic Relief Bill that it led logically to repeal of the Test and Corporation Acts.

Opinions as to the practical effect of Repeal on the Catholic Question varied, however. Some argued that it would strengthen the Catholic case; others, that it would stiffen the grateful Dissenters against Catholic claims.[18]

The government accepted Peel's proposal to offer moderate opposition. Lloyd, Peel's former tutor and continuing adviser, while not sanguinary about the ultimate chances of defeating it, urged Peel not to 'concede to the Dissenters' without first consulting some of the leading bishops – he suggested the Archbishop of Canterbury and Bishops of London and Durham – adding that 'it may be of great importance for you to be able to say afterwards that you acted with their sanction'.[19]

Lord John Russell's motion was carried by a majority of forty-four. Lloyd received letters from Van Mildert, asking 'whether we are to "succumb to clamour and vituperation" or whether we shall throw it out in the House of Lords', and from Blomfield, who, as Bishop of Chester, was rapidly establishing himself among the most able and energetic episcopal parliamentarians, wishing the bishops 'would consent to give them [the Acts] up with a good grace – and not have the repeal extorted from them, as it must be before long'.[20]

Peel took his own soundings among the bishops, concluding that Canterbury, Durham, London and Chester, 'though they may not be in precise conformity, . . incline to a permanent settlement of the Question now' and that Kaye of Lincoln, Copleston of Llandaff and Law of Bath and Wells were 'at least as favourable'.[21]

On 3rd March Van Mildert wrote Lloyd a letter which Lloyd, passing it to Peel, described as 'sensible and moderate'. He still wanted the Lords to reject the Repeal Bill, if only to give time for a better measure to be drawn up and presented with full governmental and episcopal support; he suggested that such a measure might originate in the Lords. His main concern, however, was that an appropriate means be devised for securing the ascendancy of the Established Church. He assured Lloyd, 'All I am anxious for, is to have some demonstration of affection & respect for the Church, in the Upper House, & on the part of the Govt. as a counterpoise or a check to the increasing spirit of disaffection to it in the Commons . . .'[22]

The need for the government and the bishops to agree an acceptable substitute for the sacramental test led to a meeting at Lambeth on 15th March, between Peel, both Archbishops, and the Bishops of Llandaff, Durham, London and Chester.

Peel wrote afterwards to Lloyd, 'We settled a declaration – which I think will go down in the House of Commons which we can carry against the dissenting interest there and will in my opinion or at least ought under all circumstances to be satisfactory to the Church.'[23]

Peel's declaration, drafted in the light of the Lambeth discussions, formed the main component of an amendment accepted by Lord John Russell for incorporation into the Repeal Bill at the first committee stage on 18th March.

The amendment dissatisfied Van Mildert for two reasons. In the first place, Peel's declaration bound the office holder not to use any power or influence possessed by virtue of his office to 'injure or subvert' the Established Church or to 'disturb it in the possession of those rights and privileges to which it is by law entitled'.[24] Van Mildert had argued at Lambeth for the omission of the qualification 'by virtue of my office', on the grounds that nobody sincerely well-affected to the Establishment would be unwilling to make the unqualified declaration; he failed to persuade Peel. In the second place, the Bill as amended gave the Crown discretion to determine who should or should not be required to make the declaration, a provision which had apparently not been agreed at Lambeth.[25]

Van Mildert pointed out that an unsympathetic Minister could exercise this discretion so widely as to vitiate the whole purpose of having a declaration. 'Or, the effect may be, that in some instances it may be enforced, in others dispensed with – of which, the consequence would soon follow, that to enforce it in any instance, would be deemed invidious & offensive.' The only effective remedy, Van Mildert held, would be to make the declaration mandatory in all cases.[26]

Having determined by enquiry that 'some of the most discreet, moderate, & influential members of our Church' shared his anxieties, Van Mildert wrote urgently to Archbishop Manners-Sutton before descending on Lloyd; he arrived 'at the same moment' as a note to Lloyd from Tournay, Warden of Wadham, making the same two points.[27]

Lloyd's position of mediator between Peel and Van Mildert was now a painful one, and his letters reveal his discomfort:

It is really of extreme importance to give what satisfaction you can to the high party both in the Country and the House of Lords – Van Mildert is manifestly alarmed lest the Bishops should be accused of truckling – he told me that two or three members of the H. of L. had said to him 'So I hear you have deserted us' & had added 'I am sorry you should have left us to fight the battle without you.'[28]

Peel and Van Mildert, in their turn, were each in difficult positions. Peel was being asked to amend a formulary of his own drafting after it had been publicly accepted by all parties, a solecism verging on the unthinkable; he was also irritated that Van Mildert should be so critical of a document based on agreements to which Peel 'understood him distinctly to be an assenting party'.[29] Van Mildert was nevertheless a valuable potential supporter whom Peel needed to conciliate if possible.

Van Mildert found himself caught between the government and the ultra-Tories, each of whom claimed to be defending the best interests of the Church, but whose chosen courses of action were mutually exclusive. His instinct was to side with the government, heirs of the Liverpool administration whose working relationship with the Hackney Phalanx had been so long and fruitful, but, to do this with a quiet mind, he had to satisfy his conscience that the proposed declaration really was a safe replacement for the sacramental test. Refusing the call to fight to the end in defence of the Church's rights made him deeply anxious. Peel's inflexibility towards the two criticisms only increased his disquiet.

The Bill's second committee stage was timetabled for 24th March. On 23rd March, having received no word, Van Mildert wrote to Peel direct. At about the same time the hapless Lloyd, who had been 'very unwell for the last week & confined to the house', visited by no-one but Van Mildert and Tournay, attempted to improve matters by sounding Peel out on the possibility that Van Mildert might put up an amendment to the Bill in the House of Lords. He went so far as to suggest a possible wording.

Peel jumped to the understandable conclusion that this idea had originated with Van Mildert and, furious, wrote back to Lloyd accusing Van Mildert of being terrified by the lay peers. He flatly refused to 'be a party to any amendment that the Bishop of Durham may move [in] the House of Lords'.[30]

Lloyd returned a cool reply, denying that Van Mildert had even known of the suggestions about an amendment. He was anxious that

Van Mildert should be able to give the measure full and warm support, he explained, partly because Van Mildert's sentiments were 'generally in unison with those of the Church of England', partly 'from my personal regard for him and my gratitude for his uniform kindness to me'.[31]

In the meantime Peel had written a patient letter to Van Mildert, reminding him that the declaration had been drawn up in good faith after very full consultation with the Bishops, explaining the impossibility of amending it and giving the reasoning behind the provisions for discretionary exemption. It would, Peel argued, 'bring the Declaration into ridicule' if it had to be subscribed by every Crown official, however menial or unrelated to Church matters his work might be. Exercise of the discretionary power would be regulated in detail, but by 'the King in Council from time to time' rather than by statute; this was the fruit of an amendment secured by Peel himself the previous evening.[32]

On 28th March Van Mildert 'called on Mr. Peel and had nearly half an hour's conference'. The discussion was amicable, and Van Mildert came away satisfied that he could support the measure as it now stood – 'though', he wrote to Lloyd, 'I apprehend we must expect some hard knocks from our high-church friends in the Upper House'. The letter closed with an affectionate enquiry after Lloyd's health: 'I hope your Leeches did their duty . . .'[33]

The Bill came before the Lords for its second reading on 17th April. Van Mildert, as he had agreed, rose to defend it, truthfully assuring their Lordships that he had 'laboured with great earnestness and sincerity, to satisfy myself that the measure now proposed may be acceded to, with safety and with credit to the Established Church'. The bulk of his speech was employed in defending the principle and practice of Establishment. Denying that a man's religious opinions could be considered irrelevant to his fitness for political office, Van Mildert defended the Bill on the grounds that by laying down in its preamble the permanent and inviolable establishment of the Church of England, and by substituting a serviceable political test for a religious test which was 'no longer a decisive proof of church-membership, nor, indeed, was it ever entirely so', its actual effect would be to preserve the Church's ascendancy.[34]

The speech reflected a less than total enthusiasm for the Bill, which Van Mildert hinted could do with further improvement in committee; he was careful to vindicate this alteration to the law governing Establishment 'on such grounds only as should fully warrant me in resisting any farther encroachments, which may hereafter be grounded upon this measure . . .'[35]

The bishops turned out in force to support the Bill. Among those who spoke in the debate were the Archbishop of York, offering Manners-Sutton's apologies through serious illness; Kaye of Lincoln; and Blomfield. Like Van Mildert, Blomfield defended the original framers of the Test and Corporation Acts against imputations of making unworthy use of the Sacrament, explaining the abuses as a latter-day phenomenon.[36]

The ultra-Tory peers were fully as angry as Van Mildert had predicted, accusing the bishops of suspiciously rapid changes of opinion, and of *naiveté* in supposing they could preserve the Established Church by tearing down her defences.[37] The attacks roused Van Mildert to a far more spirited defence of his position: he assured his critics that 'the alliance between Church and State did not originate with the Test laws', and that the question was 'not whether the fortress shall be surrendered, but whether the outworks shall remain as they were, or be reconstructed on a somewhat different plan'. His anxiety about the Bill was concerned, he explained, not with its provisions, but with those among its supporters who might view it as 'an incipient measure only, opening a way for some ulterior objects'.[38]

Anxious to avoid misrepresentation, Van Mildert had his speeches printed for private circulation, with the usual editorial assistance and moral support from Joshua Watson. He was concerned that his clergy should 'know what I actually did say, and judge of me accordingly'. He admitted privately to Watson that he still found the Bill 'anything but satisfactory', adding 'God knows, this whole proceeding has been a bitter pill to me, from the effects of which I shall not soon recover.'[39]

In May, Burdett again raised Catholic Relief in the Commons. This time the majority was six in favour. The Lords discussed a similar motion on 13th June, rejecting it by a majority of forty-four; but Wellington's speech made it clear that he was now personally convinced Relief must pass, and waited only for acceptable safeguards to be devised. Daniel O'Connell's election for County Clare made it brutally clear that unless Catholics were admitted to Parliament, the whole basis of parliamentary representation in Ireland risked destruction. Wellington's speech hinted strongly that the next Catholic Relief Bill would be government-sponsored.

Lloyd wrote to Peel on 15th June:

Now I tell you a secret. After the Debate on Tuesday, the B. of Durham took me home in his carriage . . . I said 'You will live now to see this question pass.' 'Perhaps so,' he answered, '& if this Administration chuse to bring forward the Measure, I have no objection; it will be a very different thing coming from them.' I only tell you this confidentially. My own opinion is with him.[40]

What Peel, himself still bent on resignation if the government should produce such a Bill, made of this extraordinary story can only be imagined. It is incomprehensible that Van Mildert could have made anything approximating to the remark Lloyd reports. In 1825, Van Mildert had committed himself publicly to opposing the principle of Catholic Relief, leaving himself no room for manoeuvre at a later date. He was unsatisfied with the government's handling of the far less contentious Repeal Bill. The cautions in his Repeal speeches against making that Bill the basis for any further tamperings with the privileges of Establishment clearly referred to Catholic Relief. Apart from this letter of Lloyd's, there is no indication that Van Mildert ever deviated from uncompromising opposition to every measure for political emancipation of Roman Catholics.[41]

In July, Manners-Sutton died. Writing to the King about the choice of a successor, Wellington identified Howley and Van Mildert as the two bishops 'who by talents, qualifications, and reputation, stand the highest'. Van Mildert 'would be preferable'; Howley, however, had the seniority, and Wellington recommended the King to prefer him, 'lest resentment might lead to a coolness between the persons filling the sees of Canterbury and of London'.[42] Howley's see of London was given to Blomfield.

Van Mildert's staunchness against Catholic claims may well have been the true reason for Wellington's choice. Although Howley had also committed himself against Relief, Chadwick suggests 'Wellington may have thought that if he was bound to have an archbishop opposed to Catholic Emancipation, it was best to have one who looked so easy to frighten'.[43] Van Mildert was also a much more effective public speaker, and his prestige with the parochial clergy was second to none.

After a slow start, Howley had been drawn into close involvement with the Hackney Phalanx, and the Phalanx greeted his elevation with pleasure – also with a determination to stiffen him for the coming battle. Van Mildert wrote from Auckland:

The unaffected grief & concern which I could not but feel on the loss of your late invaluable Predecessor . . . is much alleviated by the confident persuasion that the same undeviating & firm adherence to the genuine principles of our Church-Establishment . . . will characterise his Successor, & enable us, under Providence, to uphold those principles & those interests against the lukewarmness of it's friends, & the machinations of it's enemies, from both of which, we have, at the present crisis, but too much reason to apprehend extensive injury.[44]

Park was more blunt, reminding Howley that he was now to be 'spiritual head of the first Protestant Church . . . of the World', and calling upon him 'to advance the Glory of God, the welfare of the Church against all Popery, heresy & schism . . .'[45]

In August Wellington wrote to the King that 'rebellion was pending in Ireland; that in England the government was faced with a House of Commons it dared not dissolve which contained a majority who believed the only solution was Catholic emancipation'.[46] Wellington had himself opposed this solution in the past, but was now ready to yield to the inevitable. Peel, more deeply committed to the 'Protestant' interest and made doubly vulnerable by his position as Member for Oxford University, continued to struggle.

Wellington consulted some of the leading bishops in November, and reported them adamant against 'concession'. At the end of the year Lloyd was at Addington with three bishops, probably Howley, Blomfield and Van Mildert, and reported that they would not consent to Catholic relief in any form. 'Your individual position was not mentioned', Lloyd wrote to Peel, adding 'I must . . . take some time to think.'[47]

By 15th January, Peel was ready to accept the King's challenge and remain in office in order to see through the Catholic emancipation measure which he had come to believe was the government's only possible course. The choice, he explained to Lloyd, was no longer whether the Catholic Question should be settled, but whether or not the settlement should be 'favourable to the Protestant Establishment'.[48]

The decision cost Peel his seat as Member for Oxford University. At the end of January he consulted Gaisford and Dean Smith of

Christ Church in confidence as to whether, in view of his intentions on Catholic Emancipation, he should offer his resignation. 'Thunderstruck and very sad', they felt it essential to the integrity of his position.[49] In the ensuing by-election Peel was beaten by Sir Robert Inglis, and the Tory party managers had hastily to arrange a pocket borough for him. 'Phillpotts, who persisted in voting for Peel, became "the great rat" to the Oxford Orthodox.'[50]

Peel moved for Catholic Relief on 5th March. The Government's Bill offered a number of safeguards intended to preserve the position of the established Churches of England and Ireland: Catholics would continue to be excluded from specified high offices particularly closely concerned with ecclesiastical responsibilities, Catholic Members of Parliament would have to take a special oath, and other minor restrictions were imposed.[51] On this occasion the oath, again drafted by Peel, contained no qualifications: Catholic Members were to 'disclaim, disavow, and solemnly abjure any intention to subvert the present church establishment as settled by law within this realm' and 'solemnly swear' never to 'exercise any privilege to which I am, or may become entitled, to disturb or weaken the Protestant religion or Protestant government in the United Kingdom'. Furthermore, each must undertake to defend to the utmost of his power 'the settlement of Property within this Realm, as established by the Laws', and additional political security was furnished by the companion measure raising the property qualification for the Irish electoral franchise from 40s. to £10, thus removing much of the popular vote.

If Van Mildert had been willing in principle to accept an oath as a guarantee of well-affectedness on the part of Roman Catholics, this formulation contained more to commend it to him than that exacted from Protestant Dissenters. His opposition was, however, set at a level which no oath could hope to satisfy. He felt compelled to keep faith with the doctrine that Papal allegiance corrupted.

'I know not . . . how I can alter my conduct', Eldon wrote in 1825, 'without declaring the Revolution of 1688 to have been rebellion, and the throne to have been filled for a century by usurpers.'[52] Van Mildert faced the same impasse, but for him the stakes were higher still. He had also to justify the Reformation.

Peel was now convinced that Catholic Emancipation must come; his integrity as a statesman forced him to stay in power and do all he could to minimise the damage to the Protestant Establishment. Van

Mildert, too, was a statesman in his way; he had the best title of any bishop then alive to represent the mind of the Church of England. His position, however, gave him no power but persuasion with which to influence the course of political events, and negotiating with Peel over the Test and Corporation Acts had taught him a sharp lesson on the limits of persuasion. Faced with a measure which he abhorred, and which his contact with the lower clergy convinced him was widely regarded as betrayal by a previously friendly government, Van Mildert saw no possible gain from compromise. His own integrity thus forced him to a doomed but unflinching opposition to the Bill. Lloyd's position as intermediary had become untenable.

On 2nd April the Roman Catholic Relief Bill was presented to the House of Lords for its second reading, and Lloyd rose to defend it. The existing state of affairs was, he argued, impossible to maintain; although he personally 'should have seen with far greater pleasure, opinions taking a different course', 'the rising talent of the country' now favoured emancipation, while those who still opposed it had 'reached that time of life when most men have seceded from the busy scene of human life – when far the greater part, indeed, have been called away, altogether, from this sublunary scheme of things'.[53] From a man as young by episcopal standards as Lloyd, this was an argument of superlative tactlessness, which he capped by declaring his belief that the welfare of the Church would not be safe in the hands of those who opposed the Bill.[54] Lloyd may not have intended this judgement to include the Archbishops of Canterbury, York and Armagh or the Bishops of London and Durham; he said nothing to exempt them from it.

Lloyd's central contention was that Catholic emancipation must be seen as a matter of secular politics rather than of theology, and that the proper currency of argument was therefore utilitarian: 'every action which is not sinful in itself may be argued . . . on the grounds of their conduciveness to the public happiness and the public good'. Lloyd argued that admitting Catholics to a share in government was not sinful, and even if it was, the sin had already been committed by repealing the legislation aimed at entire suppression of the Roman Catholic faith. If Catholicism was tolerable, it could not be sinful; the question of admission to the legislature was therefore one of expediency.

For himself, Lloyd claimed entire conviction that, should the Lords reject the Bill, a similar measure would nevertheless become law within two years or so, and the interval would see bloody war in Ireland. Refusing the Bill therefore equated to starting a war from which nothing could be gained: 'an act unchristian and unlawful'.

Lloyd examined the dangers facing the Church of Ireland, and acknowledged them great; 'but the question now before us is, not whether the Church of Ireland is in danger, but whether the measure now proposed by his majesty's government is calculated to diminish or increase that danger?' Lloyd claimed 'some faint gleam of hope' from the measure, but placed more emphasis on a challenge to the Lords themselves to become the Church of Ireland's defence against spoliation.

Van Mildert was not in the House to hear this speech, due to 'indisposition'. Before he himself spoke the next day, Lloyd's arguments had clearly been reported to him in detail. Van Mildert's speech contained a series of direct personal attacks on Lloyd, which he afterwards edited out of the printed version.[55] This departure from the principles of a lifetime – Van Mildert's courtesy to opponents was renowned – sufficiently shows his anguish of mind.

He was particularly enraged to hear that Lloyd had 'sought to obtain an added sanction to his own opinions, by pointing out . . . that he was Regius Professor of Divinity at Oxford', reminding the House that three other bishops had been Regius Professors of Divinity, and took the opposite side of the question.[56] He demanded to know what evidence supported the claim that all the rising talent of the country favoured Catholic Emancipation, and poured scorn on the notion (which Lloyd had not advanced) that passing the Bill would end all dissatisfaction among Irish Roman Catholics.

Against Lloyd, Van Mildert insisted that the relationship between Church and State was inalienably a religious issue, and must be argued on principle not practicalities. At stake were the interests of 'Protestantism, and, consequently, of the pure Christian faith'; power must not be entrusted to Papists, who might then use it to tear up the Bill's safeguards and force the nation back into the papal yoke thrown off by the Reformers.

A Catholic-dominated government was not a short-term likelihood, Van Mildert recognised; but he warned against the possibility of a Catholic faction forming an influential part of some future reformist coalition. In any case, simply admitting Roman Catholics into Parliament meant 'a great and important change . . . in the very character of the Legislature itself'. Whatever might continue to be claimed on paper about the permanent and inviolable Establishment of the Protestant and Episcopal Church of England, the reality would have departed. Government and Parliament would thenceforth be not Protestant but 'mixed'; how could such a Legislature be trusted with the jurisdiction over the Established Church assigned to it by his 1825 speech?

More worrying even than the measure itself was the espousal, by a government generally sympathetic to the Church's interests, of 'the principle that there should be no civil distinctions on account of religious opinions'. This incipient pluralism threatened 'the existence of any religious Establishment whatsoever'.

Lloyd rose 'in explanation' when Van Mildert's speech ended, protesting in bewilderment that 'he has mistaken altogether the substance of my arguments'.[57] His offered clarification, of five disputed points, suggests that Lloyd quite failed to understand why Van Mildert parted company from him so decisively.

Lloyd had not, he explained, held that 'state policy should be argued on grounds of expediency alone', but that 'all measures, even of state policy, should be regulated, according to the immutable rules of morality'.

For Van Mildert, the immutable rules of morality were an insufficient regulator. There was a further prior question: whether the Establishment-relationship of Church to State would be harmed. Lloyd's speech gave no indication that he regarded the composition of Parliament as in itself part of the interests of the Church, although he assured the House that he had given 'most attentive and serious consideration' to the Bill's possible effects on the 'united church of England'. It was a logical extension of Lloyd's approach, though not one which he himself would necessarily have endorsed, to see the Church simply as one interest-group within the State, its role in the political life of the nation that of an expert witness on 'the immutable rules of morality'. Van Mildert's vision was of the State as the secular aspect of the Church.

The division, a government victory, split the episcopate. Nine bishops voted with Lloyd for the Bill, eighteen with Van Mildert against it. The nine 'rebels', besides the inevitable Bathurst of Norwich, included the Irish bishops of Derry and (by proxy)

Kildare, and the three bishops of Evangelical sympathies: Ryder of Lichfield; C. R. Sumner, a protégé of George IV, whose translation to the noble diocese of Winchester at the tender age of thirty-seven caused scandal;[58] and his brother J. B. Sumner, Blomfield's successor at Chester, who also held a Durham prebend. Lloyd's former colleagues, the 'Hackney' bishops, voted solidly against. John Banks Jenkinson, who besides being Bishop of St David's (and Lord Liverpool's cousin) was Dean of Durham, voted with Lloyd.

The Bill passed its third reading on Friday 13th April, and received the Royal Assent on Monday 16th. The bitterness it stirred up in Established Church circles damaged many relationships. C. R. Sumner, finding himself under pressure, used his Charge of 11th August to assure his clergy that on a question of so much importance he could 'follow the leading of no human authority', and that his decision had been 'formed in the closet, on my knees before God!' His Council, Dean Rennell of Winchester told Norris, advised him to leave 'the whole clause concerning his prayer on his knees in his closet before he voted for the Popish relief bill' out of the published version.[59]

Two years later, Bishop Jebb of Limerick regarded the Bishop of Derry as unfit to represent the Irish bishops because he had

voted in Parliament for the destruction of our Church, as I think the affirmative of the Popery question has been. The mischief was done, when the Test act was abolished; but many, or at least some honest men, were there beguiled. I don't deny, that one or two were weak enough, not to see the inevitable consequences of the popish measure; but I fear, the mass of the renegades have not even that miserable excuse to offer. I never was on terms of intimacy with the Bishop of Derry; and I confess myself to wish, for the future, as far as possible, to avoid all communication with him.[60]

Saddest of all was the fate of Charles Lloyd. His role in the debates exposed him to particular unpopularity, the more so since he had dared to say that he did not believe Roman Catholics to be truly guilty of idolatry.[61]

Lloyd wrote to Peel on Sunday 15th April, 'What I said of Popery and Idolatry, together with the Circumstance of Van Mildert having attacked me very roughly has got among the Clergy & thrown some doubt on my Theological opinions . . .' He sent Peel a draft pamphlet defending himself, insisting that Peel show it to nobody, but asking for advice on whether to publish or at least print it.[62]

On 2nd May Lloyd attended the Royal Academy dinner at Somerset House and caught a chill. He died at his lodgings on 31st May. He was forty-five.

Edward Churton, who had known and loved him, wrote: 'The whole question was not equal in value to the life of the man who was thus made the victim of honest compliance with a mistaken principle.'[63]

Churton testifies to Joshua Watson's grief on hearing of Lloyd's death. Of Van Mildert's response he says nothing.

1830 was another difficult year. For Van Mildert it began with 'the first attack of a painful inward complaint, which afflicted him, more or less, almost continually during the remainder of his life'.

In June, George IV died. The ensuing general election left the Wellington administration in power, but with an uncertain majority; the loyalty of the ultra-Tories, still nourishing a sense of betrayal over Catholic Emancipation, was no longer beyond doubt. Pressure was building for the 'third chapter of the revolutionary trilogy',[64] the reform of parliamentary representation.

In September Edward Churton wrote an optimistic letter to Norris, twitting the Patriarch with despairing too much of the country: 'I am sorry to see you augur so unfavourably of our new Parliament . . . I thought I perceived an accession of strength on the side of right principles. I wish to see a government either Whig or Tory . . . What I dread most is that which we have seen too much of lately, the spirit of accommodation and expediency.'[65] Churton also thought the 'generally good' harvest offered the promise of a less disturbed winter.

History dealt harshly with both his judgements. The autumn brought widespread agricultural rioting and machine-breaking, and the Wellington government collapsed in November, to be replaced by Lord Grey leading a coalition of Whigs, Canningites and disillusioned ultra-Tories.

In the last days of Wellington's administration, Bishop Majendie of Bangor died. Translating Christopher Bethell on to Bangor after an episcopal reign of six months, Wellington bestowed the diocese of Exeter on Henry Phillpotts.

Grey, who could hardly forbid his old enemy's consecration, refused to proceed with the formalities until Phillpotts surrendered his other preferment as Dean of Chester and Rector of Stanhope.

Phillpotts protested: the annual revenues of Exeter averaged a pitiful £1,571. In December 1830, Grey wrote to Van Mildert suggesting that Phillpotts should exchange Stanhope for a residentiary canonry at St Paul's.

Van Mildert had not forgiven Phillpotts for his Catholic Relief treason, but given his own history, he could hardly fail to sympathise with Phillpotts' predicament. He demurred to the particular request, urging Grey to heed the 'universal' demand of a resident incumbent for Stanhope, but instead persuaded W. D. Darnell to exchange Phillpotts his Durham sixth prebend. The correspondence was cordial; Van Mildert found Grey 'frank, disinterested and gracious'.[66]

Grey seems to have pursued a policy of conciliating the High Church bishops at this time, championing Howley in a February debate on clergy residence as 'most anxious to remedy abuses', and describing the Archbishop's views as 'very moderate and liberal'.[67]

In March 1831 the Grey government brought in the first Reform Bill amid a torrent of public petitions. Given a second reading by a majority of 302 to 301, it was withdrawn on 21st April following a Government defeat in committee, and Parliament was prorogued on 22 April with extraordinary scenes in both Houses.

The snap general election which followed strengthened the pro-Reformers, with public demonstrations of a more or less violent nature in many parts of the country. Reform was popular in Durham: Charles Thorp reported to Van Mildert in April that 'The property of the Co[unty] is against, – the numbers and noise *greatly* in favour of the Reform, and the general feeling strongly that way.'[68]

Thorp tried a bit of prudent politicking, exploiting the Newcastle barrister James Losh's confidential relationship with Brougham, now Lord Chancellor. In September, as the second Reform Bill navigated the Commons, Brougham sent Losh a letter for Thorp to show Van Mildert in confidence, protesting his disposition 'to do all the little I can for the Church as by law established' and urging that 'Everyone who feels for the establishment must tremble to think of the effect of the bill being thrown out in the Lords – for if it is so, rely on it, the Bishops will be made to bear the blame . . . The *roar* of popular *fury* will be directed against the Bench, & I foresee the very worst consequences.'

The Bill could not, Brougham warned, be defeated, but only delayed and then carried by popular agitation 'in a hostile and

domineering manner and to a far greater extent'; if 'a few fathers of
the Church were to take a sound and wholsome [sic] course,' seeking
to amend the Bill rather than to overthrow or delay it, 'more would
be done for both Aristocracy and Hierarchy than all else man could
devise'.[69]

Brougham might claim attachment to the Established Church,
but Losh's covering letter to Thorp laid bare the gulf between his
conception of Establishment and Van Mildert's: 'I perfectly agree
with him in thinking the Church of England the best of existing
Church Establishments. And were it liberated from Tithes and its
Liturgy from some useless things which give offence, it should have
my best wishes.'[70]

Thorp's reply assured Losh that 'you have no reason to apprehend resistance to burning changes and reforms from our body';[71]
but Van Mildert received Brougham's epistle coolly, writing to
Thorp

Lord B . . . will be grievously disappointed . . . if he supposes that my vote
for the Parliamentary Reform Bill can be purchased by fears and menaces
of the impending fate of the Church. I never can believe that the Church
will be more safe or last one year longer by supporting that measure which
can answer no purpose but to whet the appetites of the radicals and atheists
& to give them an increase of power which no Govt. (certainly not the
present) would long be able to resist . . . And pray be careful how you hand
me over to these high Whig Gentry from whom I am very desirous to keep
at a respectful distance.[72]

Despite the still-precarious state of his health, by which he had been
driven to the desperate expedient of warm baths,[73] in mid-September Van Mildert conducted his second Visitation as Bishop of
Durham. His Charge was an open and explicit summons to his
clergy to stand firm in the hour of trial. In language strongly
reminiscent of his Boyle Lectures, Van Mildert warned of 'the
dangers and difficulties which beset our path, the conflict we have to
sustain with enmity of no ordinary kind'. Infidelity, Atheism, Fanaticism, Popery, Socinianism, Dissent, Lukewarmness and Apathy
were in monstrous alliance, bent on the overthrow of the Church of
England; crisis approached; 'the vigilant Pastor' must combat the
'fiends of blasphemy and disorganisation'.[74]

Against this lurid backdrop, Van Mildert advised his hearers to
avoid raking up dead controversies, specifically over the Test Laws
and Catholic Emancipation, and against combativeness in general,

warning them that 'rash encounters' led only to embarrassment. Instead, as in his 1827 Charge, he urged strenuous diligence in discharging their pastoral duties. He deliberately omitted any mention of Parliamentary Reform.

A correspondent of Christopher Wordsworth's heard part of the Charge delivered, reporting himself 'much delighted with its high principles – and with the courage and dignity in which those principles were avowed'.[75]

Van Mildert took no part in the 1831 parliamentary debates. He was excused attendance at William IV's coronation on 8th September for health reasons, his part in the ceremonial taken by the Archbishop of York. He was absent when the second Reform Bill came to the Lords on 3rd October; the *Morning Post* mistakenly reported that he had taken his seat in the House.[76] At the crucial division on 7th October, however, his proxy vote was recorded against the Bill.

Grey opened the Second Reading debate, praising the 'prudent forethought' which had led the bishops to adopt 'measures of amelioration' and begging them to consider 'their situation with the country' should the Bill's defeat 'be decided by the votes of the heads of the Church'. Howley, the only bishop to speak in the debate, gave this plea as direct an answer as he was capable of:

. . . if it were their Lordships' pleasure to pass this Bill, he would sincerely rejoice, and no man more than himself, if the apprehensions which he entertained of its effects should turn out to be groundless. If, on the other hand, their Lordships threw out the measure, and popular violence, which he did not expect, should unfortunately follow, he would be content to bear his share in the general calamity.[77]

The majority against was 199–158, and it escaped nobody that, had the twenty-one bishops who opposed it voted the other way, the Bill would have passed its second reading. Only the venerable Whig Bathurst of Norwich and the newly appointed Whig Maltby of Chichester voted in support.

The ensuing public fury, with the bishops as its main target, fulfilled all predictions. On 11th October Lord Suffield declared in the House of Lords that the bishops had happily supported 'arbitrary and oppressive' government in the past, turning against the administration only when 'a liberal Government produces a measure for the benefit of the people at large, and for the extension and security of the liberties of the country . . .' Blomfield and Copleston of Llandaff rose to remonstrate before Phillpotts sailed magnificently to the offensive: 'Was this charge an instance of liberality; and did the members of his Majesty's Government by these remarks intend to incite and encourage violence?'[78]

There was violence. Although no episcopal blood flowed, the Bristol riots at the end of October saw the Bishop's palace sacked and burnt, Phillpotts' palace at Exeter was put under armed guard, the Bishop of Bath and Wells' carriage was stoned, and a number of public appearances were prudently cancelled. On Guy Fawkes Day 1831, 'the effigy of the local bishop replaced Guy Fawkes or the Pope, and at Clerkenwell all twenty-one bishops were consumed in a holocaust'.[79]

Van Mildert, as one of the notorious twenty-one, was not spared. He wrote to Henry Douglas, 'We have had our share of turmoil, & the compliment has been paid me of burning me in effigy in sight of my Castle gates, with threats of demolishing windows, & so forth.'

He found himself 'marked out . . . even by the Gentry and Magistrates of the County, in their inflammatory harangues to the populace as an object of public execration, in consequence of which, I have not only received gross insults here, but have reason to believe that it was intended and still is to watch an opportunity of doing me personal violence'. When he left for Harrogate at the beginning of November he observed wryly to Thorp that he might find himself 'waylaid or knocked on the head', and later told Henry Douglas that 'had I passed through Darlington, I was to have been way-laid and personally maltreated'.[80]

James Losh, taking part in Newcastle and Durham public meetings on Reform, was dismayed by the force of feeling. 'I think the speakers attacked the Church and the Bishops rather too *coarsely*,' he wrote after the Durham meeting on 31st October, adding 'not perhaps more severely than they deserve'. Losh, a Unitarian who favoured disestablishment, on this occasion found himself 'unwilling to add to the violence ag[ain]st the Church', and declined to speak.[81]

When the Reform Bill returned to Parliament in the spring of 1832, the intense pressure of public outcry and political lobbying on the Bishops over the winter soon showed effects. Blomfield, absent the previous October on the plea of mourning for his recently deceased father, chose the Bill's first reading to separate himself decisively from his High Church colleagues by declaring his intention to vote for the Bill and oppose any mutilating amendment.

Van Mildert set out his own position in a speech on 9th April. He attributed the Bill to 'a restless disposition – a love of innovation – a wish to destroy institutions because they were ancient – a desire to set the subject over the ruler, and to trample the ruler under the subject'. It would not serve the 'religious and moral interests of the country'; it would not better the conditions of the poor. He denied with sincere indignation that the bishops 'thought only of their own interests, and that they cared not for the welfare of the lower classes'.[82] To Van Mildert's world-view, government had simply no part in the divinely-assigned responsibilities of the 'lower classes', and nothing but demagoguery on the part of unscrupulous and self-seeking Radical agitators could make it appear so. Giving the masses a taste for political power could yield only evil results.

On 13th April Blomfield, the Archbishop of York and eight other bishops, including the Dean of Durham, joined Bathurst and Maltby in the majority that secured the Bill's second reading. On 7th May the Lords carried a mutilating amendment with the support of thirteen bishops and three archbishops, York's unintentional. On 8th May Grey asked King William for a promise to create enough new peers to force the Bill through the Lords. The King refused. Grey resigned.

On 9th May the King began negotiations with Peel and Wellington about forming a Tory administration pledged to bring in a reform measure. After a week of public turmoil and sterile attempts to form a Cabinet, Wellington admitted defeat. The King reluctantly agreed to create new peers if necessary, and the Grey administration returned to power. The Reform Bill passed its third reading on 4th June with only twenty-two dissentient votes, and not a bishop among them.

'I never saw the House so overwhelm'd with a sense of its utter helplessness, humiliation, & degradation', Lord Bristol wrote to Christopher Wordsworth.[83]

Reform was passed; but the bishops were not forgiven. In early August Howley's primary visitation at Canterbury was mobbed. The crowd, he wrote soothingly to his wife, was 'partly abusive but seemingly good natured', and the pelting his carriage received 'broke no windows, except one of a house with a stone intended for us'; the bodywork suffered 'no contusions that will not disappear with sufficient scrubbing';[84] but the incident was symptomatic. Public hostility to the Established Church continued. The fiery trial was at hand.

CHAPTER 6

Launching the Ark

At 7 pm on 5th April 1831, the surgeon Thomas Greenhow read to the Newcastle upon Tyne Literary and Philosophical Society a paper entitled 'The expediency of establishing in Newcastle an academical Institution of the Nature of a College or University for the promotion of Literature and Science, more especially amongst the Middle Classes of the Community, briefly considered.'

The meeting was enthusiastic. James Losh, a vice-president of the Society and a shareholder in the new University of London, moved that Greenhow's paper be published and a further meeting convened to debate it.

Like its London prototype, opened in 1828, the Newcastle University was to offer 'useful knowledge' such as modern foreign languages, scientific and technological disciplines, law and medicine, possibly also classics, but definitely eschewing divinity, and was to be open to students of any religious allegiance.[1]

In the animated public discussion which followed, Charles Thorp, who as a Trustee of the Society probably received a free copy, clearly mulled over Greenhow's plan attentively. On 7th June Greenhow produced a second and more detailed paper for the Special Meeting, which appointed a Committee 'to draw up a prospectus of the proposed College, and to issue an address to the public'.[2]

On 11th June, the *Newcastle Courant* carried a major article PROPOSED ACADEMICAL INSTITUTION IN NEWCASTLE. The same day, Thorp wrote from Bamburgh Castle to Van Mildert at Hanover Square:

. . . I would fain bring before you the project of a University to be attached to our College. A slight extension of the establishments & a few Professorships founded by the body in the Cathedral would effect the object. It would give to the Dean & Chapter strength of character & usefulness –

149

preserve the Revenues to the church & to the north – & prevent the
establishment of a very doubtful Academical institution which is now
taking root in N'Castle. I trust you will not think me a projecter beyond
what the times require.[3]

There is no definite evidence that this inspiration was Thorp's own.
The facilities of Bamburgh Castle, centre for the activities of the
Lord Crewe Trustees, included apartments for the Archdeacons and
a library; other clergy also stayed there from time to time. Canon
David Durell, Sub-Dean of Durham, was at Bamburgh when consulted about the University project late in July. Whether he was
there in June, and party to earlier discussions, is not known.[4]

In 1941 Edward Hughes, working from the Thorp Correspondence, conjectured that Van Mildert originated the plan and first
took Thorp into his confidence with his letter of 26th June 1831.
Discovery of the 11th June letter in the Jenkyns Papers undermined
this scenario. A. J. Heesom, reviewing the available evidence in
1982, further called attention to Southey's 1829 *Quarterly* review of
Surtees' *History of Durham*:

Among the best intentions of Cromwell . . . was that of erecting a Northern
College at Durham. The plan was never matured, either as to discipline or
endowment. Oxford and Cambridge, which were both in possession of the
sectarians, petitioned against it; and, at the Restoration, 'it totally dis-
appeared amongst some worse things built on the same rotten foundation'.
The time, it may be hoped, is not far distant, when a northern university
will be founded; and in lasting honour will the memory of that excellent
lady be held, who has made known her intention of contributing to it with
a munificence unequalled in later times, and unsurpassed in former ones.[5]

Heesom takes the 'excellent lady' to be a flesh-and-blood enigma;
another possibility could be a reference, *pace* the Elect Lady of 2
John, to the Established Church.

The Hackney Phalanx was heavily involved in the founding of
King's College, London, as a counter to 'Godless Gower Street';
Van Mildert contributed £500.[6] Given that 'a northern university'
was mooted in High Church circles as early as 1829, with an explicit
Durham connection, it is hard to think Van Mildert gave the matter
no consideration before the summer of 1831; while Thorp's June
letter is decidedly spare for a first mention of so earthshaking a
proposal. One explanation might be that Van Mildert had already
discussed possibilities with Thorp in a general way, and Thorp was
signalling him that it had become necessary to act at once.

Jenkinson maintained in 1836 that he 'certainly was given to understand that the first suggestion of establishing a University at Durham came from the Archbishop of Canterbury'. This is contradicted by the fact that on 9th August Van Mildert asked Jenkinson himself to 'open the matter, in strict confidence, to the Abp. of Canterbury'. Van Mildert's comment to Thorp on 10th August, that he was 'anxious that the Archbishop shd. now, or soon, be apprized of what is going forward', adding 'It wd. give him great satisfaction, & his suggestions might be of great use', hardly suggests the original idea had come from Howley.

If it is correct that the June, July and August correspondence represented a putting on written record of earlier confidential oral negotiations, then Howley is likely to have been involved from an early stage. The use of his name was however typical of the way personal and official prestige were deployed to strengthen the proposals; on 19th August Jenkinson explicitly hoped to use Howley's support as a lever on the Chapter. The question of precisely who was the first to see the Durham possibility seems likely to remain unanswerable.[7]

No reply from Van Mildert to Thorp's June letter is extant. Since he left London for Harrogate soon after, Van Mildert may have preferred to wait until he could talk privately to Thorp; a letter from Doncaster dated 21st June does not mention the 'great topic'. By the end of July he was back at Auckland Castle. After thorough consultation, Thorp returned to Bamburgh to broach the project secretly with Durell.

From the beginning of the correspondence Van Mildert committed himself unreservedly to the University scheme, urging Thorp to develop it as quickly as possible into

a producible shape – so as to anticipate, not only any mongrel attempt at Newcastle, but any fierce attack upon Church-Dignities, from the H. of Commons, where there is great reason to apprehend a movement, as soon as the Reform Bill is disposed of – & it is not at all improbable that your Chapter may be selected for the first onset. Whenever you are prepared, with a plan, or outline, I can answer for its being pressed in high quarters without delay.[8]

Durell also responded favourably, writing to Van Mildert on 25th June

It is probable that our enemies might have respect for the measure as it accords with the intention of their predecessors in spoliation. That considerable sacrifice must be made is unquestionable, & I hope the Dean & Chapter will consider it as a premium paid to secure the remainder. You cannot, I think, offer to the public any plan more suitable than that suggested by your Lordship . . .[9]

Forced to rely heavily on this cynical materialist argument in securing the Dean and Chapter's support for the project, Van Mildert was never wholly comfortable with it. Durell, he observed to Thorp, wanted the university 'rather as a peace-offering to the public, than for it's own sake. I incline to view it in both lights.'[10]

Van Mildert adopted a background role in the initial stages. It was agreed by 25th July that Thorp should approach the Dean, to whom Durell had already sent the gist of the proposals, and Gaisford. Van Mildert urged strict secrecy, for 'special reasons' which he would not commit to paper.[11]

Gaisford was in Wiltshire, the Dean at Abergwili Palace, with a postal lag of four days in each direction; and Thorp was dilatory, not writing to Gaisford, despite repeated nagging, until 29th July. Van Mildert had Durell write to the Dean on 28th July; Thorp wrote on 2nd August.

Van Mildert grew increasingly impatient. 'I shall be ready to step in immediately, as soon as you think fit', he told Thorp on 27th July. By 6th August he was writing to Gaisford on his own account, and even considering communicating direct with Archbishop Howley. Time was pressing. He was particularly anxious 'that the Abp. of York shd. be made privy to it as soon as possible, in order to prevent his being ensnared in any other device that may interfere with our purpose'. Proposals for a York university had been circulating at least since 1826: it was vital 'that there shd. be no similar project started as from Bishopthorpe, likely to compete with us for public favour'.[12]

The response was mixed. Gaisford doubted the viability of 'a foundation upon the plan of our old Universities, and embracing the full range of studies pursued in them', preferring a 'superior school, and a place where the poorer candidates for orders might acquire instruction suitable to their intended profession'. The Dean, while expressing strong approval for the project and willingness 'chearfully [to] give it my most cordial support', warned Thorp ominously not to overrate the Chapter's means.[13]

Although Van Mildert thought it a matter of 'main importance' to have Gaisford's co-operation, particularly 'considering his high position as an Academic', the plan continued to be for a full University. Jenkinson felt nothing less would 'give satisfaction to the public, nor consequently answer the end in view'; Thorp warned Gaisford that the establishment of 'a Northern Collegiate or Academic Establishment' could not be long delayed, 'seeing the great want there is of such an institution, and the ardent desire which manifests itself in several places, York, N'Castle, and as we hear Liverpool, to obtain it. We may have such an institution . . . in our own hands, or those of our adversaries.' It was no unworthy objective to provide 'the rising families of our towns mines & manufacturers' with an alternative to the dubious benefits of Edinburgh and Geneva – and, Thorp added darkly, London University.[14]

Van Mildert immovably intended Durham University to be an Anglican foundation; but his aim was always higher than what Lord Durham called 'a mere manufactory for the lower members of the Church, for the creation of curates (a very useful branch of the Church, he would admit)'. Van Mildert saw an important role for Durham in nurturing learned candidates for Orders – in February 1834, with Howley's endorsement, he wrote to all his fellow bishops inviting them to accept Durham graduates as ordinands on the same footing as graduates of Oxford and Cambridge[15] – but the University was to be much more than a theological college. He also looked to producing a learned laity – men genuinely rooted in the Church of England, equipped to take leadership positions in the secular life of the nation. He hoped, as the pressure mounted to open Oxford and Cambridge fully to Dissenters, that a University wholly funded by Church monies might prove better able to remain faithfully Anglican.

As the political changes of the day cut deeper into the foundations of the Church–State relationship, Van Mildert built his Ark, hoping there to preserve the true vision of a University as a place of godly learning.

It saddened Van Mildert that Gaisford had reservations, but losing Gaisford from the Chapter was a worse blow. His wife, Van Mildert's foster-daughter, had died in 1830; he was unsettled in Durham and homesick for Oxford. In April 1831 Van Mildert preferred him to the eleventh and richest Durham prebend, giving his former Stall to Thorp; by the end of the summer Gaisford had negotiated an exchange with Samuel Smith, Dean of Christ Church.

Gaisford took office at Christ Church in time for the new academic year, and Smith took the Golden Prebend.

Van Mildert wrote wistfully to Henry Douglas, 'I could not but regret losing him from Durham, but for a purpose, so creditable to him, so beneficial to the University & the Church, as well as to his own family prospects, it would be selfish to express any other feeling than that of pure satisfaction.'[16]

The loss was bitter. Gaisford's international reputation would have been a priceless asset to the new University, besides the 'delight and satisfaction' Van Mildert had derived from their 'frequent correspondence . . . Seldom do so many excellences combine to form so complete and admirable a character as his.' Van Mildert remained loyal to the friendship, defending Gaisford against Douglas indignation when in 1832 he married Jane Catherine Jenkyns, whose brother Henry was a Christ Church don.[17]

Jenkinson agreed with Van Mildert about the need for haste; so, when Van Mildert wrote to him on 12th August, did Howley. Their anxiety was purely pragmatic: they wanted 'to secure the whole credit of the proposal to the Church of Durham, so that it may not appear to be the result of any previous attack'.

Howley proposed that 'the first notice the Government should have of the measure should, if possible, be from the application of the parties for their aid in carrying it into execution; and that from that moment the design should be made generally known'.

Jenkinson recognised that 'before such application can be made, the plan must receive the consent of the Chapter', and was apprehensive about how long that might take, although he hoped that Howley's support would help expedite matters.[18]

By the end of July Thorp and Van Mildert had agreed a draft plan for the staffing and finance of the proposed University.[19] The Dean and Chapter were to be 'the directing body'; the Bishop was to be visitor, with 'efficient not nominal controul' over their management. Van Mildert wondered whether a University ought not to have a Chancellor, but this was not taken up.

There was disagreement over what the senior University official should be called. Thorp suggested Principal; Van Mildert, fearing it might 'seem to trench upon the superiority of the Dean', preferred Sub-Dean. Master was also proposed. The title eventually adopted, Warden, first appears in a letter from Van Mildert to Jenkinson at the end of November. There was to be a 'Tutor – who may be Vice-Principal . . . to superintend the studies'; Van Mildert favoured constituting him 'Censor also, for purposes of discipline'.

More disagreement arose over the range of subjects to be offered. Thorp, mindful of the 'useful knowledge' called for by Greenhow, suggested Professors of Mathematics, Natural Philosophy, Modern Languages, History, and preferably 'Chymistry, Natural Hist. & Botany' and Political Economy as well, besides the indispensable Divinity and Classics. Gaisford urged a more traditional estab- lishment: 'Divinity, antient languages, mathematical and Natural philosophy I consider essentials, the numerous tribe of Medical Sciences with names terminating in ogy I consider non-essentials and excrescences – they are amusing and to a certain degree instruc- tive, but are not wholesome discipline for the mind.'[20] The relatively modest scheme presented to the chapter in September proposed only three Professors – Divinity, 'Greek and Latin' and 'Mathematics & Natural Philosophy' – with 'Readers in other Branches according to circumstances'.[21]

Thorp proposed an intake of twenty scholarship students and twenty 'others within walls paying'. By September there was no upper limit stipulated for 'ordinary students', and a third category had been added: 'Occasional Students admissible to one or more Courses of Lectures' at the discretion of 'the Dean and Master (Principal)'.

The proposed financial arrangements were twofold. The Prin- cipal and the Professors of Divinity and Classics were to be remuner- ated by annexing Durham prebends to their respective offices. As negotiations proceeded, the first two remained constant, but a draft dated 25th August gave the third Stall to a Professor of 'Hebrew- and-Oriental-Literature' and the September scheme proposed giving Stalls only to the 'Master or Principal' and the Divinity Professor. Gaisford felt that providing 'working' professors with Stalls was preposterously over-generous, a view shared by Howley and, at a later stage, Lord Chancellor Brougham.

The need to ensure that the professors would 'work' generated some heat. Thorp's proposal in the 25th August scheme that 'the Divinity and Hebrew Professors shd. have each a Reader paid from their Stalls' was vetoed for fear of encouraging professorial idleness. Jenkinson urged the particular need for the Greek Professor not to 'be a sleeping, nor even a superintendent, Partner'. His unfavourable comparisons between the Professors at 'St. David's College', who were 'in fact all working, & hard working, Tutors' and those at Oxford and Cambridge[22] can scarcely have endeared him to Van Mildert.

The remaining finance was to be found by one of two options: a one-fifth levy on the revenues of each Stall and of the Deanery, after the next vacancy; or reassignment of capitular property. Thorp thought it impractical to impose a levy on the existing Chapter: vested interests must be protected. He hoped that the project could be financed in the short term by a voluntary increase of the Chapter's annual vote to the Education Fund, from £300 to £1,800.

It was Gaisford who first identified the deferred levy scheme as a political non-starter: it would hardly appear 'over generous to saddle successors with burdens wh. we are ourselves unwilling to bear'. This argument immediately convinced Van Mildert, who opposed the levy from then on. Van Mildert was also anxious not to concede any damaging precedent for altering the constitution of the Chapter.

By the end of August, the plans were deemed sufficiently well advanced for Jenkinson to notify the rest of the Chapter, in general terms, what was afoot.[23] The project had already been revealed to the semi-retired Archdeacon of Durham but not the Bishops of Chester, Exeter and Bristol, all of whom were Durham prebendaries.

Phillpotts of Exeter told Wellington in September that Van Mildert was 'rather colder in [his] demeanour towards me than formerly, in consequence of the proceedings on the Roman Catholic question'.[24] While holding similar theological and political views, the two men had little in common temperamentally. Van Mildert shared the sentiments of Blomfield, who, trying in 1823 to defend Phillpotts' no-holds-barred pamphleteering, confessed to feeling 'a pang when I see a minister of the gospel enter into the field of political controversy, and indulge in the language of bitterness, on which side soever he may be ranged'.

According to Howley, Phillpotts' first reaction was to mishear the Durham proposal as relating 'to a School', and to dismiss it as unlikely to result in any advantage. Although Howley thought him 'well inclined to the larger plan', Phillpotts had little enthusiasm for a new University. He complained to the Church Commissioners in 1836 that the superabundance of educated persons over employment opportunities only spread discontent, and that he had done his best to urge a theological seminary as more use both to the Durham diocese and to 'the whole of the northern part of England'. Phillpotts blamed the decision to found a University on the Chapter's 'deference and high respect' for Van Mildert. He was one of the three bishops who refused to accept Durham degrees as a sufficient qualification for Orders: in pursuit of his own preference for a theological college, he insisted on 'a B.A. degree from Oxford or Cambridge together with a Durham Divinity Certificate'.[25]

John Bird Sumner of Chester was another Catholic Relief delinquent, and worse yet, had Evangelical sympathies. Van Mildert, his temper shortened by the battles for control of the SPCK, deplored 'the rapid incroachments of the party, (for it is mere party-spirit) in every direction. Even the radicals themselves are scarcely more bent upon doing us mischief than this smooth & plausible & undermining confederacy.' The Dean later argued against giving Sumner more detailed information than other Chapter members, on the grounds that 'it might place him in an awkward position if Gilly [a known Evangelical] or others not in the secret should, as they very probably will, converse with him on the subject'.[26]

Bishop Gray of Bristol had acted on Van Mildert's behalf during the Durham magistracy affair, but Gaisford and Van Mildert doubted his discretion,[27] and secrecy was paramount.

On 31st August Jenkinson wrote to the Chapter in strict confidence, telling them of proposals for 'an enlarged system of education to be connected with our College' and promising them further details before 'the ensuing September Audit'.[28]

Van Mildert had hoped to be able 'to announce, (or rather to intimate, however darkly,) the intention of the thing' at his episcopal visitation in mid-September, but to his great disappointment, matters were still not far enough advanced to make that appropriate.[29]

Jenkinson's enthusiasm for the project had already peaked. The distance between Durham and Abergwili made it difficult to keep him closely involved with developments. He had other preoccupations that summer, too: in mid-August his eldest son's right thumb was blown off through playing with gunpowder. By 31st August he was commenting tetchily on the lack of clarity in Thorp's outline plans, and expressing definite reluctance to see the Chapter's annual contribution go higher than £1,800. He was persuaded to stretch this to £2,000, but the version of the scheme which he circulated to the Chapter on 22nd September alarmed him so badly that he added a covering letter explaining why he felt 'unable to give it his unqualified support'. The new plan, Jenkinson claimed, differed materially from the one he had originally undertaken to propose. He thought it would 'affect too largely the present income of the Chapter'; an annual vote of £2,850, or even £3,450, was now being mentioned. He also objected strongly to the reduction from three to two annexed Stalls.[30]

Despite Jenkinson's rapidly waning enthusiasm for the project – he told Blomfield in 1836 that he 'was against it from the very first' – matters had now gone too far to draw back. Jenkinson was not present at the Chapter meeting on 27th September, but he sent a recommendation which the Chapter unanimously accepted, 'to pass a vote which will enable him . . . to take whatever preliminary measures may be necessary, in order that the Institution may be brought . . . into early & useful operation'. They also voted to thank Van Mildert for his 'liberal intentions' and optimistically declared themselves 'ready to receive for the benefit of the Academical Institution any aid that may be offered'.[31]

Van Mildert, delighted with the reports he received on the Chapter meeting from Thorp, Durell and Gilly, that year's Sub-Dean, now expected the Dean to communicate the University plans to the Prime Minister.[32] In the event it was Howley who on 4th October sent Lord Grey a first outline of the proposals; on 5th October Grey received a letter from Van Mildert explaining matters in more detail. The project was presented as an 'Academical Institution at Durham' modelled on 'the Colleges of Oxford and Cambridge, . . Christ Church in particular, which is, in like manner, connected with that Cathedral', intended to provide a full university education 'more particularly to the Northern Counties, . . having a Principal, Professors, Tutors &c. with Endowments for a certain number of Students'. Grey's response was prompt and suave, assuring Van Mildert that 'it has seldom been my good fortune to receive a communication which gave me such unqualified pleasure', applauding both the objective and the manner of its prosecution, and promising every assistance in his power.[33]

News of the Durham proposals soon leaked across the Tyne. The *Newcastle Chronicle* was scathing:

The auspices and influence under which the College at Durham has been announced are not what we think will answer the demands and wishes of the neighbourhood and the wants of the country. The exclusive restrictions which it is intended to impose upon the students must prevent a very large mass of the wealthy and intelligent classes of the district from taking advantage of the instruction it offers; while the influence and profession of the individuals by whom it is proposed . . . tend strongly to encourage the belief that it will be conducted too much for theological objects, and we fear in too clerical a spirit, and too much on the plan and in the system of the old-established Universities, to answer public expectations. . . [34]

The Newcastle Literary and Philosophical Society's annual report in February 1832 declared that the Durham proposals had not 'at all superseded the desirableness of an Institution like that proposed for Newcastle'. A Newcastle prospectus was printed on 5th June 1832, with plans to raise 'capital of £15,000 in twenty pound shares'; on 24th January 1833 a public meeting at Newcastle Guildhall, presided over by the Mayor, formed a 'Joint-Stock Company' to establish the college; but although the Company later reappraised its capital needs at £5,000 not even that much was forthcoming.[35] In March 1833 James Losh wrote bitterly, '. . . if the public took any serious interest in the plan, I have no doubt of its success. But the Newcastle and North[umberlan]d public does not rise in my estimation.'[36]

The Durham Great Chapter was to meet on 20th November. Despite Van Mildert's arguments, the majority still favoured funding the University from their successors' income rather than their own. The prospect that this myopic greed might sell a strategic pass in the battle to stave off redistribution of Chapter revenues haunted the Bishop, for whom a major point of ecclesiological principle was at stake.

On 19th November Van Mildert lost his temper, apparently at a meeting with Thorp, Durell and Dr Smith, the former Dean of Christ Church. He threatened to write to Grey mooting 'awkward questions'. The next day, his 'ill-humour . . . having somewhat subsided', he wrote a long, patient letter to Durell 'as Senior Member of the Chapter of Durham now in residence', explaining the unwisdom of the 'one-fifth plan'. The letter, which Van Mildert also showed to Thorp and Smith, set out his own intentions. Besides undertaking to annex 'two, or perhaps three stalls to offices in the new institution' and buying 'a house contiguous to Durham Castle' for rent-free occupation by 'such College officers, whether Professors or Tutors, as the Chapter may wish to place in it', he would subscribe 'One thousand pounds towards the Outfit of the establishment'. Moreover, if the Chapter would 'agree to extend their annual expenditure to Three Thousand, instead of Two, I will pledge myself to contribute annually another Thousand, so long as my Incumbency continues, & that the See is not deprived of it's Revenues.' The letter was duly read to the Chapter on 20th November, and its terms accepted. Abandoning 'the prospective tax upon the Stalls', the Chapter resolved to proceed 'by the enfranchisement of property to the amount of £80,000 – equal to £3,000 per annum', from its estates in South Shields.[37]

This, however, necessitated an Act of Parliament. Van Mildert had wanted to avoid that if possible, warning Thorp that 'if it once gets into the H. of Commons, Messrs. Hume & Co. will be for cutting up root and branch, instead of lopping off a sufficiency for the supplies'.[38]

Jenkinson felt the same anxiety. By 28th November he had still not written to Grey about the Chapter decision, telling Thorp that a parallel letter from Van Mildert would be advisable. Jenkinson feared the Act would enable Grey to impose his own ideas on the University: Grey had advocated 'a more equal & more advantageous distribution' of revenues, and worse still favoured taking a larger slice out of future Chapter income. Jenkinson hoped Van Mildert's influence might suffice to prevent this, particularly given that 'the whole offer is now so very handsome'; but he was increasingly ill at ease with the whole affair. He replied almost snappishly to Van Mildert's enquiry on 29th November that he had not yet written to Grey, and that it was 'too late for me to write by this day's post. I have been engaged all the morning & I have still much to do . . .'[39]

When Van Mildert returned to London in early December, a letter from Grey followed him down, regretting the staunchness of Van Mildert's opposition to 'any prospective measures which might . . . have rendered the plan now in contemplation more extensively useful'. Grey, acknowledging that alienating future Chapter revenues could involve 'some change in the existing constitution of the Capitular Body', urged that this would 'diminish in no degree the influence and authority of the Church; but on the contrary greatly

. . . promote them'.[40] Van Mildert assured Thorp that Grey would 'find me immoveable on this point', and immovable he remained.

In early 1832 an Evangelical plot loomed. Canon Gilly, who had told the 17th December Chapter meeting that he intended 'to give a course of public Lectures, gratuitously, on some Branch of Ecclesiastical History, with the sanction of the Chapter, every year during his term of residence', now wrote to Van Mildert on 17th January proposing that 'some friends' should give the University an endowment 'to promote the cause of Protestantism, either by a Professorship, or a Lectureship, or something similar to the Office of [Christian] Advocate at Cambridge', intended to 'shew historically that God has never left himself without a witness, but has at all periods provided for the circulation of the Gospel without the corrupt agency of the Church of Rome'. Van Mildert declined. Introducing a 'Professorship of Protestantism, distinct from that of Divinity' was 'superfluous: the one surely includes the other', while a Lectureship compromised the Divinity Professor's authority. Most of all he disliked the Christian Advocate proposal. He felt 'requiring, year by year, something to be produced in refutation of Romish errors' could lead only to unproductive acrimony.

Gilly then laid the correspondence before the Chapter, who had Jenkinson beg Van Mildert to reconsider. Besides their anguish at seeing Dr Gilly's 'very wealthy' friends spurned, they feared the rejection would discourage other 'similar acts of munificence'.

Jenkinson's plea that Oxford and Cambridge benefited from a plurality of Divinity Professors without 'any inconvenient consequences whatever' left Van Mildert courteously obdurate. Turning Jenkinson's own argument about 'working professors' neatly against him, Van Mildert replied, that might be appropriate for a large and ancient foundation where the Professors were not 'required, or expected, to give elementary instruction to Students'. Durham University was different. If two working Professors – or a Professor and Lecturer – differed in their views, 'the results might be perplexity, rather than edification, to the Students'. Besides, Van Mildert thought, no-Popery 'would scarcely require an entire course of Lectures; nor, if it did, could be produced again, year by year, as a permanent institution'.[41]

To Thorp he was more direct:

I know not *what sort of friends* Mr. Gilly has, who are disposed to be such magnificent benefactors. *Sed timeo Danaos.* The party he is connected with (including other members of the Chapter with himself) would, I doubt not, be very ready to contribute largely for the sake of that *influence* among us which may subserve their purposes. In the project, as stated to me, I instantly saw the danger of our being in the outset tangled with a party whose zeal perpetually outruns their discretion, and a probability of turning our Institution (which ought to be most strongly characterised by sobriety and wisdom) into an arena for those unseemly displays of energy which are daily breaking forth in disputatious meetings and answering, as I conceive, no good practical purpose . . . [42]

The would-be boarders were duly repelled.

Gaisford and Tournay continued to argue against making the new institution a full University with the power to confer degrees and faculties, pleading that it set a precedent for 'a similar grant to the self-styled *London* University'. By now, however, the Chapter had accepted that nothing less than a full University would be glamorous enough to preserve their revenues against Radical attack. Van Mildert felt 'no great uneasiness' about the London University threat:

That Institution is manifestly on the decline; and if it were to hold up its head again & advance further pretensions, it can only be opposed on that strong ground of its expressly disclaiming religious instruction in Church of England principles, which . . . ought to be considered as an absolute disqualification, for such privileges as actually carry with them certain Ecclesiastical as well as Academical rights. But be it so or not I do not see why we should forego a benefit we have fairly a right to expect because others, having no such claims may choose to assert them.[43]

Dean Jenkinson continued to grumble about the terrible financial burden on the Chapter, an irritant made more poignant by Van Mildert's own growing financial anxieties: he wrote to Thorp at the end of January, 'I . . . shall have extreme difficulty, if not impossibility, in meeting all the demands of this year without selling out from the small reserve in the Funds, which I had, with much anxiety, laid by as a provision in time of need. But I am willing even to do this, & trust to Providence for the result.' Ironically enough, *The Times* later that year published a poem on how St Jerome returned to earth and found many things amiss with the Church of England, among them 'that pious soul Van Mildert/Much with his money-bags bewildered'.[44]

The proponents of the Newcastle university plans did not readily accept the exclusion of Dissenters from the Durham foundation. As the Durham University Bill came before Parliament, a meeting of Newcastle Dissenters chaired by James Losh petitioned for admission to the honours and privileges of the new University;[45] Lord Durham and, later, Joseph Hume took up their cause.

The Bill was introduced into the House of Lords: 'supposing it to have passed unhurt through that ordeal,' Van Mildert explained to Thorp, 'the fiery furnace of the H. of Commons would be so much less formidable'.[46]

The Lords considered the Bill in committee at the beginning of June. Van Mildert sat next to Lord Durham who, he reported, 'sifted the preamble and clauses very astutely but on the whole not ill-naturedly'. The main excitement focused on the exclusion of Dissenters. After 'a little smart sparring' it was agreed that Durham should adopt the Cambridge system of requiring students to subscribe the Thirty-nine Articles before proceeding to a degree but not before matriculation; this meant that Dissenters could with integrity study at Durham but not receive degrees.

The committee broke up 'in pretty good humour', but the advocates of equal treatment continued to press their case until silenced by Van Mildert's threat that if Durham degrees were opened to Dissenters he would withdraw his support, thereby ending the University's financial viability.[47]

The Durham University Bill, although 'villainously opposed by that Enemy of the Established Church, Lord King',[48] came unscathed through both Houses, its passage smoothed by Van Mildert's skilful management of the lobbying process. It received Royal Assent on 4th July.

It was now necessary to proceed as fast as possible with implementing the plans. By the end of November, Thorp was able to send Grey detailed arrangements for opening the University to students from October 1833.[49]

Among the names considered for Principal of the new University were Keble, Shepherd and G. A. Ogilvie of Balliol. By November 1831, however, Van Mildert had decided on making Thorp the first Warden 'pro tempore at least'. This was partly because, being 'already in possession of a Stall', Thorp would need no further stipend. Jenkinson agreed, complimenting Thorp's 'sound judgement and discretion', and the appointment was settled.[50]

Gaisford seems to have demurred. In December he proposed

Charles Le Bas as Warden, on grounds of age (Le Bas could 'hardly be less than 53 or 54', Thorp was 48) and attainment: ' – he being an excellent classical scholar & mathematician as well as divine, and consequently qualified to see that the other professors do their respective duties'. Despite his respect for Gaisford, Van Mildert kept faith with Thorp.

Finding 'persons of known & distinguished qualifications' for the Professorships of Divinity and Greek took longer. An early memorandum suggested Gaisford as a possible Greek Professor. The Dean of Christ Church had no intention of returning to Durham, but he devoted a good deal of time to helping Van Mildert weigh up other possible candidates, while cautioning that it might be difficult to persuade academics of established stature to 'migrate to an experimental situation'.[51] Names proposed for the Divinity Chair included Le Bas, Keble, Ogilvie (commended by Gaisford) and two of the diocesan clergy: G. S. Faber, the learned and moderate Evangelical Rector of Long Newton, whom Van Mildert in 1832 preferred to the 'plum' Mastership of Sherburn Hospital; and the red-hot Evangelical Vicar of St Nicholas', Durham, Edward Davison.[52]

By the turn of the year, interest focused on two men. Edward Gresswell of Oriel was a respected scholar, described by Gaisford as 'a man of . . . extensive learning and indefatigable application'. Claiming reluctance to see Gresswell leave Oxford, Gaisford urged his retiring habits as a drawback. The second principal contender was Hugh James Rose.

Rose, a theologian of genuine distinction, edited the influential High Church *British Magazine*. He was also an intimate of Joshua Watson, introduced to him by Archbishop Manners-Sutton. Watson esteemed Rose's 'rare qualities of heart and mind' and found great 'congeniality of feeling' with him; an opinion shared by Christopher Wordsworth.[53]

Gaisford wrote to Van Mildert at the beginning of 1832, 'I do not think that either Gresswell or Rose would do for the situation of Div. Professor. Learning probably they both possess enough & to spare. But that is not the only qualification necessary . . .' This brought an indignant rebuttal from Jenkinson, who was, 'on the most mature consideration', convinced that they were the best candidates, and saw no reason to believe them 'deficient in the other requisite qualifications'.[54]

By the end of 1832 Rose had emerged as first choice, but he took his time about making a firm decision. Van Mildert wrote to Thorp in May 1833, 'The only impediment to Mr. Rose for the Divinity Chair is the state of his health, which makes me almost afraid of the experiment, & I believe overpowers, on his part, the strong inclination which he wd. otherwise have to undertake the charge.'[55] Besides his asthma, Rose may have hesitated over the relative isolation of Durham from matters of great moment astir in London, Oxford and Cambridge, and was certainly uneasy about the new University's financial security.

On 16th July, Rose wrote to thank Van Mildert for 'the very kind offer which I have received through Mr. Watson'. He professed 'never for an instant' to have swerved from 'the strongest wish' to take the Durham Professorship, adding 'with what inexpressible satisfaction I should find myself, in these days of change, under the eye & guidance of one for whom & for whose principles I have entertained such deep, warm & unmingled respect'. He asked for more time to consider his financial circumstances.[56]

Rose told Froude at the end of July that he was 'deliberating whether to accept the Divinity Professorship at Durham'. He had by now been drawn by Van Mildert into drafting statutes for the University, writing to Joshua Watson: 'Now, however fine it is to legislate, it is also very nervous. O that I could take you down with me! Might not Durham be made a grand Theological School, where, even after the Universities, they who could afford it might go for a year or two? Think of this, and tell me anything which strikes you.'[57]

On 20th August Rose still had doubts, telling Christopher Wordsworth that he was in poor health, had laid it on Van Mildert to decide whether he should go to Durham, and had 'promised to do so, if he wishes it – But I now earnestly hope that he will not, as I am little fit for the exertion.' He wrote on the same day and in the same vein to Newman, adding that 'under circumstances of health' he would have 'coveted' the chair, since 'the duties of the Professor will so much lie in the formation of the Clergy'.[58]

By early September, it was settled. Perceval thought it 'a matter of such moment to have Rose at Durham, that one ought not to be [sic] regret it', adding a tribute to his 'indefatigable zeal' and 'sound judgment'.[59]

Appointing to the Greek Professorship also gave trouble. Van Mildert favoured Edward Churton, son of the Archdeacon of St

David's, son-in-law and curate to John James Watson, until Gaisford heard from a trusted contact that 'there seems enough of natural talent, and of acquired learning, but a considerable deficiency in steadiness, and a lack of that discretion without which talent . . . may be mischievous'.[60] Churton's brilliant younger brother William Ralph, Chancellor's Prizewinner, fellow of Oriel, 'favourite disciple of Charles Lloyd's, domestic chaplain to Archbishop Howley' and friend of Joshua Watson, would have been a much stronger candidate, but had died of consumption in 1828.[61]

Thorp suggested Dr Hampden of Oriel, Othley of Oriel, Van Mildert's chaplain C. J. Plumer, Nordgate of St Luke's and the ubiquitous Davison. Froude and Newman canvassed Rose to press the claims of another Oriel fellow, Eden; Christopher Wordsworth commended Williamson Peile of Trinity, who was appointed Senior Tutor and Censor, and also spoke well of J. J. Blunt, a former Hulsean Lecturer.

Gaisford proposed Frederick Biscoe as 'fully adequate to the situation', drawing a tirade from Jenkinson: 'The appointment of so inferior a person would be fatal to the character & credit of the new Institution. If such important Offices are filled with second, third, or fourth rate men, it will excite general dissatisfaction . . .'[62] The final choice was yet another Oriel man, Gaisford's brother-in-law Henry Jenkyns.

Canvassed as a possible Principal for King's College, London, Jenkyns had a distinguished academic record: a double First at Christ Church in 1816, an Oriel Fellowship in 1818. An Etonian, he examined for Greek prizes at his former school and assisted Dr Thomas Arnold to prepare an edition of Thucydides for Oxford University. He also published a 'well-received and highly praised' edition of Cranmer's complete works.

Jenkyns was respectably well-connected. He received a stipend from Archbishop Manners-Sutton's son Charles, Speaker of the House of Commons, whose sons he had tutored at Eton. His brother Richard was Master of Balliol. His uncle Henry Hobhouse, a lawyer and MP who had been Peel's assistant at the Home Office, became one of the most active members of the Ecclesiastical Commission.[63] The move to Durham gave Jenkyns the financial security to marry his fiancée, Hobhouse's daughter Harriet – Oxford dons forfeited their Fellowships on marrying.

At Oriel, Jenkyns enjoyed generally amicable relations with

Newman, but sided against him in two college controversies. Neither brushing with Newman nor editing Cranmer was likely to endear Jenkyns to Hurrell Froude, who greeted the news of his appointment to the Durham Chair of Greek with the comment 'What a floor the Bishop of Durham has made in thinking Jenkyns a high church man? Rose ought to have known better. However if he gives up his Fellowship in consequence I had rather spare him than Eden.'[64]

The Mathematics Chair presented different problems. The Revd John Carr, Headmaster of Durham School since 1811, was appointed Professor in June 1833, but unfortunately died four months later, 'two days after term began'. His successor was a Cambridge man, Temple Chevallier, a divine and mathematician whom Van Mildert valued, preferring him to the Perpetual Curacy of Esh in May 1835.

William Palmer of Magdalen was appointed Junior Tutor and Censor. Readers were appointed in Law, Medicine, History, Moral Philosophy and Natural Philosophy, and a Lecturer in Chemistry and Mineralogy. The Lecturer in Modern Languages, James Hamilton, was recommended by the Duke of Cumberland on the advice of Prince Frederick of Prussia. Van Mildert, noting wryly to Thorp that 'Royal recommendations' must receive 'due acknowledgements', warned Cumberland that he could not commit the Chapter's decision; but Hamilton was duly accepted.[65]

The University opened on 28th October 1833 with five Divinity Students, two of them already B.A., nineteen 'Students of the Foundation' and eighteen 'Students'. It was announced that the Divinity Students' terms would be longer than those of the 'Academic Course', that the Professor of Greek would 'read with the Students of the Academic Course, as well as with the Divinity Students, on the Philology of S[acred] S[cripture] during the whole period of study', and the Divinity Professor would also 'read with' the students of both courses throughout their studies.

Rose arrived in Durham something above a week before the students, passing through Harrogate to pay his respects to Van Mildert. Thorp returned from a trip to Bamburgh a few days later. Jenkyns visited Durham at the end of October to 'make personal enquiries' before reaching a final decision about the Greek Professorship. By Thorp's request he 'assisted at the examination of

candidates for admission' on 29th October, writing a formal acceptance to Van Mildert later that day. Jenkyns then returned to
Oxford, coming into residence at Durham the following January.[66]

On New Year's Eve Rose wrote to Jenkyns, 'I really think I may
make a very favourable report. It is a great point to have got thro'
the *first* term quietly without any necessity for severity, & to find that
many of the young men are taking great pains . . .'

Rose had already begun to find the duties oppressive, however: he
had hopes for the immediate appointment of an assistant to work
with him, 'for I am quite sure that no justice can be done to Clerical
Education by *one* man'. He also wanted Jenkyns to give an Epiphany
Term course 'on the Criticism & Interpretation of the Greek
Test[ament]', adding when Jenkyns protested that he naturally had
not meant Epiphany 1834, and that the proposal 'was with reference
to future years' – unless Jenkyns 'shd. be quite able to undertake
[the lectures] comfortably in the May term'.[67]

Rose and his wife spent a few days with the Thorp family at the
beginning of 1834. Rose reported Ryton 'a very delightful place',
but his relationship with Thorp was already showing signs of strain.
When Jenkyns came into residence Rose pressed hospitality on him,
writing diplomatically: 'The Warden is all kindness – but he is
overdone with work & the kindest thing to him is to let him be as
quiet [as] we can. I have my fears of his health now & then.'

During the year Rose delivered and published two public lectures,
'An Apology for the Study of Divinity' and 'The Study of Church
History Recommended'. The second caused controversy by vigorous disparagement of the ecclesiastical historians Milner, Mosheim
and Jortin. Newman, who shared Rose's 'very low opinion' of them,
called it 'one of the most enthusiastic compositions I ever met with
. . . I trust it will carry away, as well as inform and convince a great
many readers.'[68]

Jenkyns published his first lecture 'On the Advantages of Classical
Studies', but Van Mildert pressed him in vain to publish his second:
Jenkyns consulted his brother Richard and Gaisford, who advised
him that the lecture 'wd. be more useful if read from time to time to
new sets of students, than if committed to the press'.[69]

Rose continued to complain about the weight of his divinity
course, writing to Joshua Watson, 'They overwork me here, for
while my brother professor has two lectures a week, I have seven

days' lectures, and the Sunday evening lecture is a very distressing and weary one.'[70] Rose was not the only member of the University staff to find his work burdensome: the Chapter meeting on 15th February was forced to declare the Readership in Moral Philosophy 'vacant in consequence of the absence of Dr. Miller'.

Two tasks were becoming urgent: drawing up statutes for the University, and securing a second Act of Parliament to annex Durham prebends to the Wardenship and the Greek and Divinity Chairs. A private postscript to Rose's letter of 8th January exhorted Jenkyns to use 'any means of urging the Bishop to getting the Bill for the Stalls quickly on'; the 'many delicacies about what Stall shd be taken' were frittering away irreplaceable time. 'And tho' Govt. is in a certain way pledged to this Bishop, yet if *he* dies, they are *not* pledged to another & wd certainly court popularity by taking some [corrected to 'most'] of the D. stalls for other purposes.'

A plan agreed between Van Mildert and the Chapter in September declared that the annexation was to be managed by taking one in two of 'the first six Stalls vacant by death'. Van Mildert acknowledged to Jenkyns that this arrangement was not ideal, and by February 1834 had abandoned it in favour of taking either three 'particular stalls, as they become vacant by death or removal, or . . . the three stalls that first become vacant, whichsoever they may happen to be'.[71]

A number of interlocking problems bedevilled the issue. On the one hand, Rose in particular was anxious to have the Stalls presented as early as possible: Van Mildert was now near threescore-and-ten, his health was deteriorating rapidly, and his death might terminate the whole arrangement. On the other hand, Van Mildert wanted the most valuable prebends secured to the University, and was ambivalent about sacrificing his next three presentations – he too felt chill breath on the back of his neck.

The final difficulty, on which the second Durham University Bill foundered, concerned the possibility of Chapter preferment passing into the hands of Government. If a prebendary were to be presented to some dignity in the Royal gift, the patronage of his Stall would revert to the Crown for that turn. In July 1833, while working on the drafting of statutes, Rose had identified a threat that Government might give, say, Thorp a bishopric in order to thrust 'a person like Dr. Arnold' into the Chapter with an express brief to 'liberalize' the University. Rose prescribed drawing up the statutes governing the 'divinity department' with sufficient care and tightness to give any such future interloper 'a hard task'.[72]

Van Mildert detected a worse danger. The same technique might force a Government nominee into one of the three stalls to be annexed to University offices. 'What, if *Dr. Arnold* were to replace *yourself*, or *Sidney Smith* [sic], our Professor *Rose?*' he asked Thorp. He and Rose felt the only safe course was to secure a waiver of Crown prerogative with regard to the annexed stalls, thus putting the Durham Professorships on the same footing as the Oxford Lady Margaret Professorship.[73] Thorp, possibly feeling that no Government willing to give him a bishopric could be entirely bad, temporised.

A Chapter meeting on 15th February 1834 officially requested Thorp as Warden to draw up statutes for the University. On 15th March Thorp presented draft statutes to the Weekly Chapter, who ordered a circulation of copies to the Bishop, Dean and all the prebendaries. By the end of March nothing had been formalised, and Rose, now back in London, was becoming alarmed. He wrote to Jenkyns, 'Thorp has all but lost the Bill by chusing to persevere in declaring that the D. and Chapter were not to be parties to the Bill, tho' their consent to the B[ishop]'s always nominating the Warden & Professors is clearly necessary.'

The Chapter had passed a resolution to that effect two years previously, but 'like every other rule and statute' it was 'never put into form, & never sealed'.

Rose and Thorp were now openly at war. 'I find Dr. Tournay expressed at once the same opinion of T. when he went to Oxford last year that we are compelled to hold now', Rose told Jenkyns, adding darkly that since returning to London he had uncovered further secret Thorp machinations against the value of 'their' Stalls, going back 'above a year'.[74]

The petition for the Bill was entered at the end of March in the name of the Bishop only, then commandeered by the Diocesan Registrar and rushed back to Durham to receive the Chapter's approval and Seal on 4th April. Van Mildert left Harrogate for London early in April. On 16th April he saw Lord Grey and 'communicated our Bill to him'. Grey declared the Bill 'so entirely a matter of arrangement' between Van Mildert and the Chapter that 'no discussion can fairly be raised upon it', but protested that the Crown waiver, if secured, would leave the Warden and Professors 'excluded . . . from the prospects they might otherwise have had of higher advancement', which would be unfair.

Van Mildert discussed Grey's argument with Lord Shaftesbury, who felt the Durham prebends were prize enough to more than compensate for any loss of 'higher advancement'. The waiver could not be inserted in the Bill without Crown assent. Van Mildert reluctantly endorsed letting the Bill proceed as it stood, but clearly signalled his intention of withdrawing it at a later stage, if he could not carry his point.

Shaftesbury successfully moved the Bill's second reading on 16th April. The Committee was fixed for 29th April. Van Mildert sent Thorp a full account of events, urging him to come to London for greater ease of discussion.[75]

Thorp's reply shocked him deeply. The Warden now pressed for the waiver to be abandoned, arguing that it could only harm the University's interests if they attempted to deny Government 'that interest in the University which in the natural order of things it will possess'; 'the influence of the Crown will on the whole be useful to the University, & a great deal be lost to it by taking it away'.

Van Mildert, perplexed and distressed, patiently dismantled Thorp's arguments. 'I remember it was your own observation, that the present Ministry would assuredly avail themselves, with eagerness, of any opportunity to get a hold upon any of the University offices; &, having got it, to retain it for the purpose of eventually moulding the Institution itself to their own views & purposes.' He asked why Thorp was now 'disposed to place more confidence than heretofore in the conformity of the views of the present Govt. with ours – & certainly much more than I can bring myself to entertain'.

He also reported Grey's latest suggestion, that the Crown should keep rights over the Stalls but not the University appointments, with a 'competent Stipend' being provided from the prebendal revenues when any 'Office' was thus deprived of its emolument. Van Mildert disliked this, but asked Thorp to discuss it with 'Dr. Smith, or a Chapter, (if you can convene one soon enough)' and give counsel, repeating his plea that Thorp 'should come to town as soon as your health will permit, that we may confer more at leisure & at ease than we can in writing'. The Weekly Chapter discussed the proposal on 26th April but did not 'feel . . . competent to express an opinion upon this question which shall bind their body'. No 'new matter proposed to be introduced into the Bill' could receive authoritative consideration before 20th July.[76]

The Committee was deferred to 6th May. On the previous Saturday, 'the Chapter' had a 'conference with the Bp.' in an attempt to reach a common view. Van Mildert met with Grey on 5th May, sending a delicately worded memorandum of his 'impression that Your Lordship perceives some objections, or difficulties, in applying to the Crown to relinquish it's Prerogative'. Grey in turn claimed the impression that Van Mildert had already determined to withdraw the Bill.[77]

On the evening of 5th May, Henry Hobhouse 'met Phillpot and Thorpe [sic] at the Athenaeum. The former introduced me to the latter. I asked T. in the presence of P. how the Bill went on? P. said "The fewer Bills, the better." T. said "I really don't know how it stands." ' Staggered, Hobhouse went to Lambeth the next day to consult Rose, missing him but finding Ogilvie, who told him of the 'Chapter conference' (which increased Hobhouse's astonishment at 'Thorp's ignorance') and promised Rose would call on him, adding that Rose was 'content' to lose the Bill. Hobhouse then tried Shaftesbury, 'who thinks the Bp. ought not to proceed with the Bill, unless Ld. Grey considers, & thinks it very likely that Ld. Durham will not let Ld. G. do so, and further will persuade him to put a mitre on Dr. T's head to obtain the Sway of the University'.

At 5 pm it was announced that the Committee was 'adjourned to Friday'. Hobhouse wrote in consternation to Jenkyns: 'My dr. Henry, I fear your Bill will be strangled in the Birth.'[78]

On 8th May, urged by Shaftesbury, Van Mildert agreed to make one last approach to Grey before withdrawing the Bill. His letter of 9th May brought an instant response: Grey had not the time to see Van Mildert again, but would reopen the matter with the King at the first opportunity. He hinted that the King might not be wholly unwilling to concede.[79]

By the end of the next day, a final refusal had been given. Van Mildert, with a graceful letter to Grey, withdrew the Bill and went North at once. He was consumed with anxiety for his wife, who had suffered a stroke the previous autumn and been near to death in February. Reaching Harrogate on 12th May, he was relieved to find Jane 'better than when I left her'; he himself was 'exceedingly jaded, & . . . suffered much pain in my journey'. He left without seeing Rose, who remained in London.

From Harrogate he sent Thorp a mordant retrospective on the University Bill fiasco, explaining the withdrawal by the difficulty of securing Chapter agreement to fresh clauses before the parliamentary session ended. 'My only wish & desire now is, that I may not (shd. I live to resume the matter again another year) go up to town with an imperfect & undigested Document, but with a Bill drawn out carefully in all it's details, thoroughly canvassed & approved by a full Chapter, leaving nothing afterwards to my discretion or indiscretion . . .'[80]

The 'collision of opinions' with Thorp had hurt him deeply. He could no longer be confident that Thorp's vision of the University chimed with his own.

Rose wrote to Jenkyns on 27th May, 'In good truth, Thorp is at the bottom of all this . . . The Minister wd. not, I believe, have objected of himself. But now that an objection is taken, with Thorp constantly to urge it, how can it be got over?' Rose felt that any danger from 'conceding the point to the Crown' was likely to be temporary, but that was irrelevant. 'The Bill is gone – & you & I have not an appointment.'

Although Van Mildert had 'directed the appointments to be made out' in November 1833, 'for some reason Thorp . . . kept them back'. Rose saw himself and Jenkyns in a precarious situation: unless the Chapter had '*sealed* any Act giving the nomination to the Bishop', Van Mildert '*cannot* appoint, till they have passed a Statute giving him the power. This *cannot* be before July. And *will* they *then* give him the nomination, before he endows the offices? If not, where are you and I?'

When Jenkyns demurred from this as unduly pessimistic, Rose pointed out that they were paid from Van Mildert's voluntary contribution to the University Chest. Van Mildert had only to die, and their income could dry up at source. Rose did not mistrust the whole Chapter:

I believe many of the[m] to be most honourable men. But I am equally aware that *one* who leads them says one thing today & another tomorrow. And when I remember the way in wch. he spoke of Peile's sacrifices of income, & his *good* fortune in getting what he has at Durham, I will never put myself into his power without having bread to eat totally independent on *him*.[81]

Rose did not return to Durham. He had persuaded his brother Henry John, a Fellow of St John's College, Cambridge, to take over teaching the divinity students for the summer term.

Van Mildert evidently queried the propriety of this step, drawing a defensive letter from the Professor. Rose explained he had 'found clearly that in order to have an efficient plan of study, . . . a residence of eight months at least on the part of the students would be necessary'. Rose's own state of health would not allow him to undertake 'daily lecturing of two hours during eight months, and the residence during one part of the year, against which the medical men warned me'. He wanted to renegotiate his duties around six months' residence and teaching, with a second Divinity Professor to take over for one term each year. In order to provide a salary for the second Professor, Rose offered to 'give up a third of the proposed salary as well as a large part or, if necessary, the whole of the fees'.

Rose protested that not only had he repeatedly submitted this plan to Thorp's judgement, but Thorp had given him to understand that Van Mildert himself approved it. On that understanding, Rose had in February 1834 accepted the post of Chaplain to Archbishop Howley.[82]

Thorp confirmed Rose's account, but added that he felt the attempt to retain Rose's services had already gone too far: 'I certainly should not incline to any further concessions. The modification of residence I have suggested is quite enough . . .'[83]

Rose spent July and August corresponding with the Chapter about his financial standing and conditions of service. Dr Smith, that year's Sub-Dean, sent him the Trustees' guarantee of £600 per annum plus the divinity students' fees, and bland replies to his pleas that the working arrangements Thorp had imposed on him made his duties an impossible burden to his health.

Thorp assured Van Mildert that he had left the University arrangements open to be 'settled at a College meeting' where Rose, Jenkyns, Peile and Palmer were present, since he 'wished the regulations to approve themselves to those who were to execute them. Mr. Rose's recollection fails him in this point . . .'[84]

Selective memory lapses seem to have been a feature of the affair. Thorp told Jenkyns in November 1834 that Rose, instead of dividing the £1,000 for the two senior Professors' stipends equally, 'claimed £600 upon some understanding to which neither the Warden nor any other members of Chapter were parties'. In fact Van Mildert proposed the unequal arrangement to the Dean in November 1831, and Thorp knew of it.[85]

Thorp maintained that all arrangements with regard to the

Divinity course had been set down in the draft Statutes, which Rose had been shown 'before any one had seen them, except it was yr. L'dship'. This chimes ill with a letter from Jenkyns, undated but written before Rose left Durham, thanking Thorp for 'your notes of Statutes, which I have read with care, & communicated, as I suppose was your wish to Rose', and another from Thorp to Jenkyns, sending him 'our hasty sketch of statutes' which he hoped to put 'into better form before I return to Durham to take Rose's opinion'.[86]

Thorp thought Rose might fairly demand 'a dispensation from time to time ill health calling for it; – assistants if found necessary; – & an extension of the residence of the Div[init]y Students supposing their studies to require it', provided that these 'indulgences & exceptions' were exercised solely 'by leave of the Warden'. Rose could not be allowed to 'claim that indulgence as the rule of his own practice, when experience had proved that Durham suited his health'.

Other suggestions of status-consciousness lurk between the lines of the letter. Thorp describes himself as 'the only one of the Staff practiced in the actual government of a College', emphasises that he was the one called upon to draw up Statutes, and had apparently also assumed the right to choose Rose an assistant, 'wh[ich] he refused in a reasonable bona fide case'. Rose's bid for the 'Divinity branch' to have independent status 'apart from the other authorities' was anathema.

It was hardly astonishing if a theologian of national stature chafed under such authoritarianism. Neither was it remarkable if Thorp, finding his Northern University muscled in on by a London high-flyer with grand schemes to change the face of clergy training, felt his position as Warden compromised. The clash showed neither man at his best; but Rose's charges of unreliability against Thorp seem well-founded.

Thorp offered a rhetorical plea of guilty 'to the desire of retaining Mr. Rose', but no practical concessions.

Rose considered his position carefully. He learned from Van Mildert that 'the difficulties as to the Crown Prerogative were not the reasons for withdrawing the Bill – that Lord Grey requested it might be withdrawn for what a party concerned said were State Reasons – & which the Bishop says he is not at liberty to explain'. Van Mildert thought the legislation not finally lost: 'If it shd. be, he will still give the Stalls to the Professors, if they fall in his life & he does not see what more he can do.'

Rose was offered a formal Chapter guarantee of salary 'under all circumstances', but felt that without some movement on the question of working arrangements his position would be impossible.[87]

The first, third and eleventh stalls were now more or less definitely earmarked for annexation: but on 28th September the seventh fell vacant when Bishop Gray of Bristol died.

Although there is no direct evidence that Van Mildert ever offered Gray's stall to Rose, it is probably no coincidence that he waited until 6th October, the day after Rose wrote his resignation, before giving the stall elsewhere.

Thanking Van Mildert for 'the kindness & affection which I experienced at yr. Ldship's hand, while resident at Durham', Rose declared that he 'should have gladly returned, had it not been made impossible . . .' Durham's scope for developing 'a new system of Clerical education' still powerfully attracted him; '& yr. Ldship, from having . . . suffered so severely in health, will easily judge how much that attraction was increased by my having enjoyed at Durham, a degree of health, quite unknown to me for many years before, or since'.[88] Rose, who became Principal of King's College, London, had less than five years left before his asthma killed him.

A full explanation of Rose's decision must include frustration at being so far from the centres of action. He was, he told Jenkyns, 'a thorough Southron', and although he could and did become involved in local affairs, he pined for the national. In January 1834 Newman was sufficiently irked by Rose's absence to speak of 'running up to Durham to hold a conference' with him; by March, Rose had contrived to be back in London and was busily picking up threads.[89]

Losing Rose was a heavy blow to Van Mildert: besides his 'eloquence in the pulpit, his ability as a writer, his wisdom in counsel, his learning in controversy, and the many graces of his personal character', his public stature enhanced the University's prestige. Smith was less impressed, telling Van Mildert: 'I am sorry for anything that is to add to your anxiety but I cannot upon any other account regret Mr. Rose's resignation. I think that he has shewn such a temper as would in all probability be very detrimental to the interests of our young university, and however great his industry and talents may be they can be no compensation for a restless Disposition which would involve us in endless disputes.'[90]

Replacing Rose was difficult, the more so as the parliamentary fiasco had made the University's financial basis shakier than ever. Although Van Mildert had rallied gallantly to its defence immediately after the Bill disaster, instructing his bankers to make his contribution to University funds £1,000 every six months,[91] the departure of Rose was one desertion too many. Van Mildert well knew that Gray's vacant Stall might be (as it in fact was) the last he would ever have at his disposal. Instead of using it to lure in another distinguished theologian for the Divinity Chair, he gave it to his much-loved nephew-by-marriage Henry Douglas.

Obviously not wholly comfortable about this, Van Mildert asked advice from the Dean as well as Thorp. Jenkinson replied diplomatically: 'From the respectability of Mr. Douglas' character I have no doubt that his appointment will be acceptable and give general satisfaction.'

Thorp, according to Rose, wrote Van Mildert 'a long letter' assuring him that 'when he had once settled what stalls shd go to the Profrs, however long they might be in falling, no one cd. blame him for giving away the rest to his own friends'.

Six members of the Chapter, Douglas among them, later used this argument in modified form to the Church Commissioners: Van Mildert 'considered the appropriation of the first, third and eleventh stalls so settled that when one of the other stalls fell vacant that summer [1834] he gave it to an outsider'.[92]

The Divinity Chair was to remain vacant until 1840. During the academic year 1834–5 the divinity students were taught by Henry Jenkyns, the Greek Professor, and Temple Chevallier, the Professor of Mathematics.

Rose regarded Jenkyns as his natural successor, and Smith's letter of 4th September recommended this. During the winter of 1834 Jenkyns was already weighing the comparative financial advantages of the two Chairs, advised by his father-in-law Hobhouse. Spurred by the imminent start of another academic year, Van Mildert sent Jenkyns a formal offer on 28th September 1835; the Divinity Professorship had, he felt, 'been longer vacant than is quite seemly or satisfactory'.[93]

Jenkyns was not a public figure, but he was able, committed to the work in Durham, tolerant of Thorp, and little inclined to distract himself from his duties by meddling in the affairs of the great world. His relationship with Hobhouse moreover became strategic to the

University's interests after Hobhouse was appointed to the 1835 Ecclesiastical Commission. Van Mildert expressed pleasure on learning of Hobhouse's appointment: 'He used to be very staunch both in Church and State, & I hope still continues so: & his opinion will have weight.' To Jenkyns he added more pointedly: 'He will not be disposed, I think, to put even Deans and Chapters in jeopardy, nor to break down any of the bulwarks of our Establishment.'[94]

The one mildly surprising aspect of the choice was Jenkyns' continued friendship with Dr Arnold; but Jenkyns dissented from Arnold's heresies, and Van Mildert had always approved of remaining on amicable personal terms with men of exceptionable theology but sound moral character.

By now the question of annexing prebends to the Chairs was completely out of Van Mildert's hands, the Ecclesiastical Commissioners having taken it over within a general review of capitular finance. Jenkyns agreed to assume the duties and salary of Divinity Professor, but in order to avoid any risk of 'retarding succession to a Stall' he kept his original title of Greek Professor.

The adopting of statutes continued to hurry slowly. Jenkyns warned Thorp in November 1834, 'I do trust that the present Chapter will not separate, without sealing some code of statutes for us however short. If not, shaken as we are already, I am sure we shall fall to pieces.'

Thorp replied that he was proposing Statutes which could, 'if taken as a basis . . . be easily cut down to what we want. They are not altogether what I like, being framed rather in accordance with the vision of others than my own.'[95] On 21st November the Chapter accepted Thorp's draft and formally determined to make a fundamental statute constituting a Senate and a Convocation. On that basis they agreed to petition Parliament to grant the University a Royal Charter. Hobhouse thought the Charter superfluous, and the leisurely pace alarming: 'I hope the Charter will not keep you much longer without Statutes', he wrote to Jenkyns in December.[96]

Public affairs took an unexpected turn in November 1834 when the King sacked the new Melbourne Government and called on Peel to form an administration; but Hobhouse's judgement that 'a mere change of Ministry' would be little help with the University's political problems proved well-founded. A Charter was drafted in February 1835. Before leaving London on 10th March Van Mildert discussed the whole Charter issue with Peel, who was cordial but vague: 'he seems quite disposed to favour our views,' Van Mildert reported; '& on that point the interference of Parliament will not be required'.[97]

Reaching Harrogate on 12th March, Van Mildert found a letter from Howley which reported Peel, 'much pleased with the result of his conference with you', but as recommending that the Charter application 'should be delayed, till the threatened motions respecting Subscription to the Articles on admission to Oxford & Cambridge had been disposed of'.[98]

Van Mildert took this as indicating 'that Sir Robt. Peel is in good earnest on the matter, & desirous of putting the concerns of the Chapter on the most practicable & least hazardous footing'; but the Peel administration fell at the beginning of April, and the question of a Royal Charter was not settled in Van Mildert's lifetime.

The fundamental statute was finally agreed on 20th July 1835, and attention turned to drafting University Regulations. These were 'submitted to Convocation on Thursday, Feb. 25th, 1836', by which time Van Mildert was dead.[99]

In November 1835 Howley, urged by Van Mildert, brought the question of annexing Durham prebends to the University offices before the Ecclesiastical Commissioners; but they decided to defer considering it 'till the concerns of the Chapter were brought in due course of proceeding before the Board'.[100]

Van Mildert clung gallantly to the question, to the very end of his life. His last letter to Joshua Watson, dated 28th January 1836, mentioned having 'written somewhat largely to the Archbishop on our Durham University concerns, and the arrangement of our prebendal stalls, which, I much fear, will not go on so smoothly as when Sir Robert Peel was an Ecclesiastical Commissioner. I have stirred up the Archbishop to do what he can for us; and, knowing his good-will in the matter, I hope for the best'.[101]

Van Mildert must have asked himself, as many others were asking, whether his University could survive him. With the loss of his £2,000 annual payment, his readiness to meet unexpected expenses, his many unprogrammed extra contributions, above all his staunch conviction of the University's worth, its future now seemed to hang on the fragile goodwill of an increasingly quarrelsome and reluctant Durham Chapter. He had built well, however. By his own vision, determination, perseverance and sacrificial generosity he had swept the Chapter in spite of themselves past the point of no returning. Van Mildert's University still had a hard passage ahead; but the life he had given it was too strong to fail.

CHAPTER 7

An old almanack

On 9th May 1832, at the height of the Reform Bill crisis, Joshua Watson's doomsday scenario came true. The Radical MP Joseph Hume launched a furious Commons attack on the 'established and enormously overpaid Church', moving successfully for a detailed Return of clerical pluralism in the Church of England.[1] This was a transparent preliminary to corrective measures. The Radical assault on the Established Church was under way.

Joshua Watson had in early 1831 proposed a Royal Commission of Enquiry to obtain 'accurate information on the state of Church revenues, with a view to the suggestion of the best practical remedies for the evils of translations, of unseemly commendams, and offensive pluralities'. Significantly, he wanted no lay membership: 'Laymen would of necessity be the Minister's nominees', and Grey's nominees could not be trusted to guard the Church's interests. In practice the lay membership of Grey's Commission of Enquiry, announced on 23rd June, was unexceptionable: its most radical member was Stephen Lushington, a Whig ecclesiastical lawyer whom Liverpool had appointed to the Church Building Commission and Wellington to the Ecclesiastical Courts Commission.[2]

Van Mildert was a Commissioner, with Howley, Vernon Harcourt of York, Blomfield, Kaye of Lincoln and Bethell of Bangor: all except York associates of the Hackney Phalanx, although Blomfield and Kaye were Reform Act defectors.

The Government wanted summary findings as rapidly as possible. On 15th January, although the Commissioners were only at the stage of 'giving directions for preparing a tabular statement of the Returns that have been made, preparatory to making a Report', they agreed to give the Government 'a return of the gross & net amounts of Eccles:l property as far as they have yet been received'. Van Mildert was 'not quite well satisfied on this proceeding – but it cd. not well be put aside'. The next meeting on 21st January made its 'chief business' to 'determine on the most convenient sort of *digest*, or *tabular statements*, to be made of the Returns to the Inquiries', and Van Mildert's apprehensions sharpened. He told Thorp, 'The Govt. have obtained possession of the gross & net averages of the Returns, but without the explanations requisite to a correct judgt. upon them. This must be carefully watched, lest some sinister use be made of it. Ld. Lansdowne seemed anxious to satisfy me that no such things were in contemplation. *"Sed timeo."* All this is *confidential*.'[3]

Church Reform schemes of all complexions abounded. The Hackney Phalanx were most horrified by the radical proposals of their 'well intentioned, but highly misguided friend, Lord Henley'. Henley, Peel's brother-in-law and a devout churchman, proposed a far-reaching package including retirement pensions for clergymen at 70, abolition of all sinecures, *commendams* and canonries, conversion of all cathedrals into parish churches, a levelling of episcopal incomes accompanied by a prohibition on translations except to archbishoprics, and the exclusion of bishops from the House of Lords. Park commented darkly to Howley that some 'professed friends of the Church of England' were doing her more harm than all her enemies.[4]

The mood of the Hackney Phalanx at the end of 1832 bordered on the apocalyptic. In October Howley's archiepiscopal Charge inspired Henry Handley Norris to write him an emotional letter about 'the ordeal thro' which there is every indication that we must shortly pass', which, he added, he had 'long foreboded':

But tho' the Church of England and those who cleave to her and suffer persecution with her may pass thro' fire and water in the purification she has to undergo my confidence is that she will come forth into a wealthy place and whilst I supplicate for myself that my faith may not fail me in the hour of tryal I am no less earnest in imploring for your Grace those larger measures of divine wisdom and ghostly strength which may present you as a beacon upon a hill during the darkest moments of the storm . . .[5]

Many saw the cholera epidemic which reached England from the Continent in October 1831 as a sign of Divine judgement. 21st March 1832 was declared a national day of fasting and humiliation. A sense of impending doom oppressed many sober churchmen. The Conservative electoral disaster at the 'Reformed' general election in December seemed a further omen of Radical triumph. As they waited for the 'Reformed Parliament' to open its proceedings, churchmen of all shades from Keble to Dr Arnold were convinced that the Established Church was about to be dismantled. Blomfield, the least fanciful or fanatical of prelates, wrote to Archdeacon Glenie in Ceylon: 'What trials are in store for us God only knows, but that we shall have a hard struggle for our very existence as an Established Church, is abundantly clear . . .'[6]

In mid-January Arnold's *The Principles of Church Reform* argued that the Established Church could be saved only by conceding enough of its doctrinal basis to bring in the majority of Dissenters. Van Mildert thought 'Dr. Arnold's lucubrations . . . exquisitely absurd and mischievous'.[7]

Van Mildert composed a 'Prayer for this Church and Nation in the Year 1833', lamenting the wicked and irreligious state of the times, and thanking God that 'the sins & iniquities prevailing among us have not yet drawn upon our heads the full measure of Thine indignation, & that time is yet presented to us for repentance & amendment . . .' It seemed to Van Mildert that not only the Church but the entire 'social body' faced dismemberment. He prayed that the holders of ecclesiastical and secular authority might be preserved from 'rash enterprises which may endanger our ancient & well-tried Institutions in Church & State, & thereby open a way to the evil-minded to effect the overthrow of our dearest & most sacred rights . . .', imploring Divine assistance not only to protect the righteous and 'turn the hearts of the scoffer & the scorner . . . to contrition', but also to give the rulers 'true Christian courage . . . to put down the turbulent & unruly'.[8]

Van Mildert's health continued poor, and his mood dark. He wrote to Bruce Knight at the end of 1832:

In truth, the aspect of the times, like that which an impenetrable fog just now presents at my window, baffles all attempt at getting an insight into what we are to hope for, or to fear. Were I not compelled, *nolens volens*, to take a prominent part in public life, most gladly would I retreat to some obscure nook or corner, and bid farewell to the great world, with all its doings and misdoings.[9]

In mid-December Archbishop Howley and sixteen bishops met at Lambeth hoping to reach a common position on Church Reform. Van Mildert reported to Thorp, 'I bore my full share (if not more than my share) in the conversation – for, after all, it was little more than *conversation*, adapted to elicit our respective opinions on the most important topics without much discussion of specific measures and chiefly to enable the Abp. to communicate to the Govt. our general feelings and persuasions.' The meeting did not seek to adopt any 'particular schemes or devices of any kind'; the sixteen were a diverse group, including Bathurst of Norwich, Maltby of Chichester and five other Reform Bill 'rebels'.[10]

Although at the beginning of 1833 Van Mildert entertained 'good hope' that 'our Bench as a Body will come out of the conflict without discredit, notwithstanding some few exceptions', and reckoned 'at least 3 fourths' of those present at Lambeth 'to be actuated by the best spirit of firmness & discretion and a real desire to do with a good grace every thing safe & needful & nothing more',[11] organising any more definite episcopal pressure-group proved difficult. Howley was preoccupied with the grave illness of his son, who died at Oxford that spring; his own health broke down under the accumulated stresses.[12]

The Government kept its plans very quiet. As late as 2nd February Van Mildert told Thorp it seemed 'pretty certain that the Govt. are in no state of preparation for any measures relative to the Church, excepting Tithes', and thought that they should 'probably escape the annoyance of having Church Reform mentioned in the King's Speech'. He attended the Lords on 5th February for the King's Speech still 'wholly ignorant' of what it was to contain, but hoping to gain some 'insight . . . into the views & feelings of different parties, from the discussions . . .'

The Speech itself, pledging church reform and specifically 'a more equitable and judicious distribution of the revenues of the Church', struck him as 'all but a death blow . . . The great evil is that the Ministers seem purposely to keep us in the dark as to their intentions so that it is impossible for us to be prepared for them. God send us a good deliverance.' He told Bruce Knight on 6th February: 'Scarcely venturing to hope that I can render any essential service in the troubles we must expect to encounter, I yet trust, by God's help, to be found at my post, and not to swerve, so long as there is any *vis vitae* remaining in me.'[13]

Nobody was surprised to find reform moves beginning with the Church of Ireland. The Church Temporalities (Ireland) Bill, introduced into the Commons on 12th February, among other things amalgamated two archbishoprics and eight bishoprics with neighbours at the next vacancy, removing their revenues; reduced the revenues of the two richest sees; suspended the presentation and

removed the revenues of any parish which had been without
worship for three years; and abolished church cess, a tax levied on
the inhabitants of a parish to keep the parish church in good repair.
The proceeds of the Bill's various economies were to be administered
by a new corporation, to be called the Ecclesiastical Commissioners,
for 'such purposes as Parliament shall hereafter appoint and decide'.

To High Churchmen this was abomination. 'Why do we not
petition against the principle of the Irish Church robbery Bill?'
Archdeacon Bayley demanded. '. . . I would petition against the
principle only, and take no notice of the folly of the detail.'[14]

The Conservative leadership took a more pragmatic view. Conceding the principle, Peel began negotiations with the Government
aimed at securing the redistributed revenues to Church of Ireland
purposes.

Moderate politicians of both sides were anxious to avoid another
clash between Lords and Commons. Stanley, the Irish Secretary,
argued that a Lords rejection of the Bill 'would vastly increase the
chance of disestablishment', which the Whig leadership wanted no
more than did the Tories. In mid-February Grey, confirming that
the Government had church reform measures in train, defended the
clergy and episcopate against an attack by Lord King. He deplored
King's proposal to take tithes from Deans and Chapters and distribute them more equally among those 'who did all the work'. 'Earl
Grey's rebuke to Lord King might a little revive us,' Van Mildert
wrote, 'had not Ld. Althorp's projects for upsetting the *Irish* Church
given fresh cause for dismay . . .'[15]

Catholic Relief marked Van Mildert's Rubicon: he had worked
then through all it meant to part company with the Conservative
leadership, and no expediency politics could deflect him now.
During the spring and early summer he served as the 'beacon upon a
hill' of Norris' vision, an orientation point for bishops inclined to
oppose the Bill. The bishops met to 'talk over matters every Thursday after business at the Bounty Board', using the Dean's Yard
offices of Queen Anne's Bounty as a base; but no agreed position
emerged, and in a natural development a group of 'three or four'
took to visiting Van Mildert weekly for 'more confidential discussion': he cautioned Thorp not to 'blab'.[16]

Rumours of all kinds abounded. Van Mildert, discovering he had
been credited with saying 'that the Irish Church Bill had better not
be opposed, for that in a short time we should only have a worse',

assured Bruce Knight there was not 'a shadow of foundation for it. I quite agree with you, that a worse can hardly be; and, I believe, there are few of the Clergy who are not of the same opinion.'[17]

Van Mildert kept a keen eye on expressions of clerical opposition to the Bill. He complimented Bruce Knight on the 'noble feeling and spirit' his Welsh clergy had shown 'towards their Irish brethren', and with Joshua Watson's support advised Thorp on tactics for handling Durham clerical feeling.[18]

At the end of May the Bishops had a 'congratulatory private audience with his Majesty'. Van Mildert reported to Thorp that 'mutual professions of attachment were interchanged with many assurances of Royal favour and protection', adding darkly 'How these will be verified time must show.'[19]

On 3rd June, seven bishops caused outcry by voting against the Government on a matter not directly concerned with Church interests. Three days later Phillpotts exacerbated the situation with 'a tremendous warrior utterance about the king's duties under the coronation oath'. The King wrote to Howley 'urging the bishops, for the sake of their order and the church, not to meddle in politics'.[20] Pressure on the bishops to accept the Bill intensified on 21st June when the Government finally agreed to drop the appropriation clause, a decision regarded by the Radicals and Irish Catholics as a dastardly betrayal, and the Conservative leadership officially withdrew its opposition.

Van Mildert wrote to Thorp:

The omission of the most shameful clause of the Irish Church Bill will probably smooth its progress in the H. of Lords. Yet to my apprehension the rest of it is so incorrigibly bad that I shall never be able to give it countenance. It assumes throughout, though tacitly, such maxims and principles of legislation respecting the Church as are utterly subversive of every rational view of an Established Church, either with reference to its spiritualities or its temporalities . . . I detest the measure more than I can describe and am quite sure the Church cannot long survive it.[21]

He was more worried about the June developments' effect on his brother bishops, and in particular feared that Howley would now support the Bill. The prospect of a public collision with the Archbishop, 'the person of all others from whom I should most reluctantly differ', disturbed him so much that he considered simply staying away from the debates. He wrote to Joshua Watson: 'But I cannot help it: again and again have I considered the matter, and can see only one course open to me consistently with integrity or a safe conscience, or with my notions of sound policy and discretion . . .'[22]

On 17th July, in the second reading debate, Van Mildert made his last major speech to the House of Lords. The *Mirror of Parliament* published it. Although he described it as 'but a slender performance, little more than a skeleton',[23] it was a pivotal speech for Van Mildert personally; he was saved from realising its full cost only because he failed to sway most of his hearers.

He began by magnificently sweeping aside Grey's argument that the Dean and Chapter of Durham, by reallocating part of their revenues to finance Durham University, had set a precedent for the present measure. Van Mildert contended that since their action was 'strictly in accordance both with the spirit and the letter of the Chapter Statutes, which expressly point out the advancement of learning as one special object of their endowment as a collegiate body', it was no precedent for 'alienating the property of the Church to other purposes than those for which it was originally bestowed'.[24]

Van Mildert then detailed exactly how the Bill destroyed his conception of Establishment.

Firstly, it shifted the burden of taxation to finance the upkeep of the Church from the laity to the clergy. This traduced the principle that the Church's ministrations benefited, and were therefore the financial responsibility of, the whole community. Accepting that the worship and ministry of the Established Church were 'not matters of common interest' overthrew 'the very idea of national religion'; it adumbrated a pluralist situation, the Church of Ireland merely one denomination among many.

Van Mildert objected strenuously to investing 'what are called Ecclesiastical Commissioners . . . to a great extent, with the executive administration of the Church'. Empowering Commissioners to gather information, make recommendations for change, or administer a narrowly specialised function such as church building, was an acceptable expression of State authority. Giving Commissioners power of initiative encroached disastrously on episcopal responsibilities, an usurpation which 'seems to militate against the fundamental rights of the Church as a spiritual body'. Van Mildert foresaw the confusions of authority that would arise when a permanent executive bureaucracy was overlaid on the Threefold Ministry, and was appalled.

The suppression of bishoprics (and so many bishoprics) for the unadorned purpose of seizing their revenues was piracy. Grey's plea that half the proposed unions of sees had 'previously been in force' cut no ice with Van Mildert. Unions of sees had perfect propriety when demanded by internal circumstances and agreed by the Church authorities, particularly in pursuit of 'some spiritual advantage'. Unions 'compulsorily forced upon the Church' for reasons of temporal policy were an abomination.

Van Mildert denounced the provision for suspending presentation to parishes without worship for three years as the Bill's worst abrogation of episcopal authority. The bishops alone were responsible for ensuring that the spiritual needs of the community were properly served, and deciding whether, and if so which, parochial charges should be abandoned. Parliament had no right to interfere. Besides, the proposal specifically precluded 'any prospect of reviving Protestantism, where it happens to be most depressed', giving 'encouragement . . . to the proselyting spirit of Popery'.

The Bill, Van Mildert argued, violated the State's duty to defend the Church's secular interests because it overturned her property rights. In a striking example of the congregationalist vein underlying one strand of High Church thinking on authority, he denied that the revenues of the Church 'constitute one large common fund'. The Church was not

one entire corporation, possessing revenues which may undergo continual changes in the mode of their distribution; but is rather an aggregate of corporations, each possessing its own distinct property, with which no other can, of right, interfere. There are corporations sole, such as Bishops and beneficed clergy; and there are mixed corporations, such as deans and chapters, and other collegiate bodies, all having their respective possessions and rights, independent of the rest; and unless these inherent rights can be set aside, it does not appear how they can be justly dealt with as one common fund.[25]

Van Mildert, like Southey's *Book of the Church*, viewed the Church not as a single organisation whose resources could be internally redeployed in pursuit of institutional objectives such as efficiency or equity, but an aggregate of individual cures each a separate, sacred and inalienable trust. He was against diverting prebendal revenues to other ecclesiastical purposes, concerned not for the interests of the particular incumbent or patron, but for the structural self-understanding of the Church. His disgust with the self-regarding

attitude of some Durham prebendaries during the University negotiations shows in his comment to Peel on an 1835 plan for Chapter
reform: 'to the condition . . . that present vested interests are to be
spared . . . I attach no value whatever. To me it seems too much like
a bribe to present possessors, to tempt them to despoil their successors of rights & emoluments no less inalienable than their own. As
such, I feel something revolting in the proposition, however defens-
ible it may be upon abstract grounds of Law & Equity.'[26]

Van Mildert's 1825 speech against Catholic Emancipation
declared that spiritual jurisdiction over the Church belongs 'to the
State, as allied to the Church, and although exercised by the
Church, is derived from the State'. By spiritual jurisdiction he
understood

> the appointment of particular persons to exercise spiritual functions
> throughout the State, . . . the rules and regulations by which they shall be
> directed, . . . their respective remunerations . . ., in short, . . . every thing
> which, in Ecclesiastical, no less than in Civil Polity, it is the duty of the
> Legislative and Executive Government of the Country to provide, for the
> general benefit of the community.[27]

Bathurst of Norwich, telling Howley that 'the State has a right to
re-model the Church as to its internal arrangements',[28] was saying
no more than Van Mildert allowed. The Grey government could
fairly claim its redeployment of the Church of Ireland's human and
financial resources as within the jurisdiction Van Mildert awarded.

To this, Van Mildert's logic allowed only one answer. The Bill
itself proved that the government had repudiated the terms of
alliance on which its claim to jurisdiction over the Church
depended. The paradox in Van Mildert's conception of Establishment was this: while jurisdiction over an established Church
belonged properly to the State, any State attempting to exercise a
jurisdiction independent of the Church's apostolically ordained
leadership thereby apostatised from the Establishment relationship.
Establishment, in Van Mildert's terms, was the spiritual relationship of civil and ecclesiastical authorities in a harmony based on
mutual respect and complementary service to the same national
community. The legal framework which he had struggled to preserve was the formal expression of that relationship.

In 1829 he had asked how the Catholic Emancipation 'principle
that there should be no civil distinctions on account of religious
opinions' could 'possibly be maintained with safety to our existing

Establishments', or indeed could be 'reconciled with the existence of any religious Establishment whatsoever'. Now he had answered his own question. In a speech whose modest length and temperate language gave few clues to its radical content, he demonstrated that the spiritual reality of Establishment, as he himself understood it, was at an end. What Establishment might be made to mean in the future was an open question.

In 1829, when Catholic Emancipation was carried, Van Mildert was sixty-four: not of an age, or a temperament, to relish a radical re-evaluation of his lifetime's commitment to 'the Church of England as by law established'. Yet the argument of his Irish Church Bill speech suggests that by 1833 he was, however unwillingly, making a radical shift in directions that were, in the last analysis, disestablishmentarian.

A straw in the wind had been the exclusion of the laity from the 1831 Ecclesiastical Commission proposals. His attempt in the 1834 Durham University Bill to secure his University from the implications of Establishment moved Van Mildert further along a road he wished fervently never to have to tread. Not for him the bold speculations of Rose about a lay Synod to take over the responsibilities of an apostate Parliament; like his other self Joshua Watson, Van Mildert was disposed to 'hate democracy in any shape; but of all shapes the worst is an ecclesiastical democracy'.[29] Neither could he share the anti-materialism of Keble's 'Take every pound, shilling and penny, and the curse of sacrilege along with it – only let us make our own Bishops and be governed by our own laws.'[30] His own ministry had taught him only too clearly how much scope for doing good the Church stood to lose if 'Reform' stripped away her revenues.

His decision to oppose the Irish Church Bill was not taken lightly. The vehemence of his insistence to Joshua Watson that in conscience he could take no other course suggests he had a clear inkling how costly this path might prove.

By 17th July, he must also have known that he would lose again. Phillpotts was fighting the same battle, with ferocious relish and a total disregard for who might or might not be lined up behind him; but the support of the King, the Government and the official Opposition for the Bill was too much weight to shift. Some of the English and Irish bishops viewed the Bill as a perfectly appropriate exercise of State authority.[31] The Church was not of one mind.

In deciding his tactics, Van Mildert suffered the crippling handicap of not being Archbishop of Canterbury. His personal respect for Howley moreover forbade any challenge to the Archbishop's authority.

Newman wrote, 'I wish the Archbishop had somewhat of the boldness of the old Catholic Prelates; no one can doubt that he is a man of the highest principle, and would willingly die a Martyr; but, if he had but the little finger of Athanasius, he would do us all the good in the world.'[32]

Van Mildert commanded some of the oratorical skills Howley so transparently lacked; he had the boldness of imagination to conjure Durham University from bare conception to practical reality in little more than two years; his 'prestige was higher with the clergy than any other bishop's'.[33] His speech carried a clear challenge to the English and Irish episcopates to reclaim their authority from state usurpation; but the challenge went unheard, and having foreseen that, he made no open plea.

In the event, Howley distinguished himself in the eyes of the Oxford Movement by opposing the Bill; but clarion-calls summoning Israel to battle were not in his line, and his indecision beforehand destroyed any possibility of effective co-operation with Van Mildert.

Van Mildert wrote to Joshua Watson before the debate, 'You may be assured . . . that my utmost endeavours shall be used to give no just occasion for offence to opponents or to friends.'[34] Howley had given no firm lead for him to follow; he would not himself offer a firm lead for fear of disloyalty. Van Mildert made the explanation his integrity required, then, leaving his vote to be cast by proxy, retired to the North.

The Bill won a second reading by 157 votes to 98. Fifteen bishops voted against; eleven, including Archbishop Whately of Dublin, voted for. Minor revisions in committee were accepted by the Commons; the Bill was law by August. On 14th July, three days before Van Mildert's verdict and not restricted by Van Mildert's deliberately moderate choice of phrase, John Keble preached his Assize Sermon on National Apostasy and denounced the Irish Church Bill as sacrilege.

In the autumn of 1833 Jane Van Mildert, whose health had been fragile all year, suffered a stroke which affected her personality. Van

Mildert wrote a prayer of 'humble supplications for my beloved Wife, labouring under grievous infirmities both of body & mind . . . enable her patiently & chearfully to submit to Thy blessed Will . . . whereinsoever she may fail in her duty, Lord, shew mercy to her . . . grant her a peaceful & tranquil end, full of faith, hope . . .' and broke off in a scrawl of pain.[35] Early in 1834 Jane passed through a crisis, but by 18th February Van Mildert could tell Thorp, '. . . you will be glad to hear that the apprehensions of danger to my dear Invalid are this morning pretty well removed. She has rallied so as to come down to breakfast &, I trust, with due care, may escape a relapse. But these recurrences keep me in perpetual anxiety, & the shock I received from that of yesterday still dwells painfully in my recollection.' Henry Douglas, summoned as to his aunt's deathbed, arrived the next day, to Van Mildert's 'great comfort'. March found the Bishop 'much broken by his domestic distress'.[36]

Jane's condition gradually deteriorated. In November Bruce Knight was told, 'Mrs. Van Mildert continues much the same as for the last twelvemonth, though not likely to rally again, as in former times.' Although she outlived her husband, she was never again fit for the journey south, and Van Mildert hated to leave her: 'I am very anxious to return to Mrs. V.M., whose distress at my absence is exceedingly painful to me', he wrote to Thorp in March 1835, during one of his increasingly brief visits to London.[37]

Among the most durable legacies of Oxford Movement historiography, from Newman onwards, has been the identification of 1833 as a crucial watershed for High Churchmen.[38] For Van Mildert personally, this is to some extent tenable. 1833 marked his last great appeal to Parliament to stay from restructuring the relationship of Church and State.

G. F. A. Best[39] suggests that Howley's conversion from the moderate and modest reformer of the early 1830s to the later stout defender of radical Ecclesiastical Commission measures 'may well have had something to do with' Van Mildert's death in 1836. The decisive date may rather have been 1833. After the passing of the Irish Church Act, Van Mildert was quietly but ruthlessly sidelined from central Church policy-making. The very staunchness with which he had defended the lost understanding of Establishment won his exclusion from the negotiating processes that engineered a new concept.

He seems to have withdrawn from active involvement in the 1832 Ecclesiastical Revenues Commission, its Phalanx element strengthened during its twice-extended life by the addition of Gaisford, Christopher Wordsworth and Thorp. He was not a signatory to its June 1835 final report, a mass of statistics on the revenues of sees, chapters and benefices copiously garnished with special pleading.

Omitted from the 1835 Ecclesiastical Duties and Revenues Commission, he told Archdeacon Singleton of Northumberland: 'As to my appearance among them, it cd. have answered no good purpose, & I had rather be excused from the *responsibility*, than have been a *dissentient*, opposed probably to those from whom it wd. be most painful to me to differ. My time is nearly gone by, & I am becoming *an old almanack*.'[40]

There is nevertheless an important sense in which 1833 changed nothing for Van Mildert. He did not conceive either himself or the Church as free to lay down responsibility for the political common life of the nation. His last three years saw him increasingly marginalised, reduced by bodily weakness into serving 'when consulted, as a sort of Chamber Counsel',[41] but no whit weakened in his passionate commitment to the Church's future.

His sources of information were initially excellent. Howley kept him informed of the Commissioners' intentions; he made regular attempts to influence them by letter and, when in London, private persuasion. If his points were rarely conceded, they were always given a hearing.

As he had himself said in 1829, 'Yet I am inclined to think an old almanack not altogether an useless thing. It may be useful, not only as a record of past times, but as a guide to future times; and I apprehend that a man who should set about making a new almanack, without some knowledge of old ones, would produce but an indifferent performance. But that is not the wisdom now in vogue.'[42]

Joshua Watson also passed through a personal crisis in 1833. His resignation as SPCK Treasurer in July brought nearly twenty years of service to a pause. Bereft of his wife, his work and his sense of direction, 'The Archtreasurer' retreated for a while from the activity of his friends.

Norris, Archdeacons Watson, Bayley and Lyall, with many allies including Bishop Jebb and W. F. Hook, launched energetically into Rose's 'association for the defence of the Church', mooted after his conference with the Irish High Churchman William Palmer of Worcester College, Hurrell Froude and A. P. Perceval at his Hadleigh vicarage in late July.[43] This proved a bed of nails: Newman and Froude wanted to operate in their own style and had little patience with Phalanx methods. Palmer, who went to Hackney at the end of October to consult about the Association and set briskly to politicking with 'men of the right sort collected from various parts' by Norris, soon found the role of intermediary a comfortless one.

Watson had hidden himself away at 'Langton, near Tunbridge Wells'. Canvassed by Bayley about proposals for a general clerical declaration of confidence in Howley's leadership, probably first suggested by Rose, he gave a tepid response: he doubted whether this was 'attainable in the present state of the clergy without compromise', and feared Howley had already missed his moment by 'losing the advantage I was anxious he should make of the Ecclesiastical Commission'. When Norris wrote invoking his support for the Association he hedged:

'. . . The truth is, as I was obliged to confess the other day to the Bishop of Durham, I feel the infirmities of premature age are come upon me, and find myself so slow in apprehension and conception, in expression and action, as to be greatly indisposed to exertion either of body or mind, and to be out of humour with every person or thing that would move me to either.[44]

Norris envisaged the Association as 'a solid union of such a character, that those of their superiors who were true to their calling should find a body formed to which they could appeal, and which they could call to their support in the day of trial'. Watson protested the lack of any actual 'sanction, express or implied', from the Bishops, giving the body an embarrassingly 'unauthorized character'. Newman urged the same point, telling Palmer there would be 'an awkwardness' in

forming a Society, or Association even . . . without the sanction of the Bishops and though it is enough for satisfying our conscience to know that really they are privately with us, yet the world cannot know this, and it goes out to the world as a bad precedent, and an inconsistency in the case of those who have (rightly) made the absence of Episcopal sanction an objection to certain Societies hitherto.[45]

Newman had no wish to be answerable to 'committees, secretaries etc', accurately foreseeing the kind of censorship that a formal organisation would seek to impose on his planned Tracts. Another of his objections illuminates the vivid contrast between his approach and the Phalanx's:

And further, if we profess an Association, we are under the necessity of bringing into the government of it men who do not agree with us. We feel our opinions are *true*; we are sure that, few tho' we be, we shall be able to propagate them by the force of the truth; we have no need, rather we cannot afford, to dilute them; which must be the consequence of joining those who do not go so far as we do.

Newman favoured creative anarchy, organised if at all on a diocesan basis. He pressed Rose's Loyal Address strategy. This finally carried the day, although elements of the Association plan survived – and did create difficulty around the Tracts.

Watson later told Lyall he had 'prayed Norris earnestly to lay before his correspondents the danger alike of success or failure, for I knew not which at this time would be worst for the Church. They were, however, too far committed to be open to such counsel as would have suspended all action . . .'[46]

Cajoled by Norris with the plea 'It is no common occasion; indeed, I know not one that has occurred during our whole course of service where all the experience and judgment that can be had is so much needed . . .',[47] Watson let himself be bullied out of his retirement. Returning to his Park Street post he set to work on Newman's 'rough draft of the Address . . . sent up from Oxford'.

Park Street and Oxford immediately fell out, over both content and literary style. Newman thought his own initial draft 'too moderate, since I wrote in fear of P[almer]'s thinking me ultra'. Norris and his colleagues felt Newman was too extreme and would alienate valuable potential supporters. Palmer removed 'all mention of "extra-ecclesiastical interference"', Watson and Norris 'diluted' it further. Newman's partisan account of the redaction processes runs: 'Thus it came down to us; and written in a most wretched style. We polished it; struck out some offensive passages, and sent it back. It came down again as uncouth and almost as offensive as before. We amended it and printed it. Then circulated it far and wide.'[48]

The dissension highlighted the stresses within the nascent Oxford Movement. Palmer found his position increasingly difficult. Edward Churton went to Oxford to mediate between him and Norris: Keble 'could hardly help laughing, and did laugh and enjoy excessively afterwards, his diplomatic look and bearing'.[49]

The Address finally assumed its canonical form, although Newman thought it 'milk and water' and clergy in various places made unauthorised alterations of their own. In Durham, the third paragraph[50] caused difficulty. Norris sent up a copy to T. L. Strong for circulation in the diocese; Thorp, who had been 'well inclined' until he saw the text, vehemently opposed pleading clerical support for reform measures. A clergy assembly held at Auckland Castle at the end of November agreed; they were 'thoroughly annoyed & wish to join in the purpose of the address, but could come to no resolution & parted only resolving to consider the matter farther'. The Dean of Durham suggested qualifying the pledge with the words 'after due consideration'; Rose advised that if the Declaration's sponsors found this compromise unacceptable, the only possible solution was for Joshua Watson to write 'as strongly as he can' to Van Mildert, urging the Bishop to pressure '3 or 4 of the leading Clergy'.[51]

Van Mildert disliked the plans for a more general kind of association, and hoped that after the Address had been presented to the Archbishop 'nothing more will be thought of; unless, upon the introduction of any hostile measures into Parliament relative to the Church, it should be deemed necessary to come forward with petitions to both Houses'. He told Bruce Knight in December 1833: 'whatever the Clergy incline to do in this way, should be done spontaneously, and without even the appearance of being urged to it by their ecclesiastical rulers. For this reason, I leave my own Clergy to follow entirely their own inclination and judgment.' He declined any part in the presentation of the Address, disappointing Newman, who wrote to Bowden: 'I am sorry to hear what you say about Durham; and cannot quite understand it. At first the Bishop of D. had scruples but I was told had overcome them.'[52]

The Address was finally presented to Howley on 6th February 1834 by the Archdeacon of Canterbury at the head of a delegation of twenty-one other archdeacons, deans and clergy; among them Keble, deputising for a sick Pusey. With late additions, it attracted some seven thousand signatures.

Churton credits the idea of a parallel Lay Declaration to Christopher Wordsworth. 'Manufactured in London' without interference,[53] it was signed by more than 230,000 heads of families.

This was a classic Hackney exercise, drawing together allies of many political and theological complexions behind a broad commitment to 'promote the purity, the efficiency, and the unity of the

Church': an effective demonstration that, despite the legislative changes of the past five years, the Established Church could still command substantial public support.

The Tracts for the Times, circulating from August 1833, caused serious friction between Hackney and Oxford. 'I have no great veneration for *Tracts*', Christopher Wordsworth told Joshua Watson in November 1833, adding that if the Association were to 'circulate Tracts . . . I can have nothing to do with it.'[54] The very word recalled the Lincoln's Inn Fields débâcle.

Norris made himself thoroughly unpopular with Newman, Froude and Keble by insisting that the Tracts be given up for the sake of Address and Association. 'Old Norris wrote to my Father to announce that the "tract system was (he was happy to say) abandoned." We must throw the Zs overboard: they are a small and, as my Father says, daily diminishing party', Froude wrote to Newman.[55]

Joshua Watson was more tolerant of the Tracts, associating them with the passionate Hutchinsonianism of his own and his friends' youth; he inclined to be 'very lenient . . . to the excesses of young men'. He remained on good terms with Keble and Pusey, and while he thought Newman 'wanted guidance, but could not find, or acquiesce in the counsels of, a needful guide', in 1835 he gave a 'most munificent subscription' to the chapel at Littlemore.[56]

1833 marked some changes for the Phalanx. Joshua Watson's withdrawal from SPCK ended an era. Despite all the year's *Angst*, however, the work continued. The Phalanx had by no means despaired of maintaining Establishment. Watson's Lay Declaration included a ringing assertion 'that the consecration of the State by the public maintenance of the Christian Religion is the first and paramount duty of a Christian People' and committed its signatories to 'do all that in us lies' to 'uphold unimpaired in its security and efficiency' the Establishment relationship.

The National Society, SPG missions and the Church Building Society continued to make demands on Phalanx time and money. As the schools work had provided a spur towards church building, so after Van Mildert's death the extending of church-room prompted endeavours to pay more assistant clergy. In 1836 the Evangelicals founded the Church Pastoral Aid Society; Watson and Norris retaliated in 1837 with the last of the Hackney societies, the

Society for the Employment of Additional Curates in Populous Places.

Blomfield, who as early as 1832 was urging Howley of 'the necessity of a mixed Commission of Clergymen & Laymen to consider what measures should be adopted in the way of Church Reform whether as to the establishment of a consistent scheme of discipline, or the arrangement of ecclesiastical property', and even that possibly 'this Commission should be permanent, and invested with the power of initiating all legislative measures affecting the Church in it's spiritual character, or in it's secular provisions, or both',[57] spearheaded the group of former Hackney associates who now elected to take a pragmatic view of co-operation with the Whig government. After Van Mildert's virtual withdrawal from episcopal power-politics, Howley was sucked inexorably into Blomfield's slipstream. During Peel's short ministry of 1834–5, both were centrally involved in discussions whose upshot, in February 1835, was the Ecclesiastical Duties and Revenues Commission.

A. B. Webster's 1954 study of Joshua Watson claims the Ecclesiastical Commission as Hackney's greatest achievement. It took up the traditional Phalanx pattern of a mixed body of leading clergy, bishops and eminent laity, and built it centrally into the life of the Church. The principles to which the Commission worked were the same utilitarian goals of efficiency, equity and practical effectiveness which had guided Hackney's public work, and apart from the obligatory Archbishop of York, the bishops originally appointed to the Commission were all Phalanx associates.[58]

There were significant differences, however. It was no accident that Hackney always included all the bishops; Van Mildert's protest against divorcing authority over church affairs from the apostolic episcopate did no more than restate what the Phalanx had always held in practice. The pattern was broken when Liverpool refused to make all the bishops Church Building Commissioners. The Ecclesiastical Commission, tussling vigorously with Van Mildert and others after him, could claim some precedent in the National Society's battles with Shute Barrington; but it hardly qualifies as a true-bred Hackney offspring.

Joshua Watson, unhappy with Howley's handling of the Ecclesiastical Revenues Commission, had no warmth for the new body. Blomfield and Howley ignored his advice, backed by Van Mildert, to begin with a clergy questionnaire in order to bring 'the grounds of the changes in agitation . . . before the public before legislation was attempted'. Knowing how shaky Peel's majority was, they were in a hurry.

Watson and Van Mildert coined the nickname 'the Ecclesiastical Divan', and observed the Commission's proceedings with detached cynicism. 'Although I have had an Ecclesiastical Commissioner here, daily going in & coming out for a fortnight,' Watson wrote to Van Mildert at the end of 1835, 'yet I have done little more than laugh at the expected secrecy of printed papers & copied resolutions, when our friend has come home every afternoon with his packet stamped with the talismanic words, *Strictly Private.*'[59]

Van Mildert contended to the end of his life that the Commissioners' fundamental strategy of internally redeploying ecclesiastical revenues did violence to the Church. He had made an empirical and utilitarian defence of Anglican pastoral ministry the peroration of his 1827 Durham Charge, but it was never a position he found comfortable. Like Newman in Tract One, he revolted at making 'present palpable usefulness, producible results, acceptableness to your flocks . . . the tests of your divine commission'. Far more natural to him was the 1831 Charge's climactic assertion of 'the Protestant Church of England' as 'a genuine branch of that holy Catholic Church, of which it is promised that "the gates of hell shall not prevail against it"', warning his clergy: 'The charge consigned to us is too precious to be bartered away for popularity, or to be yielded from mere deference to public opinion.'

He could never have written Tract One, with its insistence on individual personal authority; but his resistance to the Ecclesiastical Commissioners pushed him steadily further from Blomfield's accommodation to State remodelling of Church structures. Newman in Tract One appealed directly from the local to the catholic, passing over the national level which traditionally defined the uniqueness of Anglicanism; from that step inevitably arose the thirst for a universal catholicism appeased, if perhaps not finally quenched, by his submission to Rome. Van Mildert had never previously been pressed to question the model of a specifically Anglican authority resting on the double foundation of Reformed Catholic theology and time-proven Establishment practice. Now that he found the due British political process in conflict with apostolic order, he made it abundantly clear which, for him, took priority.

His 1834 Assize Sermon defined the purpose of Establishment as keeping the State faithful. National peace, prosperity, security, justice depended on adherence to 'Christian principles and Christian conduct'; the Church was charged with the prophetic vocation to challenge rulers with their ultimate allegiance to God, whatever temporal unpopularity that might entail. 'An irreligious Government, an irreligious Legislature, a nation whose rulers and subjects discard from their polity and their jurisprudence a sense of duty to the Most High, as the prime source of every blessing, public and private, social and individual, would be a degrading anomaly in the history of mankind.'

Van Mildert was never blind to the presence of abuses in the life of the Church, nor slow to do what his ecclesiology permitted to amend them; he always defended the social utility of the Church's ministrations; but he grounded this utility on the Church's Divine commission to keep faith with the past for the sake of the future. He wished to see the Church rendered 'more conducive to the spiritual interests of the State; more stable as well as more perfect; better adapted to the exigencies of the present day, yet still resting on its ancient basis, as that which alone can ensure its conservation to the latest ages'.[60]

The Commissioners' reform strategies appalled him by their theological inadequacy. They disrupted the 'ancient basis', but did not seem to him to be guided by either the light 'flowing from *Divine Revelation*' or the vision of a future state governed by God's will.

Van Mildert argued against suppressing prebends and diverting their revenues to central ecclesiastical funds, on the double ground that removing gradations within the hierarchy weakened the Church's mission in a highly stratified society, and that breaking the local ties of the Church's historic endowment removed an important source of funding from 'charitable institutions of every kind' and 'works of national utility'. If the revenues of Deans and Chapters must be redeployed, at least let their constitution and structure be left unmutilated, and their revenues be applied to 'those parishes or districts already connected with them', with the rightful owners allowed some discretion in deploying the diverted resources.[61]

Peel's long and patient reply argued from pure expediency. Cathedral dignities were a good thing in the abstract, but not good enough to counterweigh the spiritual destitution of the great urban centres. How could the Church justify paying £9,000 annually to the Dean of Durham, 'with no other Ministerial functions than those which belong properly to the Dean', when any advantage derived from this 'great aristocratic appointment' must be set against 'the alienation of thousands from the Church, who witness this appointment and witness at the same time, populous districts in the neighbourhood of Durham, overrun with dissent from the Church because there is no adequate provision for the performance of the Rites of the Church?'[62]

Whatever its merits as an analysis of Methodism, this was an argument finely judged to weigh with Van Mildert: his experiences as a Church Building Commissioner and on the Bounty Board committee for impoverished livings had taught him the scale of need. One in particular of Peel's observations, 'Additional Churches subscribed for – but not built because there is no Endowment', targeted the very weakness Van Mildert had originally noted in the Church Building schemes. Peel did not, however, meet Van Mildert's objection that these shared objectives could be met 'without any disruption of our Ecclesiastical System'.

Van Mildert commended Peel's action in annexing a conveniently vacant Westminster prebend to the 'very populous and spiritually ill-provided parish of St. Margaret's' as precisely the kind of reform he was advocating; it left the 'integrity of the Chapter . . . untouched'. Peel's proposal to annex a Durham prebend to the Vicarage of Newcastle upon Tyne was a cherished project of Van Mildert's own.[63]

Van Mildert hated to see contemporary Radical rhetoric about Cathedral dignities as 'mere retreats for indolent, useless, & worldly-minded Clergy' damage their genuine usefulness. He wanted Chapter reform based on a just appraisal of existing potential, as well as fair recognition of existing abuses.

Besides high-minded ecclesiological debate, he also diligently fought the Durham Chapter's corner, with particular concern for University interests.

Van Mildert still trusted Peel as an ally, telling Thorp 'Sir Robt. Peel is in good earnest . . . & desirous of putting the concerns of the Chapter on the most practicable & least hazardous footing . . . After all, we must see it is impossible to be confident that any measures well guarded, & favourable to the Church, will pass through the H. of Commons; of whom a very large proportion will be dissatisfied with any thing short of confiscation or spoliation.'[64] He even hoped he might have convinced Peel of the need to preserve Chapter structure.

When the Ecclesiastical Commission's first report was published on 19th March, Van Mildert tackled Howley over the proposals to equalise episcopal revenues. He opposed creaming off a surplus from the richer sees, arguing that notwithstanding the proposed unions of sees, this would be insufficient to give the poorer sees the target figure of £4,500 per annum and provide for the proposed new sees of Manchester and Ripon, unless the archbishoprics were 'diminished' (undesirable) or the sees of London, Durham and Winchester reduced below £10,000 (inconceivable). He urged the Commissioners to think instead of annexing cathedral dignities to the poorer sees.[65] If episcopal revenues must be diverted, let 'the Bishop . . . direct the appropriation . . . to such special purposes as he deemed most beneficial to his own Diocese, whether in augmentation of Livings, or building & endowing Churches & Chapels, or the increase of Glebe Houses & Schools, or the relief of distressed Clergy, beneficed or unbeneficed, or in any other way most needed in the districts committed to his charge . . .'

Van Mildert, himself fully committed to promoting all these objects with the scope his vast revenues allowed, could make this plea with integrity. It was doomed partly because sacrificial generosity was not the commonest component of the contemporary episcopal character, partly because those with political authority over the Church refused his characterisation of the Church as an aggregate of inviolably separate individual cures. Peel and Blomfield classed the Church as a single organisation in sorry need of overhaul; to 'bring it into the condition of a mere stipendiary Establishment', anathema to Van Mildert, was for them a desirable means to deploy Church revenues more equitably and efficiently.

At the beginning of April Peel's government fell, defeated on Lord John Russell's motion to appropriate surplus Church of Ireland revenues to general educational purposes in Ireland. Melbourne returned to power.

The following January Van Mildert picked up 'a rumour . . . that, because four residentiaries suffice at St. Paul's, therefore the rest may be reduced to that number'. He could glean no solid information; he had drifted too far now from the centre of events. 'But the mist must soon be cleared away, and our destiny disclosed.'[66] Before the second Ecclesiastical Commission Report confirmed his worst fears, Van Mildert was dead.

The tension between Bishop and Commissioners bore unexpected fruit in 1838, when Canon William Selwyn of Ely published a pamphlet *Substance of an Argument . . . against those clauses of the Benefices Plurality Bill which confer additional powers on the Ecclesiastical Commissioners*. It includes a complete correspondence between 'W. Dunelm' (Van Mildert's autograph as Bishop of Durham) and 'the Ecclesiastical Commissioners for England', beginning on 3rd August 1838. G. F. A. Best finds the spurious correspondence 'so exceedingly lifelike and circumstantially presented that only the most careful reader will mark that it is, in fact, completely imaginary'.[67] It is hard to think Selwyn seriously intended deception; those contemporaries who still revered Van Mildert presumably realised he was more than two years dead. Selwyn followed Van Mildert's teaching on the nature of the Church and her endowments; maybe he felt this justified raising his departed master's spirit to fight in his cause.

Joshua Watson, like Van Mildert, was now drifting away from the mainstream of events; in the summer of 1835 he even took his daughter Mary touring in Scotland. On the way they stopped to visit Van Mildert in his castle. Van Mildert was delighted: 'It will be a gratification to me beyond all price that you have seen Auckland and me together before one, or the other, or both, may be levelled with the dust.'

The emotion was bittersweet. Watson wrote afterwards of the

strange conflict of affections . . . it had been better for us both if the visit had been made before the widowed feelings, as it were, of both of us had robbed the meeting of half its charm. But . . . it must ever be a great joy to have seen your Lordship at Auckland, and to have shewn Mary her own early friend, and one of the oldest of her father's remaining friends, in the full possession of the homage which it is in the power of the State to render to the Church, and in the receipt of the honour due to the public and private virtues of the Christian divine.[68]

Van Mildert himself was more than ambivalent about his palatine life-style: the enormous and costly web of employees, the two packs of foxhounds, the constant lavish hospitality. In 1835 he gave Howley a stiff hint that if the revenues of Durham were to be cut, the pomp of the Palatinate ought to be the first casualty.[69]

The occasion was marked by Van Mildert presenting Edward Churton to the desirable living of Crayke. Watson had earlier, at his wife's plea, solicited help for Churton, 'the only request I ever preferred on private grounds', when he needed to move on from being his father-in-law John James Watson's curate at Hackney. Van Mildert considered him for the Greek Chair at Durham, but his references were not good enough; in 1834, probably at Van Mildert's urging, Howley gave him Monks-eleigh.[70]

At the end of 1835, Van Mildert sent his last Christmas letter to Bruce Knight, with his customary gift of £100 for distribution in the Diocese of Llandaff. 'My good friend, fare you well: with the best old-fashioned salutations of the approaching hallowed season, (including a Bishop's blessing to you and yours,) believe me always sincerely and affectionately yours. W.D.'[71]

In early February he caught a 'low fever' with 'fits of shivering and pain . . . The next day he was better; but shivering returned at night, and from that time his vital powers gradually declined. His constitution, worn out by labor, anxiety, and local maladies of long standing, sunk under an attack which did not at first seem to threaten fatal consequences.' He was absent from the public dinner which 'the inhabitants of Bishop Auckland' gave his secretary Robert Archibald Douglas-Gresley on 2nd February 'as a mark of their respect for him'. This had to be held in the Assembly Room at Auckland Castle, the original venue, the Talbot Inn, being too small for the numbers who wished to attend.

'The Chairman proposed the health of the Bishop of Durham, which was acknowledged by the Revd. T.L. Strong, who bore testimony to the exemplary piety and profound learning of the Reverend Prelate, and concluded by stating, that although it had pleased the Almighty to afflict him in body, he was yet as vigorous as ever in the exercise of his judgment and understanding.'[72]

On Sunday 14th February Van Mildert joined 'with much fervency and devotion' in the prayer Strong offered at his bedside; then his mind wandered, leaving him 'in such a state of stupor, as to be totally unable to keep up his attention, for more than a minute together'. On 21st February, 'apparently without the slightest pain or distress', he died the quiet death of exhaustion. Later that Sunday morning the Cathedral and Durham city parishes offered prayers for his recovery 'under the belief that his Lordship was then living'.[73]

During substantial renovations to the chapel at his beloved Auckland Castle, Van Mildert had a vault constructed at the northern end of the cross aisle 'for his own body and that of Mrs. Van

Mildert';[74] but even in death his private wishes were sacrificed to public ends. The Dean and Chapter had him buried in Durham Cathedral, within the altar-rails.

On the night of 29th February, Van Mildert's body was removed to Durham Castle; but plans to hold a grand funeral procession from Castle to Cathedral were scuppered by 'the tempestuous state of the weather'. Instead, 'the corpse was removed to the Galilee Chapel' to lie peacefully by the dust of the Venerable Bede until the appointed time. The next noon, on a wild Durham day, Van Mildert's final and most magnificent ceremonial pageant was staged. The *Durham Chronicle*, which had no motive for exaggeration, records: 'Nearly the whole population of the town . . . repaired to the Cathedral at the appointed time; where, after considerable delay, the funeral procession was formed, and moved from the chapel to the choir . . . the choristers singing "I am the resurrection and the life," &c., as it advanced.'[75] The members of the University walked in the procession; some sixty uninvited clergy added themselves to the invited mourners as a mark of respect.

The Times, which had not loved Van Mildert in life, pronounced him in death 'a brilliant ornament of the Church of England' whose 'loss will be deeply felt both among the clergy and the laity, the rich and the poor'.[76]

The *Durham Chronicle* obituary, presented at the head of the 26th February 'Deaths' column without any mark of distinction, was a masterpiece of hostile respect: '. . . Dr. Van Mildert, who was of Dutch extraction, owed his elevation, not to birth or high extraction – for his parents were in humble circumstances, and he was himself for many years a poor curate – but to his own talents, which were considerable. He was the author of some able volumes of sermons, which are admitted by those who differed from him to possess great merit . . . He was a determined but conscientious opponent of Catholic emancipation, and a constant supporter of Tory politics in his place in the House of Lords. His charities, in the augmentation of poor livings &c., since his translation to the See of Durham, are understood to have been very considerable.'

At the Spring Assizes Lord Denman, who politically had little in common with Van Mildert, paid tribute: 'His piety and learning placed him among the highest names of England; while his numerous acts of charity and munificence, and his love of truth and justice, made him entitled to their warmest gratitude and praise.'[77]

If Van Mildert's opponents were generous in their commend-
ations once he was safely dead, his friends were lavish.[78]

After the tributes came more solid memorials. Thorp chaired the
memorial fund committee. The resulting statue, by 'Lough, a
sculptor in whose prosperity Joshua Watson took a lively interest',
stands in the Chapel of Nine Altars in Durham Cathedral. A Van
Mildert Scholarship was also endowed at Durham University.

Van Mildert College, founded in 1965, keeps his name part of the
modern Durham University, and there are a number of less well-
known commemorations: as recently as November 1979, a stained
glass window depicting Van Mildert was consecrated in the parish
church he built at Etherley near Bishop Auckland.

'His work is ended, and he has gone to his rest', *The Times*
observed, not without satisfaction. Among those who had known
him, however briefly, he was long remembered.

Whatever his personal sufferings, Van Mildert never ceased to rise
to social occasions. A Canon whom Van Mildert had ordained priest
in the grimmest year of all, 1834, more than half a century later
recalled 'that to me memorable day' when 'the newly-ordained
clergy were invited to dinner at Auckland Castle; and on presenting
ourselves we were ushered into a large apartment, where we awaited
the coming of the bishop. Presently the door opened, and he entered
– a slight and graceful figure – followed by his chaplains . . . He
went round the circle which we made to receive him, bowing to each
in turn, and addressing a few words to those with whom he was
personally acquainted. We were entertained with becoming splendour, and while partaking of his lordship's venison, &c., I saw that
his own repast consisted of a basin of broth or gruel, which he sipped
occasionally. At the same time, his conversation with those near him
was as animated as if the beverage had been of a much more
exhilarating description.'[79]

James Losh, who as a Unitarian and a Whig found Van Mildert's
1831 Charge grossly offensive, was thawed by his personal charm: 'I
dined and drank coffee with the Bishop . . . I was treated as one of
the *Law dignitaries* and had much conversation with the Bishop as to
the new University etc. The Bishop, tho' old, infirm and deaf, did
the honours of his hospitable and splendid entertainment, in a very
graceful and gentlemanly manner.'[80]

All his life Van Mildert made and kept friends, as interested in
their families as themselves. The warmth of concern he showed for

an extraordinary range of people is one of the most attractive things about him. His friendships lasted. His 'young friend' of 1814, T. L. Strong, was at his death-bed twenty years later. In 1821 Van Mildert turned down a solicitation from Howley in order to keep his promise of a Christ Church Studentship to 'my friend Mr. Dyke in Kent, who, with a family of Fifteen Children, looks forward to this provision for his second Son with some solicitude'.[81] In 1832 he preferred Thomas Hart Dyke to the 'plum' Rectory of Long Newton. His friendship with Bruce Knight was lifelong; while the network of interlinking friendships that was the Hackney Phalanx provided the means, support and inspiration for most of his lifetime's ministry.

From that pattern of fellowship and committed service Van Mildert conceived his vision of the Church. He dreamed the Church of England as the soul of the State, as the servant of every citizen, as the custodian of true learning and wisdom, as an act of loving homage offered to God in the consciousness of unworthiness but with a confidence founded on Divine Grace. Never blind to the disparities between the Church as he dreamed and as he knew her, he spent his time, energy and (when he had any) money trying to bring her into closer conformity with his vision of her true nature and mission; but he never lost the passionate love for the Church of England, her liturgy, her history, her faithful membership both lay and clerical, which first drew him into her ordained ministry.

After Van Mildert there were no more Prince Bishops. His death allowed Melbourne's Whig government to sweep away the last decayed remnant of the Patrimony of St Cuthbert. This would have caused him neither surprise nor much regret; he commented on an 1834 proposal to extend his geographical jurisdiction, 'I shd. be very sorry if the good people of Berwick were to be brought under the authority of the Prince Palatine. But there can be no fear, in these times, of such an addition being given to such a Functionary.'[82]

Van Mildert measured his own achievements by a different yardstick. He set out his aims in a prayer he wrote while grappling with the task of producing the right Charge to his clergy in the troubled year 1831: 'Crown my labours, O Lord, I beseech Thee, with such success as will most promote Thy glory, the good of Thy Church, and the salvation of myself and others; for the sake of Jesus Christ, Thy Son, our Lord.'

Notes

INTRODUCTION

1 R. W. Church, *The Oxford Movement*, London (1892), p. 12.
2 C. P. S. Clarke, *The Oxford Movement and After*, London (Mowbray, 1932), pp. 17–20.
3 G. F. A. Best, 'The mind and times of William Van Mildert', in *Journal of Theological Studies*, New Series, vol. XIV, part 2, October 1963, pp. 360ff.
4 E. R. Norman, *Church and Society in England 1770–1970* (Oxford University Press, 1976), pp. 71–2.
5 Van Mildert to Joshua Watson, 2nd April 1806; E. Churton, *Memoir of Joshua Watson*, Oxford (Parker, 1861), vol. I, pp. 69–70.

1. THE LITTLE DUTCH CURATE

1 On Hutchinsonianism, see above, pp. 40–2; also J. C. D. Clark, *English Society 1688–1832: Ideology, social structure and political practice during the ancien regime* (Cambridge University Press, 1985), pp. 218–19.
2 Clark, *English Society*, pp. 186–8, sets out the evidence for Dr Johnson's Jacobite sympathies.
3 *Ibid.*, p. 126 and passim, particularly Chapter 3.
4 C. Daubeny, *A Guide to the Church, in Several Discourses*, London (T. Cadell and W. Davies, 1798), p. 148.
5 Churton, *Memoir*, vol. I, p. 20. Boucher befriended John James (see above, pp. 14–20), marrying his widow after James' tragically early death.
6 (J. A. Park), *Memoirs of William Stevens, Esq.*, London (1812), pp. 54, 59, 117; G. F. A. Best, *Temporal Pillars: Queen Anne's Bounty, the Ecclesiastical Commissioners, and the Church of England* (Cambridge University Press, 1964), pp. 122, 134.
7 Genealogical notes in Van Mildert Papers, probably in Van Mildert's own hand: Durham University Add. Ms. 974.207V2. R. A. Cochrane, 'William Van Mildert, bishop of Durham 1826–1836' (Durham University M.Litt. thesis, 1950), pp. 2–12, exhaustively documents the history of the early Van Milderts.

8 Churton, *Memoir*, vol. 2, p. 264.
9 C. Ives, *Sermons on several Occasions, and Charges, by William Van Mildert, D.D., Late Bishop of Durham. To which is prefixed a memoir of the Author*, Oxford (J. H. Parker, 1838), pp. 6, 15, 154.
10 Van Mildert to Thomas Grant, 21st April 1795: Durham University Library Add. Ms. 274.207V2L4; Grant married Nancy Ives in 1776. Cornelius Van Mildert's will commends Ann Williams' 'constant careful attendance on my late daughter Rachael'.
11 P. Virgin, *The Church in an Age of Negligence: Ecclesiastical Structure and Problems of Church Reform* (James Clarke, 1989), pp. 141, 221; p. 215, quoting diary of Revd William Jones of Broxbourne, entry for 27th Jan. 1803.
12 (W. C. Farr, ed.), *Merchant Taylors' School*, Oxford (Blackwell, 1929), pp. 55–9.
13 The Queen's College Batells Book 1779–91, pp. 135–8.
14 M. Evans, ed., *Letters of Radcliffe and James*, Oxford (Oxford Historical Society, 1888), p. 50.
15 R. H. Hodgkin, *Six Centuries of an Oxford College*, Oxford (Blackwell, 1969), pp. 165–6; J. R. Magrath, *The Queen's College*, Oxford (Clarendon, 1921), p. 145; Ives, *Memoir*, pp. 9–10.
16 *Letters of James*, pp. 177–8; C. C. Gillispie, *Genesis and Geology*, New York (1959), pp. 31–2; W. Jones, *The Works of the Right Reverend George Horne, D.D., Late Lord Bishop of Norwich; to which are prefixed Memoirs of his Life, Studies, and Writings*, second edition, London (Rivington, 1818), pp. xxiii, 11. Horsley and Jones were both Fellows of the Royal Society.
17 Van Mildert to E. Mendes Da Costa, 10th June 1784: Durham University Library Ms. Add. 274.207V1. Oxford University refused Da Costa, a Portuguese–Jewish conchologist, permission to read a course of lectures on fossilology in 1774. He provided Van Mildert with letters of introduction to several dons.
18 Virgin, *Age of Negligence*, p. 135, and table XII, p. 283.
19 *Letters of James*, pp. 160–1.
20 *Letters of James*, p. 143; Gillispie, *Genesis and Geology*, pp. 20–1; V. H. H. Green, *Religion at Oxford and Cambridge*, London (SCM Press, 1964), p. 179.
21 W. R. Ward, *Victorian Oxford*, London (Cass, 1965), pp. xiii, 2; C. E. Mallet, *A History of the University of Oxford*, London (Methuen, 1927), vol. III, p. 142; on Oxford Jacobitism, Clark, *English Society*, pp. 153–6.
22 L. Stone, ed., *The University in Society* (Princeton University Press, 1974), vol. I, pp. 38–9; V. H. H. Green, *A History of Oxford University*, London (Batsford, 1974), p. 109; footnote, p. 115.
23 *Letters of James*, pp. 233–4.
24 W. Stephen, *History of the Scottish Church*, 2 vols., Edinburgh (David Douglas, 1894, 1896), vol. II, p. 545. See also Park, *Stevens*, pp. 131–51.

A typographical error on p. 135 separates Bishop Abernethy Drummond of Brechin into two.

25 Van Mildert's first sermon: Van Mildert Papers.

26 Robert Finch, D.D., a fellow Taylorian, was Rector of St John the Evangelist, Westminster, and treasurer of SPCK 1775–1802.

27 Cochrane, 'Van Mildert', p. 44.

28 Durham University Library Add. Ms. 274.207V21S4 has nos. 119 (dated 20th May 1792) and 200 (dated 18th May 1794).

29 Quoted in Clark, *English Society*, p. 223.

30 G. Horne, *A Charge intended to have been delivered to the Clergy of Norwich, at the Primary Visitation of George, Lord Bishop of that Diocese*, Norwich (Yarington and Bacon, 1791), pp. 39–40. See also W. R. Ward, *Religion and Society in England 1790–1850*, New York (Schocken Books, 1973), pp. 12, 15.

31 For a detailed account of General Douglas and his father, William Douglas of Fingland, see P. W. L. Adams, *A History of the Douglas Family* . . ., Bedford (The Sidney Press, 1921), pp. 361–2, 334–5.

32 Philip Douglas to Van Mildert, 27th Sept. 1791: in Adams, *Douglas Family*, pp. 449–50.

33 Horne, *Charge*, p. 34.

34 Maltby to Earl Grey, 5th Nov. 1838: papers of 2nd Earl Grey.

35 J. Hunt, *Religious Thought in England in the Nineteenth Century*, London (Gibbings, 1896), p. 85. Similarly the Whig Sir James Mackintosh, who in 1791 had written *Vindiciae Gallicae* as a refutation of Burke's *Reflections on the French Revolution*, in 1800 'entirely recanted its sentiments, declaring that he now "abhorred, abjured, and for ever renounced the French Revolution, with all its sanguinary history, its abominable principles, and for ever execrable leaders, and hoped to be able to wipe off the disgrace of having been once betrayed into an approbation of that conspiracy against God and man"'. J. H. Overton and F. Relton, *The English Church from the Accession of George I to the end of the Eighteenth Century*, London (Macmillan, 1906), p. 220.

36 J. Stevenson, *Popular Disturbances in England 1700–1870*, New York (Longman, 1979), pp. 67–8, 71–2, 77–8, 171. In March 1768, when Van Mildert was two, a 'Wilkes and Liberty' mob, rioting in St George's Fields, was fired on by Government forces.

37 *London Chronicle*, vol. LIV, no. 4204 (Wednesday 8th October 1783). For the proclamation of Peace, see vol. LIV, no. 4207 (11th Oct. 1783).

38 W. Van Mildert, 'Janus Clusus', dated 10th Oct. 1783: Durham University Library Add. Ms. 274.207V2108.

39 Horne, *Charge*, p. 28.

40 W. Van Mildert, 'Rights of Men, a new ballad': Durham University Library Add. Ms. 274.207V2108.

41 Daubeny, *Guide*, p. 120.

42 *The Times*, 3rd Oct. 1789, p. 2, column 2; 12th March 1792, p. 3, column 2.

43 J. McManners, *The French Revolution and the Church*, London (SPCK, 1969), chapters 10–12; E. J. Hobsbawm, *The Age of Revolution 1789–1848*, London (Weidenfeld & Nicholson, 1962), p. 95.

44 R. A. Soloway, *Prelates and People: Ecclesiastical Social Thought in England 1783–1852*, London (Routledge & Kegan Paul, 1969), pp. 38–9.

45 B. Porteus, *A Charge delivered to the Clergy of the Diocese of London, at the Visitation of that Diocese in the year MDCCXCIV*, London (Rivington, 1794), p. 29.

46 W. Jones, *A Letter to Three Converted Jews, lately Baptized and Confirmed in the Church of England*, London (F. & C. Rivington, 1799), p. 3. See also Ward, *Religion and Society*, p. 44, and J. A. De Jong, *As the Waters Cover the Sea: Millennial Expectations in the Rise of Anglo–American Missions 1640–1810*, Amsterdam (1970), chapter v.

47 De Jong, *Millennial Expectations*, pp. 163–4, 202, 213.

48 Horsley to the St David's clergy, May 1793: letter reprinted in (D. Jones), *Tracts published under the signature of the Welch Freeholder*, London (c. 1794), tract vi, pp. v–x.

49 Daubeny, *Guide*, pp. 86–7.

50 See Clark, *English Society*, pp. 231–4, 263–76. Bowles and Reeves were both friends of Stevens.

51 W. Stevens to J. Skinner, 1st May 1797: Park, *Stevens*, p. 138.

52 *The Charges of Samuel Horsley, late Lord Bishop of St. Asaph: delivered at his several Visitations of the Dioceses of St. David's, Rochester, and St. Asaph*, Dundee (1813), pp. 40–1, 43: from Horsley's 1790 St David's Primary Visitation Charge.

53 W. Van Mildert, travel diary, 1792: Van Mildert Papers; abridged version, ed. A.T.S. Bradshaw, in *Durham University Journal*, vol. LXXI, no. 1, pp. 45–53.

54 Van Mildert to Henry Douglas, 26th Nov. 1831: in Adams, *Douglas Family*, pp. 552–3.

55 Information supplied by the Grocers' Company. The other candidate was a Rev John Sharp.

56 Churton, *Memoir*, vol. 1, pp. 54–5.

57 *Ibid.*, p. 59.

58 *Ibid.*, pp. 92–3. Cobbett was at this time a 'bellicose anti-Jacobin journalist', to the extent of refusing to illuminate his house in honour of the 1801 peace declaration, and having his windows broken by a London mob in consequence. E. P. Thompson, *The Making of the English Working Class*, London (Penguin, 1968), p. 83.

2. 'VAN'

1 The full title of the benefice was St Mary-le-Bow with St Pancras Soper Lane and Allhallows Honey Lane. Before the Great Fire these were

three small adjacent parishes. The Fire took Soper Lane along with its church, and Honey Lane became a market. Only St Mary-le-Bow was rebuilt, 'one of Wren's loveliest churches, famous for its bells [and] for the romanesque crypt that had given its name to the Archbishop of Canterbury's provincial court': Best, 'Van Mildert', p. 358. The rebuilding, begun in 1671, was finished in 1680; Van Mildert noted an arcade omitted from Wren's original plan. The site had archaeological interest: 'The Steeple is founded on the old Roman Causeway, which lies about 18 feet below the Level of the present street: & the Church on the Walls of a Roman Temple.' Documents relating to the Parish of St Mary le Bow, London, Van Mildert Papers.

2 W. O. B. Allen and E. McClure, *Two Hundred Years: the History of The Society for Promoting Christian Knowledge, 1698–1898*, London (SPCK, 1898), p. 149.

3 W. Van Mildert, handwritten pamphlet 'Account of the Evening Lecture at Bow Church, drawn up from Authentic Documents, for His Grace, the Lord Archbishop of Canterbury, by W:V:M: April 1797', Van Mildert Papers.

4 B. H. Coleman, 'Anglican church extension and related movements c. 1800–1860 with special reference to London', Cambridge (Ph.D. thesis, 1968), p. 69.

5 Cited in J. Hunt, *Religious Thought*, pp. 11–12.

6 W. Van Mildert, 'Account of the Evening Lecture at Bow . . .' and 'Sequel to the Account of the Evening Lecture at Bow Church drawn up by W:V:M: April 1800', in Van Mildert Papers.

7 Ives, *Memoir*, p. 19.

8 E. A. Varley, 'A study of William Van Mildert, Bishop of Durham, and the High Church movement of the early nineteenth century', 2 vols., Durham (Ph.D. thesis, 1985), vol. 1, pp. 66–7.

9 Virgin, *Age of Negligence*, pp. 193 ff., p. 290, table XVIII.

10 'By some incautious conduct, during his time of mourning, he brought on an eruptive fever, which incapacitated him, during many months, for clerical duty, and from the effects of which he never entirely recovered; in fact, the disease, on abating, became partly chronic, and obliged him frequently to resort to Harrogate for relief, throughout the course of his after life.' Ives, *Memoir*, p. 15.

11 Archbishop's Registrar to Van Mildert, Dec. 1800, *ibid.*, p. 18.

12 Van Mildert's 'legal agent and adviser' to Van Mildert, Dec. 1800, *ibid.*, pp. 17–18.

13 *The Times*, 27th June 1801, p. 2, col. 1; 30th June 1801, p. 2, cols. 1–2.

14 Horsley, *Charges*, pp. 83–4. The quotation is from his 1796 primary visitation charge to the clergy of Rochester.

15 Ward, *Religion and Society*, p. 106.

16 Ives, *Memoir*, pp. 16–19; W. Van Mildert to Cornelius Ives, 15th Feb. 1802: Durham University Library Add. Ms. 274.207V2L447.

17 W. Van Mildert, *The Excellency of the Liturgy, and the Advantages of being*

Educated in the Doctrine and Principles, of the Church of England. A Sermon, preached in the Parish Church of St. Mary Le Bow . . ., London (1797), pp. 17–18.

18 Daubeny, *Guide*, pp. 187 & ff.

19 This argument interestingly anticipates, in undeveloped form, the teaching of Charles Lloyd, Van Mildert's successor as Oxford Regius Professor of Divinity, that the Prayer Book was 'the close English cousin of the Roman service books': G. Faber, *Oxford Apostles: A Character Study of the Oxford Movement*, London (Faber, 1933; paperback edition 1974), p. 122.

20 W. Van Mildert, *Cautions against Innovation in Matters of Religion. A Sermon, preached in the Parish Church of St. Mary Le Bow . . .*, London (1798), pp. 13–17.

21 W. Van Mildert, 'The nature & obligation of the Baptismal Vow. A Confirmation Sermon.' Durham University Library Add. Ms. 274.207V21S4.

22 Van Mildert, Waterland papers. He cites another inaccurate *Gentleman's Magazine* note. Obituary, in *The Gentleman's Magazine*, April 1836, New Series, vol. V, p. 425.

23 Extract from Boyle's will (1691), in W. Van Mildert, *An historical view of the rise and progress of Infidelity, with a refutation of it's principles and reasonings; in a series of Sermons preached for the Lecture founded by the Hon. Robert Boyle*, 2nd edition, London (F.C. and J. Rivington, 1808), vol. 1, pp. vii–viii.

24 J. J. Dahm, 'Science and apologetics in the early Boyle Lectures', in *Church History*, vol. 39 (1970), no. 2, p. 175, note 17. C. B. Wilde, 'Hutchinsonianism, natural philosophy and religious controversy in 18th century Britain', in *History of Science*, vol. xviii (1980), p. 74. Van Mildert, *Boyle Sermons*, vol. 1, pp. xxi–xxv, gives a nearly complete list of lecturers and their subjects to 1807.

25 Ives, *Memoir*, p. 20. Some later series were well received: Thomas Newton's *Dissertations on the Prophecies*, delivered 1756–8 and later published in expanded form, became a minor classic, its author receiving his lawn sleeves in 1761. Biscoe's *The History of the Acts of the Holy Apostles confirmed from other Authors, and considered as full Evidences of the Truth of Christianity* (published 1742) had its admirers, among them Van Mildert, who used it in preparing his own sermons.

26 Van Mildert, *Boyle Sermons*, vol. 1, p. 408.

27 Wilde, 'Hutchinsonianism', p. 914.

28 Varley, 'Van Mildert', vol. 1, pp. 97–104.

29 S. Gilley, 'Christianity and Enlightenment: an historical survey', in *History of European Ideas*, vol. 1 (1981), no. 2, p. 105.

30 Jones, *Works of Horne*, preface to second edition, p. xxiii.

31 *A Word to the Hutchinsonians: or Remarks on Three extraordinary Sermons Lately preached before the University of Oxford, by The Reverend Dr. Patten,*

The Reverend Mr. Wetherall, and The Reverend Mr. Horne, By A Member of the University, London (1756), p. 4: attributed to Kennicott by the British Library Catalogue of Printed Books.

32 D. Hume, *Dialogues concerning Natural Religion* (1779), Part IX, opening lines. Hume was building the argument up as a prelude to demolition; others, for example Clarke, thought it sound. See Van Mildert's summary in *Boyle Sermons,* vol. 2, Appendix, p. 12.

33 Cf. Daubeny, *Guide,* p. 145, on the tendency 'to offer incense to that idol of the natural man, human reason'.

34 Jones, *Works of Horne,* pp. xx–xxi.

35 Hutchinson maintained that God confused not the languages of the builders, but their liturgies; Van Mildert followed the orthodox translation. Van Mildert cited Hutchinson as an authority on the Plagues of Egypt and on heathen mythology (*Boyle Sermons,* vol. 1, Appendix, pp. 10–11).

36 W. Van Mildert, *Sermons preached before the Honourable Society of Lincoln's Inn, from the year 1812 to the year 1819,* Oxford (1831), vol. 1, pp. 95–8, 112; *Boyle Sermons,* vol. II, pp. 65, 72–5. Ives, *Memoir,* p. 33, notes Van Mildert's use of Paley's *Evidences.* Paley's *Natural Theology* appears on a list of recommended reading prepared by Van Mildert in 1818 (*Christian Remembrancer,* vol. XIII (1983), p. 45).

37 Van Mildert, *Boyle Sermons,* vol. II, pp. 61–5. Cf. Jones, *Works of Horne,* preface to second edition, p. xviii, for the apologetic value of analogies between 'divine things' and 'the natural creation'. Ives, *Memoir,* pp. 33–4, recounts Van Mildert's successful trial of the *Boyle Sermons* prescription (vol. 2, pp. 66–7) on a young atheist. The fourteenth lecture, 'The inability of man to frame a religion for himself', gave him endless trouble. Preparing it for publication, with Joshua Watson's moral and technical support, took him from December 1805 until April 1806.

38 See, e.g., B. M. G. Reardon, *Religious Thought in the Victorian Age: A Survey from Coleridge to Gore,* paperback edition, New York (Longman, 1980), pp. 64–72. Coleridge elaborated his opposition to Rationalism far beyond the germ embodied in Hutchinsonian thought.

39 Jones, *Works of Horne,* preface to second edition, pp. xxix–xxx.

40 Churton, *Memoir,* vol. 1, p. 73. Cf. Charles Lloyd's comment to Norris, 11th Dec. 1825: 'I used to say of Van, that he was so great in his knowledge of the exact doctrines of the Church of England, that orthodoxy oozed out of his pores, and he would talk it in his dreams.' *Ibid.,* p. 282.

41 Van Mildert, *Boyle Sermons,* vol. 1, p. xv. See, for example, his notes on 'Voltaire's Treatise, entitled La Philosophie de l'Histoire par feu M. l'Abbé [sic] Bazin' (*ibid.,* vol. II, Appendix, p. 54), on Gibbon (*ibid.,* vol. 1, Appendix, pp. 12, 71–2; vol. II, Appendix, pp. 62–3) and on 'one of those mischievous little manuals of Infidelity . . . circulated . . .

by the leaders of the Anti-christian conspiracy on the Continent' (*ibid.*, vol. II, Appendix, pp. 52–3).

42 *Ibid.*, vol. I, pp. 439–40.

43 *Ibid.*, pp. 401–2.

44 Abbé Barruel, *Mémoire pour servir à l'histoire du Jacobinisme* (1797); J. Robison, *Proofs of a Conspiracy against all the Religions and Governments of Europe, carried on in the secret meetings of Freemasons, Illuminati and Reading Societies* (1798). Beilby Porteus' *A Charge delivered to the Clergy of the Diocese of London, in the years 1798 and 1799*, London (1799), p. 8, described Barruel and Robison as 'two different authors, of different countries and different religions, and writing without the least concert or communication with each other': this was substantially correct, although the two men had in fact met. Horsley puffed them in his 1800 charge to the Rochester clergy; Tomline, influential Bishop of Lincoln, also endorsed their theses. Robison's went through five editions in two years. Van Mildert gave 'attentive consideration' to Mounier's attempt to 'vindicate, not only himself, but the whole fraternity of French and German philosophers, from the charge of conspiracy against the Christian religion', agreeing that Mounier succeeded in clearing himself, 'one of the best intentioned and ablest of the French Revolutionists', but remained satisfied of the Barruel–Robison theory's substantial accuracy. Their works 'contain such a mass of well-authenticated evidence respecting the associations on the Continent for the overthrow of Christianity, as can hardly leave a doubt respecting the general facts, whatever apprehension may arise that in the detail of the circumstances some inaccuracies may have occurred'. *Boyle Sermons*, vol. I, Appendix, p. 77.

45 Van Mildert thought there were 'several important events yet to take place . . . before the Millennium'. The reign of Antichrist signified both the Ottoman Empire in the East and the Papal See in the West; their necessary destruction might not be very distant, given the 'present political aspect of affairs'. The Two Witnesses, whose ministry had already begun, signified Western and Eastern Christendom, or alternatively 'the Protestant Churches witnessing against Papal Rome and in the East, the Greek Churches bearing testimony against Mahometans and Pagans'. Their 'figurative death and resurrection' was probably still to come. Finally came the conversion of the Jews, about whom Van Mildert was fairly liberal: while describing them as 'under the influence of that Apostate Spirit to whose suggestions they had ever been prone to yield', he also deplored the 'barbarous persecution, which the Jews from time to time experienced under Christian governments', 'such acts of cruelty and such vindictive retaliation of injuries, as disgraced the profession of the Gospel'. The remnant of the Old Israel was a wild card in Van Mildert's eschatological game: 'as it is almost impossible not to perceive the hand of God in the strange

vicissitudes that have hitherto befallen that wonderful people; so it is hardly to be doubted that they are thus miraculously preserved for some astonishing and greatly beneficial purpose, yet to be accomplished'. See above, p. 28.

46 Ives, *Memoir*, pp. 23–4. In the *Christian Remembrancer* booklists (see note 35), Van Mildert's Boyle Sermons appear on the lists contributed by Bishop Jenkinson (undated), Archdeacon Wrangham (1820), Professor Burton (undated) and Bishop Blomfield (1826). A later list of Blomfield's cites the 23rd lecture under 'Inspiration of Scripture' and the whole second volume under 'Natural Religion'. Charles Lloyd's vast list cites the Appendices for 'the Doctrines of the Jews' and the 23rd lecture against the Unitarian objection 'Fallibility of the Writers'.

47 *Dictionary of National Biography*, vol. xxi, p. 189.

48 Correspondence between Wordsworth and Norris is preserved in the Bodleian, the British Library and Lambeth Palace Library, the earliest letter dated 25th Dec. [1807]: British Library Ms. Add. 46136, ff. 178–9.

49 *The Times*, 15th March 1792, p. 2, col. 3, in a series of satirical portraits of the Prince of Wales' friends inspired by the Prince's announced intention to defray his debts by selling off his stud, depicted 'Old Q--' as 'a rat-tailed horse, with a wall eye; has been broken down, and used for several years as a hackney; he will be sold cheap'. Also known as the 'Star of Piccadilly', he died on 23rd Dec. 1810.

50 W. Howley to Lord Liverpool, 2nd July 1824: British Library Ms. Add. 38299, ff. 34–5. Manners-Sutton to Van Mildert, March 1807, in Ives, *Memoir*, p. 31.

51 Churton, *Memoir*, vol. i, pp. 75, 90. Bowles was accused of embezzlement while serving as a commissioner for the distribution of Dutch prize-money. Vindicated in a pamphlet by a political opponent, he could never shed the scandal, which broke out afresh in 1817. Van Mildert and Watson were convinced of his innocence.

52 *Ibid.*, pp. 75–6. The repaid sum went to benefit the see of Sydney. In about 1834, Van Mildert subscribed at least £200 to another private relief fund for a clergyman in difficulties, referring warmly to his own experience, and requested Joshua Watson: 'persuade the good recipient that the help administered emanates from a sense of public duty no less than from personal regard, and is therefore clear from anything that shall be painful to a sensitive mind'. *Ibid.*, vol. ii, pp. 38–9.

53 Wordsworth to Norris, 25th Dec. 1810, 4th June 1811: British Library Ms. Add. 46136, ff. 237, 242. Van Mildert was also asked to vet letters: Wordsworth to Norris, 4th September 1811: Norris Papers.

54 Best, 'Van Mildert', p. 359.

55 W. Van Mildert, *To THE INHABITANTS of THE PARISH OF FARNINGHAM in the County of Kent* (privately printed, 5th March 1810); reproduced entire in Cochrane, pp. 75–81.

56 Christopher Wordsworth wished him luck: Wordsworth to Norris (postmark 11th Oct. 1808): British Library Ms. Add. 46136, f. 191.

57 Ives, *Memoir*, pp. 34–5.

58 Van Mildert to Jane Van Mildert, 17th April 1812, in Adams, *Douglas Family*, pp. 453–5.

59 W. Van Mildert, *Lincoln's Inn Sermons*, Oxford (1831), vol. 1, pp. 102–3.

60 Ives, *Memoir*, p. 36. This is evidently an eye-witness description.

61 Van Mildert to Jane Van Mildert, 'Saturday' – 25th April, 2nd May or 9th May 1812. In Adams, *Douglas Family*, p. 455. The letter is exuberant and affectionate, threatening to join Jane and 'dear Helen' at Farningham for 'the whole week, & leave the Sons of the Clergy in the lurch . . .'

62 Diary entry for 16th May 1812: R. I. and S. Wilberforce, *The Life of William Wilberforce*, 5 vols., London (John Murray, 1838), vol. 4, p. 27.

63 This was the first of a series of eleven annual parliamentary grants to relieve clerical poverty, administered by the Bounty Board. Best, *Temporal Pillars*, pp. 205–6.

64 Van Mildert, *Lincoln's Inn Sermons*, vol. 2, pp. 501–23.

65 Churton, *Memoir*, vol. 1, p. 138.

66 Van Mildert to Jane Van Mildert, 3rd Sept. 1813, in Adams, *Douglas Family*, pp. 456–8.

67 C. Jackson to W. Howley, 20th Oct. 1809: Lambeth Palace Library Ms. 2186, ff. 1–3. Jackson finally persuaded Howley to take the Chair with the argument that 'with yr. connections the Professorship wd certainly put you forward for a small Bishoprick, such as the first you get must probably be – for it is always an advantage to a Minister to be able to dispose of the small Bishoprick without having to find a Commendam for it'. Perceval was particularly anxious that Howley should accept the offer because Howley was already a canon of Christ Church, and 'it was an object to Government at present to place a person in that Chair who had something to vacate'. Jackson to Howley, 24th Oct. 1809. Lambeth Palace Library Ms. 2186, ff. 4–5. Before Van Mildert was offered the Chair 'it had already been refused by Dr. Ireland'. Adams, *Douglas Family*, p. 458.

68 H. Carpenter, ed., *Letters of J. R. R. Tolkien*, London (Allen & Unwin, 1981), no. 178, p. 230. However Peel, in an 1825 letter to Van Mildert, refers to 'Professor Gaisford' and 'Professor Buckland': British Library Ms. Add. 40375, ff. 22–3.

69 Christ Church Chapter Book 1799– 45A, entry for 3rd Nov. 1813: Christ Church Batells Book x.c.309; the first entry relating to Van Mildert is dated 4th Nov. 1813.

70 Christ Church Chapter Book 1799– 45A, entry for 18th Nov. 1816. Van Mildert's attendance record, roughly one meeting in three, compared favourably with some fellow-canons. Three proxies were sometimes

needed to fill the quorum of five; it was not unknown for a 'meeting' to be held by one canon with four proxies.

71 Ives, *Memoir*, p. 49. Van Mildert, 'Diary for 1816', Van Mildert Papers. Van Mildert to C. Wordsworth, 26th Oct. 1813: Lambeth Palace Library Ms. 1822, ff. 236–7. Van Mildert to Henry Douglas, 20th March 1819, in Adams, *Douglas Family*, pp. 460–1, also refers to the composition of divinity lectures.

72 Lloyd to Peel, 30th Jan. 1827: British Library Ms. Add. 40343, ff. 17–8.

73 Churton, *Memoir*, vol. 1, p. 208.

74 Ives, *Memoir*, pp. 38–40.

75 Van Mildert to C. Wordsworth, 26th Oct. 1813: Lambeth Palace Library Ms. 1822, f. 236.

76 C. Wordsworth to Norris, undated: British Library Ms. Add. 46136, ff. 200–1. The catalogue suggests dating it 1809, but gives no reason, and 1813 is at least as likely on general grounds.

77 Van Mildert to C. Wordsworth, 18th Oct. 1814: Lambeth Palace Library Ms. 1822, ff. 238–9.

78 C. Jackson to W. Howley, 13th Aug. 1813: Lambeth Palace Library Ms. 2186, f. 48. Van Mildert tried to lure Gaisford into divinity, with no more success. Gaisford later refused the see of Oxford.

79 C. Jackson to W. Howley, 18th Aug. 1813: Lambeth Palace Library Ms. 2186, ff. 50–1.

80 Churton, *Memoir*, vol. 1, p. 272. Henry Tristram, ed., *John Henry Newman: Autobiographical Writings*, London (Sheed & Ward, 1957), p. 71; quoted in Faber, *Oxford Apostles*, p. 123, and abridged in S. Gilley, *Newman and his Age*, London (Darton, Longman & Todd, 1990), p. 48.

81 Van Mildert to Norris, 29th March 1819, in Churton, *Memoir*, vol. 1, p. 273.

82 *Ibid.*, p. 279. Lloyd and Van Mildert had not met before: Lloyd to Peel, Jan. 1827: British Library Ms. Add. 40343, ff. 2–4.

83 H. Marsh, *An Inquiry into the Consequences of Neglecting to Give the Prayer Book with the Bible*, London (Rivington, 2nd ed. 1812), p. 14.

84 H. Marsh, *A Comparative View of the Churches of England and Rome*, Cambridge (Rivington, 1814), p. 3.

85 W. Van Mildert, *An Inquiry into the general principles of Scripture-Interpretation*, Oxford (1815; third edition 1831), Appendix, p. 281.

86 P. B. Nockles, 'Continuity and change in Anglican High Churchmanship in Britain, 1792–1850', Oxford (D.Phil. thesis, 1982), vol. 1, pp. 96–7. Marsh was subsequently attacked by the Anglican George Glover for undervaluing the proper use of tradition and the Vincentian Rule. For further details of the controversy from 1810, see R. K. Braine, 'The life and writings of Herbert Marsh (1757–1839)', Cambridge (Ph.D. thesis, 1898), pp. 202ff. Cf. Hunt, *Religious Thought*,

pp. 33–5, and W. L. Mathieson, *English Church Reform 1815–1840*, London (Longman, 1923), pp. 13–14. Mathieson cites contemporary opinion that Marsh's intervention increased Bible Society support, and quotes Southey: 'I wish Herbert Marsh had let the Bible Society alone.'

87 Marsh, *Comparative View*, p. 132.

88 Van Mildert, *Inquiry*, p. 174.

89 *Ibid.*, pp. 221–3, 226. Cf. Daubeny, *Guide*, pp. 28, 31, 34–5: 'where we find the order of bishops, priests and deacons regularly appointed, there we find the church of Christ; and without these . . . it is not called a church'.

90 Van Mildert, *Inquiry*, pp. 224–8.

91 J. H. Newman, *Lectures on the Prophetical Office of the Church, viewed relatively to Romanism and Popular Protestantism*, London (J. G. and F. Rivington, 1837), pp. 249–50.

92 *Ibid.*, quoting Van Mildert, *Inquiry*, p. 97.

93 Nockles, 'Continuity and change', vol. I, pp. 107, 112–13; see also pp. 116–19.

94 Van Mildert, *Inquiry*, pp. 103–5. Cf. Faber's assertion, *Oxford Apostles*, p. 343, that the Oxford Movement's 'exalted conception of the Church . . . made demands upon the intellect of a much more subtle and difficult kind than the demands made by the current Low Church philosophy of salvation', and that a strong strand of High Church theology 'certainly made full use of reason'.

95 'Onesimus', *The Pulpit* (1814), quoted by Ives, *Memoir*, pp. 37–8.

3. THE PRIME OF THE HACKNEY PHALANX

1 H. H. Jebb, *A Great Bishop of One Hundred Years Ago, being a sketch of the life of Samuel Horsley, LL. D., formerly Bishop of St. David's, Rochester, and St. Asaph and Dean of Westminster*, London (Edward Arnold, 1909), pp. 224–5. Horsley left his three unmarried sisters little but a tangle of debts. The *Gentleman's Magazine* obituary, vol. LXXVI, part 2, p. 989, expressed deep emotion at the expiry of his life insurance premium two days before himself.

2 Churton, *Memoir*, vol. I, p. 97, credits inventing the name to the Hackney ally Dr William Hales, Rector of Killesandra, Ireland.

3 For example, by M. H. Port, *Six Hundred New Churches, a Study of the Church Building Commission, 1818–1856, and its Church Building Activities*, London (SPCK for the Church Historical Society, 1961), pp. 2–3.

4 A. B. Webster, *Joshua Watson: The Story of a Layman, 1771–1855*, London (SPCK for the Church Historical Society, 1954), p. 18. Webster feels the term 'pressure group' 'exaggerate[s] the self-consciousness of the Phalanx'.

5 Allen and McClure, *Two Hundred Years*, pp. 131, 258. SPCK was responsible for the Tranquebar mission in India (founded by Danes

and largely staffed by German Lutherans) and also for other modest work. Van Mildert's SPCK treasureship involved him in the troubles of David Evans, who in March 1813 told Tournay, Warden of Wadham, that he had 'lived in a State of Banishment going in 17 years' on the Scilly Isles as SPCK missionary. Evans' increasingly unbalanced letters were accompanied with bundles of salt fish intended to soften Oxford hearts: 'If you have any Friend in London who would wish to have some Fish,' he wrote hopefully to Tournay in March 1815, 'I will send any Quantity next Season . . .' Correspondence in Van Mildert Papers.

6 F. Warre Cornish, *A History of the English Church in the Nineteenth Century*, London (Macmillan, 1910), vol. I, p. 38. *A Letter to the Society for Promoting Christian Knowledge. Occasioned by two recent publications respecting the British and Foreign Bible Society, by a Member of the Society*, London (Rivington, 1805), p. 42, speaks of the Welsh Bibles as 'now republishing'. The fresh impression, 20,000 Bibles with Service Book and Psalms, was not in fact ready until 1809 (Allen and McClure, *Two Hundred Years*, p. 204).

7 *Letter to the Society*, p. 10.

8 Braine, 'Marsh', p. 210, seems to identify Sikes as the 'Country Clergyman'. The 'Sub-Urban Clergyman' is thought to have been Sydney Smith. The British Library Catalogue lists *Letter to the Society* as anonymous. The Bodleian copy has a handwritten attribution to 'the Revd. W. Van Mildert', repeated in the Bodleian Catalogue. The style is congruous with Van Mildert's.

9 *Letter to the Society*, p. 40.

10 T. F. Middleton to Norris, 4th Oct. 1813: Norris Papers.

11 Churton, *Memoir*, vol. I, p. 95. The dignitary referred to may have been Van Mildert's former referee Robert Finch, treasurer of SPCK from 1775 to 1802 and a prebendary of Westminster; or Bishop Randolph.

12 Mathieson, *Reform*, p. 14. Charles Lloyd thought Otter, who in 1836 became Bishop of Chichester, 'a neat and gentlemanly writer of English, but no theologian': Churton, *Memoir*, vol. I, p. 283.

13 Horsley, *Charges*, p. 157. Soloway, *Prelates and People*, p. 360, cites this charge as evidence that by 1800 Horsley had lost his earlier enthusiasm for education.

14 *Life of William Wilberforce*, vol. III, p. 72.

15 Inscription over the door of Lancaster's first school: *Dictionary of National Biography*, vol. XXXII, p. 39.

16 S. C. Carpenter, *Church and People, 1789–1889*, London (SPCK, 1933), pp. 70–2, has a useful summary.

17 *Letter to the Society*, footnote, pp. 24–6.

18 Warre Cornish, *History*, vol. I, p. 93.

19 C. Daubeny, *A Sermon Preached . . . June 1, 1809, Being the Time of the*

Yearly Meeting of the Children Educated in the Charity Schools, London (1809), p. 17; quoted in Soloway, *Prelates and People*, p. 371.

20 Churton, *Memoir*, vol. I, p. 103.

21 Park to Watson, 8th Oct. 1811; *ibid.*, vol. I, p. 106.

22 Webster, *Joshua Watson*, p. 34.

23 Churton, *Memoir*, vol. I, p. 91.

24 Webster, *Joshua Watson*, p. 35.

25 *Ibid.*, quoting the First Report of the National Society.

26 *Life of William Wilberforce*, vol. IV, p. 13. The only concession to Barrington was 'that any books he used (for he said he did give his schools some not in the catalogue) should be added to their stock'. In 1810, Christopher Wordsworth picked up a rumour that Barrington had 'set his face agst.' a 'religious society' at Darlington on discovering that 'it was distributing, not SPCK tracts but those of the Religious Tract Society'. Wordsworth to Norris, Good Friday 1810: British Library Ms. Add. 46136, f. 225.

27 Churton, *Memoir*, vol. I, p. 116.

28 S. B. Black, *The Children of Farningham and their Schools 1800–1900*, Kent (Darenth Valley Publications, 1982), pp. 2–4.

29 Best, *Temporal Pillars*, p. 264. See also p. 261.

30 The Duke of Wellington, ed., *Despatches, correspondence, and memoranda of Field Marshal Arthur, Duke of Wellington, K. G., 1819–32* (in continuation of former series), 8 vols., London (John Murray, 1867–80), vol. IV, p. 300.

31 *Life of William Wilberforce*, vol. IV, p. 197.

32 Carpenter, *Church and People*, p. 70.

33 G. Smith, *The Life of William Carey: Shoemaker and Missionary*, London (Everyman edition), p. 117.

34 Quoted in Hunt, *Religious Thought*, pp. 11–12.

35 *Life of William Wilberforce*, vol. 4, pp. 22–3.

36 Manners-Sutton to Wordsworth, 18th Jan. 1814: Lambeth Palace Library Ms. 1822, f. 115. Buchanan's scheme provided for an Archbishop of Calcutta, Bishops of Madras, Bombay and Ceylon, four Archdeacons, fifty European Chaplains, a hundred 'country Chaplains, to be natives or Europeans ordained in India', two hundred schoolmasters and four Colleges, at an annual cost of £144,000.

37 Middleton to Norris, 30th Jan. 1814: Norris Papers.

38 *Life of William Wilberforce*, vol. IV, p. 200.

39 Wordsworth to Norris, 3rd Feb. 1814: Norris Papers.

40 Joshua Watson to Wordsworth, 13th May 1814: Lambeth Palace Library Ms. 1822, f. 247.

41 C. F. Pascoe, *Two Hundred Years of the S.P.G.: An Historical Account of the Society for the Propagation of the Gospel in Foreign Parts, 1701–1900*, London (SPG, 1901), p. 472.

42 Middleton to Norris, 'Saturday, midnight' (presumably 17th May

1814, the date of the official farewell): Norris Papers. Webster, *Joshua Watson*, p. 123.

43 Middleton to Norris, 3rd June 1815: Norris Papers.

44 Middleton to Van Mildert, 14th Feb. 1815: Durham University Library Add. Ms. 274.207V21M5. Middleton wrote regularly to Van Mildert until at least 1819.

45 'It is from the labours of ordained converts that we expect the most favourable results.' Middleton, valedictory charge to the Revd C. A. Jacobi, a German Lutheran missionary sent out by the SPCK in 1813; quoted in Webster, *Joshua Watson*, p. 126. Jacobi 'died, much lamented, in 1814': Allen and McClure, *Two Hundred Years*, p. 283.

46 *Life of Carey*, pp. 177–8, footnote, lists the versions Carey produced. Marsh, who unlike the Phalanx supported overseas distribution of Bibles without the Prayer Book, gave public praise to Carey and the Baptist Missionary Society; Braine, 'Marsh', pp. 229–30.

47 Although both CMS and the Bible Society recognised their potential value: the 1818 CMS grant of £5,000 to Bishop's College, with a further £5,000 from the Bible Society towards the work of translating the Scriptures into Asiatic languages, exactly matched the grants from SPCK and SPG; Churton, *Memoir*, vol. i, p. 181.

48 Webster, *Joshua Watson*, pp. 115–6.

49 *Ibid.*, p. 116. Churton, *Memoir*, vol. i, p. 168, says Watson was elected Treasurer on 3rd June 1814. According to Allen and McClure, *Two Hundred Years*, p. 133, and Cochrane, 'Van Mildert', p. 110, Van Mildert's resignation was in 1815. This suggests Watson became Treasurer-elect for a period.

50 Joshua Watson to Archbishop Manners-Sutton, Dec. 1817, in Churton, *Memoir*, vol. i, p. 176.

51 Allen and McClure, *Two Hundred Years*, p. 285; Pascoe, *S.P.G.*, p. xi.

52 Churton, *Memoir*, vol. i, p. 177.

53 *Ibid.*, vol. i, pp. 151–61; Webster, *Joshua Watson*, chapter iv.

54 Stevenson, *Popular Disturbances*, pp. 91, 101–2, 155–62, 190–7.

55 *The Quarterly Review*, vol. vii, no. xiv (June 1812), p. 438. 'At this moment, nothing but the Army preserves us from the most dreadful of all calamities, an insurrection of the poor against the rich, and how long the Army may be depended on is a question which I scarcely dare to ask myself.' Southey to John Murray, 19th May 1812; quoted in E. Halévy, *A History of the English People in the Nineteenth Century*, 6 vols., London (Ernest Benn, 1949–52), vol. i, p. 333.

56 Churton, *Memoir*, vol. i, p. 177. *Life of Carey*, p. 251, gives a genesis of the epithet 'tub-preacher'. Thompson, *English Working Class*, pp. 427–32, arguing against any simple understanding of the relationship between religious and political excitement, makes clear the genuine involvement of some Methodists in political radicalism. Other denominations, for instance the Baptists, had similar involvements.

57 Christ Church Chapter Book 45A, 1799–, entry for 21st June 1815. 'The Revd. Dr. Van Mildert's pr[ivate] acc[oun]t', xxxvii.b.55, entry for Lady Day 1814. Van Mildert to Norris, 12th Nov. [1816]: Norris Papers. Churton, *Memoir*, vol. 1, p. 137. Watson's original plan for the Family Bible, a scholarly commentary prepared by Van Mildert and Middleton plus a commentary for 'cottage-readers' compiled by Richard Mant, was frustrated when Manners-Sutton committed the whole task 'to his own two chaplains, Mr. Mant and Mr. George D'Oyley'; *ibid*., pp. 126–7.

58 *Hansard*, vol. xiv, p. 857 (2nd June 1809); quoted in Best, *Temporal Pillars*, pp. 148–9.

59 *Quarterly Review*, vol. v, no. x (May 1811), p. 365.

60 'Substance of the Speech of the Earl of Harrowby, on moving for the Recommitment of a Bill for the better Support and Maintenance of Stipendiary Curates', in *Quarterly Review*, vol. x, no. xix (October 1813), pp. 54, 56; Best, *Temporal Pillars*, p. 149, citing *Hansard*, vol. xvii, pp. 770–1 (19th June 1810).

61 Joshua Watson to Henry Ryder, in Churton, *Memoir*, vol. 1, p. 217.

62 According to Cotton's obituary in the *Gentleman's Magazine*, 1867, vol. 1, p. 111, quoted in Port, *600 New Churches*, p. 9.

63 Churton, *Memoir*, vol. 1, p. 199.

64 Middleton to Norris, 11th Dec. 1812: Norris Papers.

65 Quoted in Port, *600 New Churches*, pp. 7–8.

66 Churton, *Memoir*, vol. 1, p. 182.

67 *Life of William Wilberforce*, vol. iv, p. 297, describes a public meeting held in 1816 to consider relief for Distressed Manufacturers where the rowdy part of the audience demonstrated its 'brutality' by 'bursting into laughter when the Bishop of London, being unused to public speaking, made a pause'. For Howley's shortcomings as a public performer, see O. Chadwick, *The Victorian Church*, 2 vols., London (Black, 1966), vol. 1, pp. 12, 159, 162, 453 (page references are to 3rd edition).

68 G. Pellew, *Life and Correspondence of Lord Sidmouth*, 3 vols. (1847), vol. iii, pp. 138–40; discussed by Port, *600 New Churches*, p. 11, and Best, *Temporal Pillars*, p. 149.

69 Port, *600 New Churches*, p. 12; Webster, *Joshua Watson*, p. 62.

70 Webster, *Joshua Watson*, p. 62.

71 R. Yates, *The Church in Danger: a Statement of the Cause, and of the Probable Means of Averting that Danger, Attempted: in a Letter to Lord Liverpool*. See Best, *Temporal Pillars*, pp. 147–51. Webster, *Joshua Watson*, p. 63, says Yates first attended the weekly committee meetings on 7th Nov. 1817; he later served on the Church Building Society committee.

72 *Life of William Wilberforce*, vol. iv, p. 368; Webster, *Joshua Watson*, p. 62; Port, *600 New Churches*, pp. 13–14.

73 Churton, *Memoir*, vol. 1, pp. 199–200.

74 Harrowby to Liverpool, 22nd March 1818: British Library Ms. Add. 38271, f. 35; quoted in Best, *Temporal Pillars*, p. 269.

75 Van Mildert to Peel, 30th April 1818: British Library Ms. Add. 40276, ff. 251–2. Van Mildert also feared the three turns provision might tempt church-founders 'to build slight Fabrics, or to neglect the due repairs of them', causing problems after 'the expiration of their term of patronage'.

76 Churton, *Memoir*, vol. II, pp. 154–5, gives Joshua Watson's view of the election of an incumbent at Clerkenwell. On secular elections see Stevenson, *Popular Disorders*, pp. 27–8, 164–5, 184.

77 Van Mildert to Watson, in Churton, *Memoir*, vol. I, p. 208.

78 Archbishop Manners-Sutton to Liverpool, 24th June 1818; Liverpool to Manners-Sutton, same date: British Library Ms. Add. 38272, ff. 180–2; quoted in Best, *Temporal Pillars*, p. 269.

79 Port, *600 New Churches*, pp. 98–9. Van Mildert's letter to Peel, 30th April 1818, expressed 'doubt whether the Emoluments of Incumbents in Parishes chiefly depending on the amount of Fees & Offerings are, or can be, adequately secured', and warned that pew-rents were unlikely to suffice for all the expenses charged to them. He was quite right. The 1826–7 standing committee's 'plan broke down in application because of', among others, '. . . the impossibility in some places of letting enough pews to provide a stipend'.

80 Best, *Temporal Pillars*, p. 268. This is not an unqualified compliment.

81 Webster, *Joshua Watson*, p. 64.

4. TOIL AND TRIBULATION

1 Van Mildert to H. Douglas, 20th March 1819, in Adams, *Douglas Family*, p. 460. The letter speaks of 'the irreparable loss that has been sustained in the death of the excellent Bishop of Peterborough'.

2 Van Mildert to Liverpool, 14th March 1819: British Library Ms. Add. 38275, f. 415.

3 Quoted in Braine, 'Marsh', p. 257. See also Van Mildert, *Memoir of Waterland*, p. 245, on Waterland's refusal of Llandaff. *The Clerical Guide, and Ecclesiastical Directory, compiled from the report of the Ecclesiastical Revenues Commission of 1832–5*, New Edition. London (Rivington, 1836), Table I, Revenues of Episcopal Sees. During his episcopate Van Mildert's Llandaff income averaged £1403.10s.7d. per annum: financial memorandum in Van Mildert Papers.

4 Liverpool to Van Mildert, 15th July 1820: British Library Ms. Add. 38282, ff. 298–9. (The wording suggests Liverpool expected Van Mildert to refuse.) Van Mildert to Liverpool, quoted in Ives, *Memoir*, pp. 58–9. Van Mildert had some contact with the Irish Douglases, including Lady Cloncurry, on whose behalf he lobbied Peel in 1817 (British Library Ms. Add. 40272, ff. 67, 69). The connection was not

wholly auspicious. When the Duke of Richmond offered Archy Douglas, Jane Van Mildert's cousin, the benefice of Dunlaven, Archbishop Cleaver of Dublin refused him institution on the grounds that 'Mr. Douglas had preached Catholic Emancipation, and abused the Bench of Bishops.' (Adams, *Douglas Family*, p. 376)

5 Liverpool to Van Mildert, 15th July 1820: British Library Ms. Add. 38286, f. 120–2.

6 Extract from Minutes of the Council of Lincoln's Inn, 24th May 1819, in Cochrane, 'Van Mildert', pp. 121–2.

7 Van Mildert to H. H. Norris, 29th March 1819, in Churton, *Memoir* vol. I, pp. 272–3. W. B. Maynard, 'The ecclesiastical administration of the Archdeaconry of Durham 1774–1856', Durham (Ph.D. thesis, 1973), p. 13, says that Edward Maltby, Van Mildert's successor at Durham, was a candidate for the Preachership in 1817 (presumably 1819).

8 Van Mildert to H. Douglas, 20th March 1819, in Adams, *Douglas Family*, p. 460.

9 Ives, *Memoir*, p. 51. Ives drew extensively on this correspondence, which seems not to have survived.

10 *Gentleman's Magazine*, vol. LXV (1795), part 2, p. 635; letter, dated 15th July, signed 'Juba'. *The Clerical Guide, or, Ecclesiastical Directory*, 2nd edition (corrected), London (Rivington, 1822), pp. iv–v, xv.

11 Burgess to Ralph Churton, 16th Nov. 1803: Bodleian Ms. Eng. Lett. C. 139, ff. 100–1.

12 W. Van Mildert, *A Charge delivered to the Clergy of the Diocese of Llandaff at the primary visitation in August MDCCCXXI*, in Ives, *Memoir*, pp. 489–512.

13 Ives, *Memoir*, pp. 492–4; Port, *600 New Churches*, pp. 98–9.

14 Best, *Temporal Pillars*, p. 214.

15 Ives, *Memoir*, pp. 497–8, 511: cf. pp. 57, 151; contrast the description of Van Mildert's relations with Roman Catholics.

16 Halévy, *History*, vol. I, p. 416, note 1.

17 *Hansard*, New Series, vol. IX, pp. 967–73 (12th June 1823); cf. Daubeny, *Guide*, p. 54, for the Church as 'a visible society, distinctly known by its ministers and sacraments'.

18 W. Van Mildert, *A Charge delivered to the Clergy of the Diocese of Durham, MDCCCXXVII*, in Ives, *Memoir*, p. 520. Burgess originally intended siting the college at Llanddewi-Brefi. In November 1821 the inhabitants petitioned vigorously against the change of plan, sending Van Mildert a copy of their circular: Van Mildert Papers. See D. T. W. Price, *Bishop Burgess and Lampeter College*, Lampeter (University of Wales Press, 1987), p. 51.

19 Van Mildert to Henry Douglas, 23rd Nov. 1820, in Adams, *Douglas Family*, p. 460. Henry became his uncle's domestic chaplain and curate of Ewelme; he later received a benefice in the English-speaking part of the diocese. Ives, *Memoir*, p. 53; Van Mildert to Bruce Knight

(undated), *ibid.*, p. 54. Cochrane, 'Van Mildert', pp. 152–6, quotes exhaustively from the diocesan Acta Books and Subscription Books. Of the ordinations during Van Mildert's Llandaff years, 'the surnames indicate that nearly all the candidates were of Welsh origin'; 'very few' were graduates; cf. Braine, 'Marsh', p. 258.

20 He contributed five guineas to this charity in 1821, and a further five guineas to the National Society. 'Summary of expenses on taking possession of St. Paul's'; C. Hodgson's Account with The Lord Bishop of Llandaff, 1823: Van Mildert Papers. Christopher Hodgson acted for a number of bishops, and in 1822 became secretary of Queen Anne's Bounty. Best, *Temporal Pillars*, pp. 225–6, gives some biographical details.

21 W. Van Mildert, *A Sermon Preached in the Cathedral Church of St. Paul, June 8, 1820, at the Yearly Meeting of the Children educated in the Charity Schools in and about the Cities of London and Westminster*, in Ives, *Memoir*, pp. 202–3, 215.

22 Soloway, *Prelates and People*, p. 383, arguing from Van Mildert's 1834 Durham Assize Sermon. Norman, *Church and Society*, p. 59, uncritically reproduces Soloway's opinion.

23 *Hansard*, vol. XLI, pp. 987–8. Unlike many of its denigrators, Van Mildert had read *The Age of Reason*, while preparing his Boyle Lectures.

24 *Hansard*, New Series, vol. I, p. 328.

25 *Ibid.*, vol. III, p. 1710.

26 Horsley to Fanny Horsley (daughter-in-law), 1st July 1801: Lambeth Palace Library Ms. 1767, ff. 41–2.

27 The other six divorce clause opponents were Law of Chester, Luxmoore of St Asaph, Burgess of St David's, ffoliot of Worcester, Sparke of Ely and the Bishop of Cork (*Hansard*, New Series, vol. 3, p. 1726). Law abstained at the third reading division, Marsh and the other five voted for (*ibid.*, pp. 1744–5).

28 *Ibid.*, p. 1306.

29 Stevenson, *Popular Disturbances*, p. 199.

30 *Hansard*, New Series, vol. III, pp. 1710–13.

31 Churton, *Memoir*, vol. I, p. 223; see also Stevenson, *Popular Disturbances*, p. 201, and Chadwick, *Victorian Church*, vol. I, p. 12.

32 Churton, *Memoir*, vol. I, p. 223.

33 Memorandum by Van Mildert on matters concerning Ewelme, dated 11th Dec. 1820, presumably for the information of his successor: Van Mildert Papers.

34 Van Mildert to H. Douglas, 23rd Nov. 1820, in Adams, *Douglas Family*, pp. 462–3.

35 Robert Huish, *Memoirs of Caroline, Queen of Great Britain*, London (1821), vol. II, p. 637.

36 Churton, *Memoir*, vol. I, pp. 223–4. The context implies a paraphrased letter from Van Mildert to Joshua Watson.

37 Van Mildert to Liverpool, 19th Nov. 1820: British Library Ms. Add. 38288, ff. 154–5.
38 Keppel Craven to Liverpool, 18th Nov. 1820: *ibid.*, ff. 148–50.
39 Keppel Craven to Liverpool, 21st Nov. 1820 (*ibid.*, f. 165), protests at the lack of response to his earlier letter. Churton, *Memoir*, vol. 1, p. 224, for Van Mildert's note. Van Mildert also sent copies of the correspondence to Sidmouth.
40 *The Times*, 23rd Nov. 1820, p. 2, col. 2; reproduced in Cochrane, 'Van Mildert', pp. 136–7.
41 'On a certain Prelate's Letter to the Hon. Keppel Craven –

The religion of Jesus is meekness and *love*;
The *politeness* of Oxford proverbially known:
Yet a Bishop from Oxford has labour'd to prove
His great *hate* to his Queen with a coarseness his own.
And 'this woman', to ev'ry true Briton's heart dear,
(While thousands with joy will range under her banners)
Not unaptly proposes this paradox queer –
Does your Lordship thus shew your acquaintance with Manners.'

(Lord Manners referred to the Queen in the Lords as 'this woman'.) *The Times*, 29th Nov. 1820, p. 2, col. 5; letter, *The Times*, 23rd Nov. 1820, p. 2, col. 4. Cochrane, 'Van Mildert', pp. 138–9, gives both in full.
42 Liverpool to Van Mildert, 21st Nov. 1820: British Library Ms. Add. 38288, f. 170. Cf. Van Mildert's 29th Nov. letter to Henry Douglas: 'My time is now continually occupied respecting the Queen's intended visit to St. Paul's, which exceedingly annoys me.' Churton, *Memoir*, vol. 1, p. 224, notes that Hughes was grandfather to the author of *Tom Brown's Schooldays*.
43 Soloway, *Prelates and People*, p. 41, footnote, citing Van Mildert's letter of 19th Nov. and Liverpool's reply of 21st Nov. as sources. The first part of the footnote, relating to Van Mildert's 1800 prosecution for non-residence, is no fairer and only nominally more accurate.
44 The Van Mildert Papers have both Van Mildert's Coronation invitations, for 1st Aug. 1820 and 19th July 1821, and copies of both acceptances. Adams, *Douglas Family*, p. 496, chronicles the history of the 'remarkably good' embroidered waistcoat worn by a Douglas nephew accompanying Van Mildert to the Coronation.
45 Churton, *Memoir*, vol. 1, p. 224.
46 Stephenson, *Popular Disturbances*, p. 20; Cochrane, 'Van Mildert', p. 140, quoting *The Times*, 30th Nov. 1820, p. 2, col. 5.
47 Van Mildert to Liverpool, 30th May 1823: British Library Ms. Add. 38294, ff. 230–2. The Van Mildert Papers preserve bills for extensive works at the Deanery: one presented on 5th July 1821 totalled £1699.12s.-.
48 Van Mildert had moved into the Deanery by 30th May 1823: British Library Ms. Add. 38294, ff. 230–2.

49 Churton, *Memoir*, vol. I, pp. 208ff. Van Mildert to Watson, 3rd April 1819, *ibid.*, p. 213, describes the degree as L.L.D., and Churton says Watson received it in 1819. Webster, *Joshua Watson*, p. 43, makes it a D.C.L. presented in 1820.

50 *Ibid.*, p. 240.

51 Van Mildert to Joshua Watson, June 1823. Watson told Christopher Wordsworth, 24th June 1823, that the Archbishop was 'looking well again, you will be glad to learn; and so are the elite of his corps, the Bishops of London and Llandaff'. Churton, *Memoir*, vol. I, p. 242.

52 Allen and McClure, *Two Hundred Years*, pp. 189–90.

53 *Ibid.*, pp. 154, 190. The second Anti-Infidel Committee's public appeal raised only £2382.2s.6d., including £1,000 from SPCK funds.

54 Churton, *Memoir*, vol. I, p. 11. H. T. Powell to H. H. Norris, 13th June 1831: Norris Papers.

55 *Ibid.*, pp. 20–2.

56 Rose to C. Wordsworth, 20th Aug. 1833: Lambeth Palace Library Ms. 1822, f. 214.

57 Newman to W. Palmer, Oct. 1833; I. Ker and T. Gornall, eds., *The Letters and Diaries of John Henry Newman*, Oxford, vol. IV (1980), p. 68.

58 A. P. Perceval to Newman, 10th March 1834; *ibid.*, p. 200, footnote.

59 Newman to J. W. Bowden, 1st April 1834; *ibid.*, p. 228.

60 Newman to Keble, undated; *ibid.*, p. 234. Newman dubbed the Watson/Norris faction 'the old Bartlett Building school'; *Letters of Newman*, vol. V (1981), p. 214. See also W. K. Lowther Clarke, *A Short History of S.P.C.K.*, London (SPCK, 1919), p. 47.

61 Quoted in Ives, *Memoir*, p. 138, date somewhere around April 1834.

62 A second edition appeared in 1843, a third in 1856. Extracts from the 1856 edition were republished in 1896. It included one volume selected from the previously unpublished materials Van Mildert's extensive researches turned up: 'such . . . as . . . might be acceptable to the public, and not tend to diminish the author's reputation'. *The Works of . . . Daniel Waterland . . . To Which is Prefixed a Review of the Author's Life and Writings, by William Van Mildert, D.D., Lord Bishop of Llandaff*, 10 vols., Oxford (Clarendon Press, 1823), vol. I, pp. 4–7. For details of Van Mildert's researches see Varley, 'Van Mildert', vol. II, pp. 276–8.

63 Best, 'Van Mildert', p. 357. For a sample of Van Mildert's skill, see the discussion of the differences between Johnson and Waterland on the Unbloody Sacrifice (*Works of Waterland*, vol. I, pp. 204–5).

64 Van Mildert collected more material on Clarke than would fit into the biography, and regretted its exclusion: 'Outline of a plan for Memoirs of the Life & Writings of Waterland': Van Mildert Papers. Asked in 1825 by 'a friend', evidently charged with reviewing 'the new Edition of Waterland' for the *Quarterly*, to suggest 'any topic of observation which it might be desireable [sic] to bring forward', he outlined a fuller discussion of Clarke's position, wanting to show that Clarke was 'a very

sincere Xtian, conscientious, & pious,' who 'meant to be, & believed himself to be, a Trinitarian', and that 'his work is not without it's merits and it's utility. A more substantial refutation of Sabellianism, and the errors bordering upon it, can hardly be desired; and errors of that cast, it should be remembered, were rife in his days . . ' Van Mildert added an anecdote of Clarke's writings persuading Horsley to embrace Trinitarianism rather than Arianism. Draft letter by Van Mildert, unaddressed, dated Jan. 1825: Durham University Library Add. Ms. 274.207V21W2: part in Ives, *Memoir*, pp. 63–6.

65 Van Mildert to another unnamed friend, undated, in Ives, *Memoir*, pp. 62–3; *Works of Waterland*, vol. I, p. 265.

66 Nockles, 'Continuity and Change', vol. I, pp. 112–13.

67 Clark, *English Society*, pp. 415–16.

68 Churton, *Memoir*, vol. I, p. 65. On the importance of Waterland in the development of High Church theology, see Nockles, 'Continuity and Change', vol. I, p. 112.

69 *Works of Waterland*, vol. I, p. 261. Van Mildert, for instance, disagreed with Waterland on the proper interpretation of John 6: *ibid.*, p. 213.

70 *Ibid.*, p. 263.

71 'The last letter I had from Mary gives a more favourable account of the poor Bishop. I trust his valuable life may still be preserved some little time longer; though I fear he has too shattered a frame to give his friends a hope of his continuing for any length of period!', Elizabeth Douglas to Henry Douglas, 30th Oct. 1823, in Adams, *Douglas Family*, pp. 549–51.

72 Poem 'January 27th 1824, after undergoing a severe surgical Operaton': Durham University Library Add. Ms. 274.207V2108.

73 *Hansard*, New Series, vol. XII, pp. 446, 1104–64. Van Mildert to H. H. Norris, 8th May 1824: Norris Papers. Ives, *Memoir*, p. 56. Cochrane, 'Van Mildert', p. 154, for the absence of any ordination by Van Mildert in 1824 and details of the Letters Dimissory issued instead. He went to Harrogate in July, and by 18th July was well enough to preach there: *ibid.*, p. 168.

74 Van Mildert to Joshua Watson, 'at the close of 1824'; Churton, *Memoir*, vol. I, p. 247.

75 George IV to Liverpool, 11th March 1826. A. Aspinall, ed., *The Correspondence of George Prince of Wales 1770–1812*, 8 vols., London (Cassell, 1971), vol. VIII, p. 455. The Bishop of Durham had quasi-viceregal powers dating back to the Saxon 'patrimony of St. Cuthbert'. By 1826 these were much reduced in scope, but Van Mildert was to prove they could still be effective.

76 Van Mildert to Liverpool, 25th March 1826: British Library Ms. Add. 38301, ff. 152–3. Howley to Liverpool, 27th March 1826: British Library Ms. Add. 38301, ff. 154–5.

77 Best, 'Van Mildert', p. 360.

78 E. Hughes, ed., *The Diaries and Correspondence of James Losh*, 2 vols.,

Durham (Surtees Society, 1962–3), vol. II, p. 68; diary entry for 5th August 1828.

79 The official nomination was made on 27th March, the *congé d'élire* and letter recommendatory issued on 5th April, the canonical election took place on 14th April, the Confirmation on 24th April. Documents in Dean and Chapter Archives, Durham; reproduced by Cochrane, 'Van Mildert', pp. 179–82. This was creditable but not exceptional haste; during the 1831 Reform crisis, Lord Grey caused scandal by filling a vacant see with such alacrity that the *congé d'élire* arrived before the late bishop's funeral: Chadwick, *Victorian Church*, vol. I, p. 25, footnote 2. Howley was enthroned by proxy on becoming Archbishop of Canterbury in 1828.

80 Hughes, *Losh*, vol. I, p. 44; diary entry for 7th May 1826.

81 Diary of Robert Archibald Douglas-Gresley, 11th–14th July 1826; in Adams, *Douglas Family*, pp. 464–5; also Cochrane, 'Van Mildert', pp. 186–90. The *Durham Advertiser* of 3rd June 1826, quoted by Cochrane, expected the Bishop's arrival on 27th June.

82 Van Mildert to Bruce Knight, 27th March 1826, in Ives, *Memoir*, pp. 72–3.

83 Thorp claimed Charles Lloyd as an 'early friend', who introduced him to Peel when Thorp was 'as a Justice of the Peace placed in circumstances of some difficulty' – Thorp to Peel, 13th January 1842: British Library Ms. Add. 40500, f. 41. Van Mildert told the Lords in 1832 that he had not met Thorp before his own arrival in Durham: *Hansard*, Third Series, vol. XII, p. 1173. Thorp was already acting as 'Official to the Archdeacon of Durham' before Van Mildert arrived in the diocese: The Acts of the Rt Revd William Van Mildert, D.D., Lord Bishop of Durham [Durham Acta Book], entry for 4th July 1826, reproduced by Cochrane, 'Van Mildert', p. 199. Prosser, 'a favourite target of the radical press', reputedly lived 'in retirement on his estates in Hereford', coming into Durham residence for the bare minimum his canonry required. 'The evidence indicates that he deputed his duties to Thorp at an unknown date during the 1820's': Maynard, 'Archdeaconry of Durham', pp. 20–1, 137. Prosser was moderately active in Chapter business; he was Sub-Dean in 1825–6.

84 Adams, *Douglas Family*, p. 486; Van Mildert to Thorp, 25th April 1833, Thorp Correspondence, vol. I, f. 125. The name Gresley was assumed at the wish of a wealthy benefactress.

85 Van Mildert to Dr Samuel Butler, 28th May 1835, turning down his request to give Crayke to Rev Edmund Paley, eldest surviving son of Archdeacon Paley and son-in-law to Dr Apthorp.

86 Virgin, *Age of Negligence*, p. 160. The theme recurs repeatedly.

87 Van Mildert to Thorp, 12th July 1832; Thorp Correspondence, vol. I, f. 90. William was preferred to Haltwhistle in 1829. His crime was possibly to have Reforming sympathies.

88 Van Mildert to Peel, 10th March 1825, suggesting Gaisford for the next

available Christ Church canonry: British Library Ms. Add. 40374, ff. 221–2.

89 In January 1832, Van Mildert sent Thorp '10 or 20 copies (I forget which) of my nephew *Cornelius* Ives's Sermon – which, if you approve, I request you to distribute . . . I should be glad to have your opinion of them.' Thorp Correspondence, vol. 1, f. 80. The underlining presumably emphasises that this is not William. Cornelius, later his uncle's biographer, published a *Compendious History of the Church of God* in 1820.

90 Archibald (Archy), son of Jane Van Mildert's eldest brother, was born and bred in Ireland. Rector of Cootehill and a celebrated preacher, he was noted for his exceptionally warm 'relations with the Roman Catholic population among whom he dwelt'. Philip Henry, older son of Jane's second brother, served a short curacy but for health reasons never accepted a living. Philip William, the Master of Bene't's son, studied at Christ Church during Van Mildert's time as Regius Professor, owing his Studentship to his uncle; he became Vicar of a Lincolnshire living, but Van Mildert seems never to have offered him preferment.

91 Van Mildert to Henry Douglas, 14th March 1833, in Adams, *Douglas Family*, p. 557. The Van Milderts' relationship with their 'nephew Harry Douglas' was particularly close. The Bishop was godfather to Henry's eldest son Willy; the correspondence reveals a number of gifts to both father and children, a close interest by both Van Milderts in the children's welfare and much mutual affection.

92 A. J. Heesom, *The Founding of the University of Durham*, Durham (Cathedral Lecture, 1982), pp. 15–20, gives a convenient summary of the controversies. Cf. Maynard, 'Archdeaconry of Durham', pp. 145–6. Maynard misidentifies Lambton's constituency.

93 Among other manoeuvres: Hugh Percy, who 'married the Archbishop of Canterbury's daughter and became Dean of Canterbury in 1825', became Bishop of Rochester briefly before being translated on to Carlisle later in 1827; J. B. Sumner, who in 1828 succeeded Blomfield as Bishop of Chester, acquired the Durham Second Prebend; Wellesley cashed in his St Paul's prebend for the Durham preferment. Canning wrote to the King on 13th June 'The Bishop of Durham consented on Tuesday, to the *double move* in his Lordship's Cathedral; against which he had exhibited for some time manifest symptoms of reluctance; conceiving (not quite correctly) that he was thus giving away *two* pieces of preferment instead of one.' A. Aspinall, ed., *The Letters of King George IV, 1812–1830* (Cambridge University Press, 1938), vol. III, p. 251. Van Mildert may have had other hesitations: it was he who would have to defend the massive pluralism. Wellesley was already Rector of St Luke's Chelsea, vicar of Thetfield, chaplain of Hampton Court and chaplain to the Court of St James'.

94 R. S. Watson, *The History of the Literary and Philosophical Society of Newcastle-upon-Tyne (1793–1897)*, London (Scott, 1987), pp. 66–86. The

account of the Masonic rites helps show why intelligent men believed the theory that Freemasonry was part of a conspiracy to impose man-made substitute religion in place of the Christian faith, with Liberal 'useful knowledge societies' functioning as idolatrous temples. The parallels between the other junketings for 'the Royal Duke' and those of 1827 for 'the Great Captain' are striking.

95 *Durham County Advertiser*, Saturday 6th Oct. 1827. The *Advertiser* had Tory sympathies; James Losh, who did not, commented: 'It is very clear that the Duke of Wellington's visit to the North had a political motive, but at Newcastle certainly, and I believe everywhere else . . . this was completely unsuccessful.' Hughes, *Losh*, vol. 2, p. 54.

96 Invitations preserved in the Van Mildert Papers include 'Mrs Van Mildert At Home to the Ladies'.

97 From Van Mildert's notes for his speeches, which he evidently elaborated extempore. Two drafts survive, between which the Wellington speech was considerably revised: Van Mildert Papers.

98 Best, 'Van Mildert', p. 356. 'Archdeacon Charles Thorp' is suggested as a second alternate; but Thorp, a more cautious character than Phillpotts, knew the value of 'a politic letter to a local liberal leader' (Best, *Temporal Pillars*, p. 276).

99 Second draft of speech notes. The *Durham County Advertiser*, 6th Oct. 1827, reported the speeches at length.

100 Howley to Strong, 17th Oct. 1827: Bodleian Library Ms. Eng. Misc. c. 361, ff. 15–16 (Strong Papers).

101 Van Mildert to Thorp, 19th Dec. 1831; Thorp Correspondence, vol. 1, f. 71.

102 E. Welbourne, *The Miners' Unions of Northumberland and Durham* (Cambridge University Press, 1923), pp. 28–9.

103 Van Mildert to Brougham, 18th April 1831; quoting J. R. Fenwick, presumably to Thorp, 12th April 1831. Thorp to Fenwick, 13th April 1831: Van Mildert Papers. Cf. Fenwick to Thorp, 14th April: 'The poor Miners are entitled to have an impartial Tribunal to which they may resort, in case of difference with their Employers; they have had it hitherto I hope, but if their Employers Agents are to be Magistrates, will they have, or at all events will they believe they have it.'

104 See Norman, *Church and Society*, p. 87, commenting on Van Mildert's 9th April 1832 speech to the Lords.

105 Brougham to Van Mildert, 2nd Feb. 1831: Van Mildert Papers.

106 Welbourne, *Miners' Unions*, p. 30.

107 Annotation on copy of letter from Brougham's Secretary of Commissions to the Durham Clerk of the Peace, 9th April 1831: Van Mildert Papers. William Williamson had been considered but omitted because he 'was supposed to be non-resident and therefore not likely to be useful'.

108 Van Mildert to Brougham, 5th Feb. 1831: Van Mildert Papers.

109 Bishop [Gray] of Bristol to Van Mildert, 1st March 1831: Van Mildert

Papers. On 17th April Gaisford wrote to Van Mildert, 'I wish some contrivance could be devised towards gagging my Lord of Bristol. I am afraid his propensity for talking will ere long produce some very serious mischief.'

110 Leonard Edmunds to John Dunn, 9th April 1831; Dunn to T. H. Faber, 11th April 1831: Van Mildert Papers. Fenwick to Losh, 14th April 1832; Losh to Brougham, 15th April 1832; Hughes, *Losh*, vol. 2, pp. 190–2.

111 I. W. Williamson, Chairman of the Quarter Sessions, to Van Mildert, 16th April 1831; Burdon to Van Mildert, 18th April 1831; Clavering to Van Mildert, 14th April 1831; Resolutions passed at a Meeting of Justices of the Peace, Gateshead, 16th April 1831: Van Mildert Papers.

112 Van Mildert to Brougham, 15th April 1831; Leonard Edmunds to Dunn, 15th April 1831; Dunn to Van Mildert, 17th April 1831: Van Mildert Papers. Dunn went at once to consult Thorp, Fenwick and two other Durham magistrates, also making a personal visit to Faber at Auckland; on their advice, he dispatched the Commission of the Peace to his London agents as instructed, but simultaneously wrote a full report to Van Mildert enclosing a copy of the second letter.

113 Gaisford to Van Mildert, 17th April 1831: Van Mildert Papers.

114 Van Mildert to Brougham, 18th April 1831; Brougham to Van Mildert, 18th April 1831; Van Mildert to Brougham, 19th April 1831; Van Mildert to Messrs. North & Smart, Solicitors, 19th April 1831: Van Mildert Papers.

115 Quoted in C. E. Hardy, *John Bowes and the Bowes Museum*, Newcastle (Frank Graham, 1978), p. 38.

116 Van Mildert to Thorp, 18th, 31st Jan., 15th March 1833 (and many between): Thorp Correspondence, vol. 1, ff. 95, 101, 114.

117 Visitation and confirmation in Durham on successive days, with public dinners at Durham Castle on both evenings. Visitations planned at Newcastle, Berwick, Alnwick, Morpeth and Auckland, confirmations at Chester-le-Street, Newcastle, Ryton, Hexham, Rothbury, Wooler, Berwick, Bambrough, Alnwick, Morpeth, North Shields, Sunderland, Hartlepool, Stockton, Sedgefield, Auckland, Barnard Castle, Wolsingham and Stanhope. Illness forced Van Mildert to cancel the Chester-le-Street confirmation; whether any other part of this gruelling schedule was abandoned is not known. Schedule of visitation and diary fragment, in Durham University Library Add. Ms. 274.207V21P8.

118 F. K. Brown, *Fathers of the Victorians* (Cambridge University Press, 1961), p. 31.

119 Letterbook of Shute Barrington, 1802–18: Durham University Library. Barrington belonged to 47 Societies, was President of five, Patron of two, Vice-President of twelve and Governor of six. Maynard, 'Archdeaconry of Durham', pp. 9–12.

120 Van Mildert to Bruce Knight, 17th Oct. 1826, in Ives, *Memoir*, p. 77.

121 Episcopal Archives, Auckland Castle. When appropriated pews and space reserved for schoolchildren were taken into account, this figure fell to three per cent. Maynard, 'Archdeaconry of Durham', pp. 382, 386–7.

122 Hughes, *Losh*, vol. II, p. 118. An 1833 press report put his total giving at £9,000, but this he repudiated, telling Thorp: 'It is an exaggeration in the first place,' (changed to 'a great exaggeration') '– and in the next place, lays me open to much annoyance. Since it appeared my table has been daily covered with pecuniary applications of all sorts . . .' Thorp Correspondence, vol. I, f. 109.

123 Van Mildert, *Charge*, in Ives, *Memoir*, pp. 533–4.

5. AND TUMULT OF HER WAR

1 Beilby Porteus, notebook for 1805, p. 42: Lambeth Palace Library Ms. 2105.

2 Chadwick, *Victorian Church*, vol. I, p. 9; pp. 7–17 for background to the 1828 Bill.

3 *Hansard*, New Series, vol. V, pp. 241–359 for the 1821 debate; vol. VII, pp. 1263–4 for the 1822 vote; vol. IX, p. 1481, for Bathurst's speech on the 1832 Bill. Bathurst first voted for Catholic Emancipation in 1808; so solitary was his crusade that he sometimes had trouble finding another bishop willing to hold his proxy. Mathieson, *Reform*, p. 47.

4 *Hansard*, New Series, vol. XII, pp. 817–42 for the 1824 debate.

5 *Ibid.*, pp. 1104–65.

6 Ives, *Memoir*, pp. 67–71.

7 *Hansard*, New Series, vol. XII, pp. 1326–35, 1361–3; vol. XIII, p. 139.

8 W. Van Mildert, *Substance of A Speech, delivered in the House of Lords, on Tuesday, May 17, 1825, by William, Lord Bishop of Llandaff, on a Bill for THE REMOVAL OF CERTAIN DISQUALIFICATIONS OF the Roman Catholics*, London (Rivington, 1825), pp. 8–17.

9 Horsley, *Charges*, pp. 42–3.

10 Van Mildert, *Inquiry*, pp. 151–2; quoted in Nockles, 'Continuity and Change', vol. I, p. 293.

11 See above, pp. 33–4; also Nockles, 'Continuity and Change', vol. I, pp. 32, 41–2. V. F. Storr, no Hackney supporter, is clear that the group, 'while not despising the connection of Church and State, regarded the Church as in essence a purely spiritual organisation, and independent of the State in all matters relating to doctrine or spiritual authority': *The Development of English Theology in the Nineteenth Century*, London (Longmans, 1913), pp. 79–85.

12 *Substance of A Speech*, pp. 3–7. On sacral royalism in High Church conceptions of the Church–State relationship, see Nockles, 'Continuity and Change', vol. I, pp. 7–16, 23; cf. Clark, *English Society*, p. 135.

13 N. Gash, *Peel*, London (Longman, 1976), pp. 80–1.

14 Ives, *Memoir*, p. 80.

15 Clark, *English Society*, p. 391, quoting Eldon's biography.

16 *Ibid.*, p. 393.

17 *Ibid.*, p. 394.

18 *Hansard*, New Series, vol. xvii, passim. For a summary, see Lord Holland's speech proposing the Second Reading, p. 1479. Many Durham Methodists sided with the High Churchmen against Catholic Relief.

19 Gash, *Peel*, pp. 96–7; Lloyd to Peel, 10th Feb. 1828: British Library Ms. Add. 40343, ff. 140–1.

20 Lloyd to Peel, 2nd March 1828: *ibid.*, ff. 189–90.

21 Lloyd to Peel, 4th March 1828: *ibid.*, ff. 205–6.

22 Van Mildert to Lloyd, 3rd March 1828; Lloyd to Peel, 4th March 1828: *ibid.*, ff. 203–4, 201.

23 Peel to Lloyd, Most Private, 15th March 1828: *ibid.*, ff. 212–13.

24 *Hansard*, New Series, vol. xviii, p. 1194.

25 So Lloyd concluded; though not at the meeting, he had ample opportunity to discuss it with those who were. Lloyd to Peel, 23rd March 1828: British Library Ms. Add. 40343, ff. 246–7.

26 Van Mildert to Peel, 23rd March 1828: British Library Ms. Add. 40396, ff. 69–70.

27 Lloyd to Peel, 21st March 1828; Tournay to Lloyd, same date: British Library Ms. Add. 40343, ff. 239, 241. Van Mildert probably wrote to Manners-Sutton on 19th or 20th March; Lloyd expected the Archbishop already to have shown Peel the letter.

28 *Ibid.*, f. 240.

29 Peel to Lloyd, Saturday (22nd March 1828): *ibid.*, ff. 243–5.

30 Peel to Lloyd, 25th March 1828: *ibid.*, ff. 248–53.

31 Lloyd to Peel, 26th March 1828: *ibid.*, ff. 254–5.

32 Peel to Van Mildert, 25th March 1828: British Library Ms. Add. 40396, ff. 65–7.

33 Van Mildert to Lloyd, 30th March 1828: British Library Ms. Add. 40343, f. 264.

34 *Hansard*, New Series, vol. xviii, pp. 1491–7.

35 Van Mildert to an unnamed friend: letter accompanying a printed copy of Van Mildert's speeches on the Bill; in Ives, *Memoir*, pp. 86–7.

36 *Hansard*, New Series, vol. xviii, p. 1508.

37 See, for instance, the speech of Lord Eldon, following immediately on that of Van Mildert: *ibid.*, pp. 1497–502.

38 Quoted in Ives, *Memoir*, pp. 90–1.

39 Van Mildert to Joshua Watson, 30th April 1828; in Churton, *Memoir*, vol. i, pp. 298–9.

40 Lloyd to Peel, 15th June 1828: British Library Ms. 40343, f. 284.

41 Van Mildert's obituary in *The Gentleman's Magazine*, New Series, vol. v, pp. 425–7, stated that he 'changed his sentiments on the Roman

Catholic Question, in compliance with the Minister of the day . . . the Editor, on being apprised of such a flagrant error, thought fit to insert his acknowledgment of it only amongst his "Minor Correspondence" . . .' (Ives, *Memoir*, p. 107, footnote). *The Georgian Era: Memoirs of the most eminent Persons who have flourished in Great Britain, from the accession of George the First to the demise of George the Fourth,* 4 vols., London (Vizetelly, Branston & Co., 1832), vol. 1, p. 524, 'utters the same inexcusable mistake'. It may be a garbled reference to Van Mildert's support for Repeal.

42 Wellington to George IV, 21st July 1828: Wellington, *Despatches*, vol. IV, pp. 549–50.

43 Chadwick, *Victorian Church*, vol. 1, p. 13; pp. 11–12 for a character portrait of Howley.

44 Van Mildert to Howley, 26th July 1828: Lambeth Palace Library Ms. 2185, ff. 17–18.

45 Park to Howley, same date: *ibid.*, f. 15.

46 Gash, *Peel*, p. 111.

47 Lloyd to Peel, Private, 1st Jan. 1829: British Library Ms. Add. 40343, f. 327.

48 Peel to Lloyd, 15th Jan. 1829: *ibid.*, ff. 329–31.

49 Lloyd to Peel, 3rd Feb. 1829: *ibid.*, ff. 338–9.

50 Clark, *English Society*, p. 399; Henry Hobhouse to Richard Jenkyns, Master of Balliol, 11th Feb. 1829: Jenkyns Papers, VIA.24. Hobhouse defended Peel vigorously, on 9th Feb. declaring him 'as firm a Friend as ever to the Church'.

51 Chadwick, *Victorian Church*, vol. 1, pp. 17–21, summarises the Bill's provisions, including the full text of the oath.

52 Eldon to Rev Matthew Surtees, Feb. 1825; quoted in Clark, *English Society*, p. 352.

53 *Hansard*, New Series, vol. XIX, pp. 75–92.

54 'I look around, my Lords, and among those who are opposed to these measures I see none, in whose hands I think, the undivided management of those interests would, under present circumstances, be safe.' *Ibid.*, p. 79.

55 *Substance of SPEECHES delivered in the HOUSE OF LORDS, on the subject of THE ROMAN CATHOLIC RELIEF BILL, on April 3d., 7th, & 8th, 1829. By WILLIAM, Lord Bishop of Durham.* Not published. London (1829). The copy in the Van Mildert Papers has a manuscript note: 'Send a Revise of the whole to the Bishop of Durham', to which another hand added 'tomorrow . . . May 20. 1829'. The text bears editorial markings in Van Mildert's handwriting, principally deleting the attacks on Lloyd, pp. 11, 20–1, 30, 41. Van Mildert's decision to edit them out was clearly taken before Lloyd's death on 31st May.

56 Van Mildert himself and Howley at Oxford, Kaye of Lincoln at Cambridge. Van Mildert might have added Marsh of Peterborough, former Cambridge Lady Margaret Divinity Professor.

57 *Hansard*, New Series, vol. xix, p. 156.

58 Lloyd to Peel, 28th Dec. 1827: British Library Ms. Add. 40343, ff. 96–8.

59 Rennell to Norris (17th Nov. 1829): Norris Papers. Rennell disapproved of the omission, feeling that it suppressed a significant clue to the Bishop's character.

60 Jebb [to Norris], Good Friday 1831: Norris Papers.

61 *Hansard*, New Series, vol. xix, pp. 82–3.

62 Lloyd to Peel, 15th April 1829: British Library Ms. Add. 40343, f. 400.

63 Churton, *Memoir*, vol. i, p. 293. Churton implies that not even Joshua Watson visited Lloyd during his last illness, although the lodging was 'not far from Park-street'.

64 Gash, *Peel*, p. 157.

65 Churton to Norris, 30th Sept. 1830: Norris Papers.

66 Van Mildert to Grey, 11th Dec. 1830; Van Mildert to Grey, 21st Dec. 1830; Grey to Van Mildert, 22nd Dec. 1830; Van Mildert to Grey, 23rd Dec. 1830; Van Mildert to Grey, 30th Dec. 1830: papers of 2nd Earl Grey. See Churton, *Memoir*, vol. ii, pp. 3–4; cf. Best, *Temporal Pillars*, p. 275.

67 *Hansard*, Third Series, vol. ii, pp. 482–3.

68 Stevenson, *Popular Disturbances*, pp. 219–20; Clark, *English Society*, pp. 400–7; Thorp to Van Mildert, 16th April 1831: Van Mildert Papers.

69 Brougham to J. Losh, Aug. 1831 [copy dated 10th Sept.]: Thorp Correspondence, vol. i, f. 47. The exchange of letters is reprinted in E. Hughes, 'The Bishops and Reform, 1831–3', in *English Historical Review*, vol. lvi (July 1941).

70 Losh to Thorp, 9th Sept. 1831: *ibid.*, f. 47. Losh, a Unitarian, later attacked Van Mildert for speaking with 'contempt and harshness of all persons who do not believe in the Trinity': Van Mildert to Thorp, 23rd June 1832: *ibid.*, f. 86.

71 Thorp to Losh (draft), 12th Sept. 1831: *ibid.*

72 Van Mildert to Thorp, 10th Sept. 1831: *ibid.*, f. 61.

73 Thorp Correspondence, vol. i, ff. 15, 18, 23; Van Mildert's letters frequently refer to his continuing ill-health.

74 W. Van Mildert, *A Charge delivered to the Clergy of the Diocese of Durham*, 1831; reprinted in Ives, *Memoir*, pp. 535–72.

75 C. Wordsworth to Joshua Watson, 3rd Oct. 1831: Lambeth Palace Library Ms. 1822, f. 269.

76 Wordsworth's letter mentions the *Morning Post* report. Van Mildert wrote to Grey from Auckland on 3rd October. The Van Milderts visited Harrogate in November, then returned to Auckland, leaving for London early in December: Thorp Correspondence, vol. i, ff. 61, 68.

77 *Hansard*, Third Series, vol. vii, pp. 967–8; vol. viii, pp. 302–3.

78 *Ibid.*, vol. vii, pp. 470–4.

79 Chadwick, *Victorian Church*, vol. I, pp. 26–9; Mathieson, *Reform*, pp. 50–1. On the Bristol riots, see Stevenson, *Popular Disturbances*, pp. 221–2.

80 Van Mildert to Henry Douglas, 26th Nov. 1831, in Adams, *Douglas Family*, pp. 552–3; Van Mildert to Thorp, 2nd Nov. 1831: Thorp Correspondence, vol. I, f. 61.

81 Hughes, *Losh*, vol. II, pp. 122–3; diary entries for 25th and 31st Oct. 1831.

82 *Hansard*, Third Series, vol. XII, p. 48.

83 Marquess of Bristol to C. Wordsworth, 5th June 1832: Lambeth Palace Library Ms. 1822, f. 71. See Chadwick, *Victorian Church*, vol. I, pp. 29–32; for a summary of episcopal contributions to the debates, Norman, *Church and Society*, pp. 86–9. 'The Bishop of Bristol was so assaulted on Tuesday night coming from the House that not [sic] the Police been in great force he would have been in all probability assassinated.' H. H. Norris to C. Wordsworth, 17th May 1832: Lambeth Palace Library Ms. 1822, ff. 173–4.

84 Howley to his wife, 7th/8th Aug. 1832: Lambeth Palace Library Ms. 2166, ff. 4–5, 6–7. See also Howley to Jane Van Mildert, 12th Aug. 1832, in Adams, *Douglas Family*, p. 468.

6. LAUNCHING THE ARK

1 Like London University it looked to public joint-stock shares for starting capital. Watson, *History*, pp. 264–5. Diary entry for 5th April 1831: Hughes, *Losh*, vol. II, p. 109.

2 *Ibid.*, pp. 264–6.

3 Thorp to Van Mildert, 11th June 1831: in Jenkyns Papers IVA.

4 Thorp was at Bamburgh Castle again in October 1833; his archidiaconal duties probably took him there regularly. On the facilities at Bamburgh see review of Surtees' *History of Durham* in *Quarterly Review*, no. LXXVIII (April 1829), pp. 398–9. The Durham Chapter elected a different Sub-Dean each year at the Great Chapter meeting on 20th November.

5 *Ibid.*, p. 389; part quoted in A. J. Heesom, 'Who thought of the idea of the University of Durham?' in *Durham County Local History Society Bulletin*, 1982; Hughes, 'Bishops and Reform', p. 460–1. Both Heesom and Hughes award Durell an extra 'r'. Cromwell's plan to use 'the Deanery & the Prebendal houses for his professors and students' is mentioned in Durell to Van Mildert, 25th July 1831: Jenkyns Papers IVA. See Van Mildert to Thorp, 27th July 1831, Thorp Correspondence, vol. I, f. 5, and C. E. Whiting, *The University of Durham 1832–1932*, London (Sheldon Press, 1932), pp. 18–29. Whiting, p. 32, cites 'a tradition that Bishop Van Mildert took the initiative in founding the University, and had great difficulty in persuading the Chapter to move in the matter'.

6 Churton, *Memoir*, vol. 1, p. 297; Webster, *Joshua Watson*, pp. 44–5; Carpenter, *Church and People*, p. 73. Charles Lloyd was no keener on the King's College proposals than Gaisford on the Durham University plan: Lloyd to Norris, 16th April, 2nd June 1828: Norris Papers.

7 Jenkinson to Blomfield, 17th Oct. 1836: Durham University Library Add. Ms. 378.4281J4. Van Mildert to Thorp, 10th Aug. 1831 (two letters): Thorp Correspondence, vol. 1, ff. 14, 15. Great care was taken in these opening manoeuvres over who wrote what, when, to whom, and in what sequence.

8 Van Mildert to Thorp, 26th July 1831: *ibid.*, f. 4.

9 Durell to Van Mildert, 25th July 1831: Jenkyns Papers IVA; cf. Durell to Thorp, 28th July 1831: Thorp Correspondence, vol. 1, f. 2. The latter includes a copy of Durell's postscript to his own letter to John Banks Jenkinson, Bishop of St David's and Dean of Durham. This postscript has wrought havoc among the historians: Best, *Temporal Pillars*, p. 275, infers 'the Dean' to be Gaisford; Whiting, *University of Durham*, p. 33, has Van Mildert, presumably thinking he was still Dean of St Paul's. Maynard, 'Archdeaconry of Durham', p. 181, awards it to 'Charles Henry Hall, Bishop of St. David's and Dean of Durham'. Hall preceded Jenkinson as Dean of Durham, a financial scandal having made it 'a great publick object' to remove him from the Deanery of Christ Church. He was never a bishop.

10 Van Mildert to Thorp, 27th July 1831: Thorp Correspondence, vol. 1, f. 5.

11 Van Mildert to Thorp, Private, 25th July 1831: Thorp Correspondence, vol. 1, f. 3. The 'special reasons' probably concerned the need to keep Radicals from learning of the scheme.

12 Van Mildert to Thorp, 6th Aug. 1831: *ibid.*, f. 12. See Heesom, 'University of Durham', p. 22, footnote.

13 Gaisford to Thorp, 4th Aug. 1831; Jenkinson to Thorp, 6th Aug. 1831: *ibid.*, ff. 10, 13. Jenkinson may have had in mind the financial difficulties of Lampeter.

14 Thorp to Gaisford, 11th and 16th Aug. 1831: *ibid.*, ff. 29, 34; Jenkinson to Van Mildert, 19th Aug. 1831: Jenkyns Papers, IVA.

15 *Hansard*, Third Series, vol. XII, p. 1213; 22nd May 1832. Van Mildert to the Bishops, 8th Feb. 1834. All but three agreed: Bishop Grey of Hereford, who declined giving any undertaking until Durham degrees proved their value; Lord George Murray, Bishop of Rochester, who abhorred 'the evils to be apprehended from admitting a greater number of the inferior orders of the people into the learned Professions'; and Phillpotts. Bishop Grey to Van Mildert, 11th Feb. 1834; Van Mildert to Bishop Murray (copy), 22nd Feb. 1834: Thorp Correspondence, vol. 1, ff. 147, 153, 169.

16 Van Mildert to Henry Douglas, 26th Nov. 1831, in Adams, *Douglas Family*, p. 552–3. The 'matters of a private nature' referred to in Van

Mildert to Thorp, 18th Aug. 1831: Thorp Correspondence, vol. 1, ff. 24, 32, probably concerned the exchange.

17 'We know very little of the Lady; but hear, in all quarters, favourable reports of her fitness for the station. We shall all anxiously hope that the little ones may find in her something to supply the want of such a parent as they have lost.' Van Mildert to Henry Douglas, 1st May 1832, in Adams, *Douglas Family*, pp. 554–5.

18 Jenkinson to Van Mildert, 19th Aug. 1831, quoting a letter just received from Howley: Jenkyns Papers, IVA.

19 Van Mildert's annotated copy of the 'original Scheme', dated July 1831: *ibid.*, IVA. Thorp's draft memorandum: Thorp Correspondence, vol. 1, f. 7a. See also Van Mildert to Thorp, 18th Aug. 1831: *ibid.*, f. 24.

20 Gaisford to Thorp, 24th Aug. 1831: *ibid.*, f. 27.

21 Copy of the Dean's proposal to the Chapter, 28th Sept. 1831: Jenkyns Papers, IVA. Numerous other drafts, some undated, are preserved in the Thorp and Jenkyns archives.

22 Jenkinson to Thorp, 9th Nov. 1831: Jenkyns Papers, IVA. Brougham to Jenkinson, 11th Jan. 1832: copy in Thorp Correspondence, vol. 1, f. 74.

23 Thorp to Jenkinson, 25th Aug. 1831; Jenkinson to Durell, Prosser and Thorp, 31st Aug. 1831: Thorp Correspondence, vol. 1, ff. 29, 34.

24 Phillpotts to Wellington, 24th Sept. 1831: Wellington, *Despatches*, vol. VII, p. 537; [Blomfield], *A Remonstrance Addressed to H. Brougham, Esq., M.P. by One of the 'Working Clergy'*, London (1832), pp. 12–13; quoted in Heesom, *University of Durham*, p. 20.

25 Van Mildert to Thorp, 27th Sept. 1831, quoting a letter from Howley; Phillpotts to Van Mildert, 17th Feb. 1834: Thorp Correspondence, vol. 1, ff. 54, 166a; Heesom, *University of Durham*, pp. 23–4, 26, 29, describes Phillpotts' hostile evidence to the Church Commissioners in 1836. Phillpotts made his second and last appearance at the Durham Chapter on 20th Feb. 1832, when the petition for the University Bill was sealed. He afterwards unsuccessfully demanded £60 travelling expenses from Chapter funds.

26 Van Mildert to Thorp, 25th July 1831; Jenkinson to Thorp, 31st Aug. 1831: Thorp Correspondence, vol. 1, ff. 3, 36. Hughes, 'Bishops and Reform', pp. 462–3, misses the Evangelical reference of Van Mildert's strictures.

27 Cf. the reported comment of Howley, that 'the Bishop of Bristol, . . . as far as I could make him out, agreed with the Bishop of Exeter'.

28 Jenkinson to the Chapter, 31st Aug. 1831: Thorp Correspondence, vol. 1, f. 55.

29 Van Mildert to Thorp, 30th Aug. 1831: *ibid.*, ff. 33, 35. A footnote referring to the University plans was inserted in the published Charge.

30 Jenkinson to the Durham Chapter, 22nd Sept. 1831: *ibid.*, ff. 51–3; Jenkinson to Van Mildert, 19th Aug. 1831: Jenkyns Papers IVA.

31 Copy of Jenkinson's proposal and memorandum of the Chapter meeting: Jenkyns Papers IVA.
32 Van Mildert to Thorp, 29th Sept. 1831: Thorp Correspondence, vol. I, f. 55.
33 Van Mildert to Grey, 3rd Oct. 1831; Grey to Van Mildert, 6th Oct. 1831: papers of 2nd Earl Grey.
34 Quoted in Watson, *History*, p. 267.
35 *Ibid.*, pp. 264–9.
36 Diary entry for 29th March 1833: Hughes, *Losh*, vol. II, pp. 150–1.
37 Van Mildert to Thorp, 20th Nov. 1831: Thorp Correspondence, vol. I, f. 62; Van Mildert to Durell, same date, and 'Minute of the Chapter of Durham, November 21st 1831', in Jenkyns Papers IVA. The date is a puzzle: according to the Chapter Minutes, the meeting was on 20th Nov. By the following summer the value of the property deal had risen to £100,000: Van Mildert to Peel, 11th June 1832: British Library Ms. Add. 40403, f. 38. The Chapter also elected Thorp as Sub-Dean.
38 Van Mildert to Thorp, 27th July 1831: Thorp Correspondence, vol. I, f. 5.
39 Jenkinson to Van Mildert, 29th Nov. 1833: Jenkyns Papers, IVA.
40 Grey to Van Mildert, 10th Dec. 1831: papers of 2nd Earl Grey. Hughes, 'Bishops and Reform', p. 469, note 4, refers this to Grey's wish to see Dissenters admitted to Durham degrees; but the chief issues in 1831 seem to have been financial. The Dissenting question became acute the following year.
41 Jenkinson to Van Mildert, 25th Jan. 1832; Van Mildert to Jenkinson, 30th Jan. 1832: Jenkyns Papers, IVA.
42 Van Mildert to Thorp, 24th Jan. 1832: Thorp Correspondence, vol. I, f. 78. See Hughes, *Losh*, vol. II, p. 117 for an attempted Evangelical coup at the 1831 annual meeting of 'the Newcastle Bible Societies'.
43 Gaisford to Van Mildert, 26th Dec. 1832: Jenkyns Papers, IVA. Jenkinson to Thorp, 13th Jan. 1832; Van Mildert to Thorp, 14th Jan. 1832: Thorp Correspondence, vol. I, ff. 75, 77.
44 Van Mildert to Thorp, 24th Jan. 1832: *ibid.*, f. 78. *The Times*, 8th Nov. 1832; quoted in Chadwick, *Victorian Church*, vol. I, p. 34.
45 Losh to Lord Howick, 16th June 1832; in Hughes, *Losh*, vol. II, p. 172. A printed broadsheet by 'W.C.W.' rejecting the petitioners' arguments, dated July 1832, is in Jenkyns Papers, IVA. Van Mildert to Thorp, 6th June 1832: Thorp Correspondence, vol. I, f. 84.
46 Van Mildert to Thorp, 14th Feb. 1832: *ibid.*, f. 82.
47 Van Mildert to Thorp, 6th June 1832: *ibid.*, f. 84; *Hansard*, Third Series, vol. XII, p. 1215. See also Whiting, *University of Durham*, pp. 39–43.
48 Cumberland to Van Mildert, 7th July 1832: copy in Thorp Correspondence, vol. I, f. 88. Earlier, in the Commons, Wilkes had decided not to proceed with a hostile amendment; Shaftesbury attributed this to 'the

very great Respect which many Individuals bear for your Character':
Shaftesbury to Van Mildert, 2nd July 1832: Jenkyns Papers, IVB.

49 Grey to Thorp, 3rd Dec. 1832: Thorp Correspondence, vol. I, f. 91.

50 Van Mildert to Jenkinson, 29th Nov. 1831; Jenkinson to Van Mildert, same date: Jenkyns Papers, IVA.

51 Gaisford to Van Mildert, 5th Nov., 26th Dec. 1831, 5th Jan. 1832: *ibid.*

52 Losh, who heard a charity sermon at St Nicholas' on 1st Feb. 1829, contrasted 'the vicar, his sons ec. of the Evangelical set' with 'Mr. Gilly a mild-mannered and liberal dignitary of the Church': Hughes, *Losh*, vol. II, p. 77. Gaisford favoured taking Sherburn Hospital to site the 'school', with the Mastership for the Principal: Thorp Correspondence, vol. I, f. 24.

53 Churton, *Memoir*, vol. I, pp. 259–60.

54 Jenkinson to Van Mildert, undated fragment: Jenkyns Papers, IVA.

55 Van Mildert to Thorp, 17th May 1833: Thorp, vol. I, ff. 131–2.

56 Rose to Van Mildert, 16th July 1832: Jenkyns Papers, IVA.

57 J. W. Burgon, *Lives of Twelve Good Men*, 2 vols., London (1889), vol. I, p. 184; quoted in Webster, *Joshua Watson*, p. 94. Froude to Newman, 30th July 1833: Newman, *Letters and Diaries*, vol. IV, p. 16.

58 Rose to Newman, 20th Aug. 1833: *ibid.*, p. 30. Rose to C. Wordsworth, 20th Aug. 1833: Lambeth Palace Library Ms. 1822, f. 213.

59 A. P. Perceval to Newman, 12th Sept. 1833: Newman, *Letters and Diaries*, vol. IV, p. 43.

60 Gaisford to Van Mildert, 27th Nov. 1831: Jenkyns Papers, IVA.

61 Churton, *Memoir*, vol. I, p. 312. Churton calls his brother 'a bright spirit, whose earthly career was too short for the great things of which he had shewn himself capable'.

62 Jenkinson to Van Mildert, undated fragment; Christopher Wordsworth to Van Mildert, 3rd July 1833: Jenkyns Papers, IVA.

63 A. S. Havens, 'Henry Jenkyns on the Thirty-Nine Articles: A Study in Nineteenth-Century Anglican Confessionalism', Durham (M.A. thesis, 1982), pp. 11, 14–21.

64 Froude to Newman, 17th Nov. 1833: Newman, *Letters and Diaries*, vol. IV, p. 112. Havens, 'Henry Jenkyns', pp. 22–34, examines the part Jenkyns played in the conflict between Newman and Hawkins.

65 Van Mildert to Cumberland, 11th July 1832; and to Thorp, 12th July 1832: Thorp Correspondence, vol. I, ff. 89, 90. The printed University prospectus of 1833, in Jenkyns Papers, IVB [A], Box 1, describes Hamilton as 'Lecturer in Modern Languages'.

66 Van Mildert to Jenkyns, 22nd, 29th Oct. 1833; Jenkyns to Van Mildert, 19th, 28th Oct. 1833. An abandoned draft of this last includes the phrase: 'I have assisted this morning at the exam. of candidates for admission.' Jenkyns Papers, IVB.

67 Rose to Jenkyns, 31st Dec. 1833, 8th Jan. 1834: *ibid.*

68 Newman to Rose, 2nd June 1834: Newman, *Letters and Diaries*, vol. IV,

p. 263; Gilley, *Newman*, p. 86. On the controversy, see Whiting, *University of Durham*, p. 44.

69 Jenkyns to Van Mildert, Feb. 1835; Van Mildert to Jenkyns, 6th Feb. 1835; Jenkyns Papers, IVB. See Havens, 'Henry Jenkyns', pp. 44–5.

70 Rose to Joshua Watson, quoted in Whiting, *University of Durham*, p. 44.

71 Van Mildert to Jenkyns, 29th Oct. 1833: Jenkyns Papers, IVB; Van Mildert to Thorp, 18th Feb. 1834: Thorp Correspondence, vol. 1, f. 116b; copy in Jenkyns Papers, IVB.

72 Rose to Van Mildert, 16th July 1833: Jenkyns Papers, IVB.

73 Van Mildert to Thorp, 21st April 1834: Thorp Correspondence, vol. 1, f. 175. The Lady Margaret Professor held his canonry by 'academical' not 'ecclesiastical' tenure, and the Crown had no right of presentation.

74 Rose to Jenkyns, postmarked 26th March 1834: Jenkyns Papers, IVB.

75 Van Mildert to Thorp, 16th April 1834: Thorp Correspondence, vol. 1, f. 173. This Lord Shaftesbury was the great Evangelical philanthropist's father.

76 Van Mildert to Thorp, 21st April 1834: *ibid.*, vol. 1, f. 175; Durham Chapter Minutes, 26th April 1834.

77 Van Mildert to Grey, 6th May 1834; Grey to Van Mildert, 9th May 1834: papers of 2nd Earl Grey.

78 Hobhouse to Jenkyns, 5th May 1834: Jenkyns Papers, IVB.

79 Van Mildert to Thorp, 8th May 1834: Thorp Correspondence, vol. 1, f. 178; Van Mildert to Grey, 9th May 1834; Grey to Van Mildert, same date: papers of 2nd Earl Grey.

80 Van Mildert to Grey, 10th May 1834: papers of 2nd Earl Grey; Van Mildert to Thorp, 10th May, [12th May], 15th May 1834: Thorp Correspondence, vol. 1, ff. 179–81.

81 Rose to Jenkyns, 27th May, 2nd June 1834: Jenkyns Papers, IVB.

82 Rose to Van Mildert, 2nd July 1834, quoted in Whiting, *University of Durham*, pp. 44–5.

83 Thorp to Van Mildert, 5th July 1834: *ibid.*, p. 45.

84 Thorp to Van Mildert, 18th Aug. 1834: Thorp Correspondence, vol. 1, f. 185.

85 Thorp to Jenkyns, 15th Nov. [1834]; Van Mildert to Jenkinson, 29th Nov. 1831: Jenkyns Papers, IVB. Cf. Gaisford to Jenkyns, 15th Aug. 1833, *ibid.*, offering him the post with 'a salary of about £400 a year' and Van Mildert to Thorp, 14th Jan. 1832, postscript: Thorp Correspondence, vol. 1, f. 77.

86 Jenkyns to Thorp, undated; Thorp to Jenkyns, 7th March 1834: Jenkyns Papers, IVA.

87 Rose to Jenkyns, 17th Oct. 1834: *ibid.*, IVB. Rose 'induced the Chapter to cut out one Statute about which Thorp was obstinate . . . viz. that the Professors shd. always deliver any courses of Lectures wh. the Chapter directed. I pointed out the *absurdity* of such a statute & they said that they agreed with me.'

88 Rose to Van Mildert, 5th Oct. 1834: *ibid.* Cf. Rose to C. Wordsworth, 30th Nov. 1833: Lambeth Palace Library Ms. 1822, f. 216v, and Newman to Rose, 20th Aug. 1834: Newman, *Letters and Diaries*, vol. IV, p. 323.

89 Newman to T. Mozley, 3rd Jan. 1834; Rose to Newman, 24th March 1834: *ibid.*, pp. 162, 224–5; Newman to C. P. Golightly, 6th Jan. 1834: Lambeth Palace Library Ms. 1946, f. 15.

90 Churton, *Memoir*, vol. II, p. 63. Smith to Van Mildert, 4th Sept. 1834: Smith Papers.

91 Van Mildert to Thorp, 20th May 1834: Thorp Correspondence, vol. I, f. 182.

92 Whiting, *University of Durham*, p. 66. Van Mildert to Henry Douglas, 14th March 1833; Jenkinson to Van Mildert, quoted in Van Mildert to Douglas, 20th Oct. 1834: in Adams, *Douglas Family*, p. 557–9; Rose to Jenkyns, 17th Oct. 1834: Jenkyns Papers, IVB.

93 Van Mildert to Jenkyns, 28th Sept. 1835; Jenkyns to Hobhouse, 26th Oct. 1834: Jenkyns Papers, VB.

94 Van Mildert to Archdeacon Singleton, 6th Feb. 1835: British Library Ms. Add. 40314, f. 62; Van Mildert to Jenkyns, 6th Feb. 1835: Jenkyns Papers, IVB. Havens, 'Henry Jenkyns', pp. 47–9, examines this aspect in detail. See also Best, *Temporal Pillars*, pp. 298, 300, 308.

95 Jenkyns to Thorp, memorandum dated Nov. 1834; Thorp to Jenkyns, 15th Nov. 1834: Jenkyns Papers, IVA.

96 Hobhouse to Jenkyns, 11th Dec. 1834: *ibid.*, IVB.

97 Van Mildert to Thorp, 7th March 1835: Thorp Correspondence, vol. II, f. 187.

98 Quoted in Van Mildert to Thorp, 13th March 1835: *ibid.*, f. 189.

99 Whiting, *University of Durham*, pp. 57–8. The Charter, delayed by continued wrangling over the status of Dissenters, was granted on 1st June 1837: *ibid.*, p. 71. The Regulations were printed in 1836: copy in Jenkyns Papers, IVB.

100 Howley to Van Mildert, 16th Nov. 1835: Thorp Correspondence, vol. II, f. 197.

101 Van Mildert to Joshua Watson, 28th Jan. 1836: in Churton, *Memoir*, vol. II, p. 48. The question of the stalls was not finally settled until June 1841: Whiting, *University of Durham*, p. 77.

7. AN OLD ALMANACK

1 *Hansard*, Third Series, vol. XII, pp. 754–8. The motion demanded 'the name of every person holding more than one dignity, benefice, church, or chapel, of the Established Church in England and Wales; stating how many, and the name of each . . ., and the gross and net annual value . . ., the number of years the incumbent has held each preferment or benefice, what duties are performed by him, what curates are

employed under him, and the amount of stipends actually paid to each
curate . . .'

2 Van Mildert studied Watson's scheme for three days then 'returned it,
declaring his own desire not to change a letter in it'. According to
Churton it was approved by Howley and Wellington but 'was stopped at
that point, not meeting the concurrence of Earl Grey': *Memoir*, vol. II,
pp. 3–6. Lushington was on Van Mildert's shortlist of influential people
to receive a private advance copy of the Durham University Bill. In 1822
he was suggested as patronage secretary at the Treasury: Hughes,
'Bishops and Reform', p. 473, note 5. One of the most active Ecclesiastical Courts Commissioners (Best, *Temporal Pillars*, p. 192, note 3), he
introduced Howley's 1831 Pluralities Bill into the House of Commons.

3 Van Mildert to Thorp, 15th, 21st Jan. 1833: Thorp Correspondence,
vol. I, ff. 94, 96.

4 Park to Howley, 26th Oct. 1832: Lambeth Palace Library Ms. 2185,
ff. 96–7. Cf. the Dean of Durham's fulminations against 'that numerous
tribe of Church Reformers . . . who are perpetually obtruding their
nostrums on the public', Jenkinson to C. Wordsworth, 4th Dec. 1833:
Lambeth Palace Library Ms. 1822, ff. 83–4. Pusey attacked Henley's
proposals to abolish cathedrals, wanting instead to have patronage
exercised to 'reconvert' them into theological schools: Mathieson,
Reform, p. 70; Chadwick, *Victorian Church*, vol. I, p. 42.

5 Norris to Howley, 25th Oct. 1832: Lambeth Palace Library Ms. 2185,
ff. 94–5.

6 Blomfield to Glenie, 21st Nov. 1832: Diocesan Letter-books of C. J.
Blomfield, Bishop of London, vol. V, pp. 1–3. The Sunderland cholera
outbreak gave Van Mildert 'much extra trouble in official correspondence as Custos Rotulorum, with the Government, & with the Magistracy, & with the Board of Health'. Van Mildert to Henry Douglas,
26th Nov. 1831, in Adams, *Douglas Family*, pp. 552–3.

7 Van Mildert to Thorp, 31st Jan. 1833: Thorp Correspondence, vol. I,
f. 101. On Arnold's proposals see Chadwick, *Victorian Church*, vol. I,
pp. 42–6. Best, *Temporal Pillars*, pp. 281–92, surveys the church reform
writings of the period; Church, *Oxford Movement*, pp. 100–4, examines
their effect on the first leaders of the Oxford Movement. Norman,
Church and Society, pp. 100–5, compares the conceptions of the Church–
State relationship propounded by Coleridge, Gladstone and Arnold.

8 W. Van Mildert, 'Prayer for this Church and Nation, in the year 1833',
Durham University Library Add. Ms. 274.207V21S4.

9 Van Mildert to Bruce Knight, 28th Dec. 1832, in Ives, *Memoir*, vol. I,
pp. 131–2.

10 Van Mildert to Thorp, 15th Dec. 1832: Thorp Correspondence, vol. I,
f. 92. The bishops present were 'London, Durham, Winchester, Hereford, Salisbury, NORWICH, Bath & Wells, Lichfield, Lincoln, St.
Asaph, Worcester, Carlisle, Llandaff, Exeter, Oxford & Chichester'.

11 Van Mildert to Henry Douglas, 1st Jan. 1833, in Adams, *Douglas Family*, pp. 556–7.

12 Van Mildert to Thorp, 8th, 31st Jan. 1833: Thorp Correspondence, vol. I, ff. 93, 101.

13 Van Mildert to Thorp, 2nd, 5th, 9th Feb. 1833: *ibid.*, ff. 104–6; Van Mildert to Bruce Knight, 6th Feb. 1833: in Ives, *Memoir*, pp. 132–3.

14 H. V. Bayley to Norris, 10th March 1833: Norris Papers.

15 Hughes, 'Bishops and Reform', p. 479.

16 Van Mildert to Thorp, 14th March 1833: Thorp Correspondence, vol. I, f. 112; quoted in Best, *Temporal Pillars*, p. 126, note 2.

17 Van Mildert to Bruce Knight, 6th May 1833, in Ives, *Memoir*, p. 134.

18 Van Mildert to Thorp, 27th Feb., 26th, 30th March, 25th April, 24th May 1833: Thorp Correspondence, vol. I, ff. 109, 117–18, 125, 133.

19 Van Mildert to Thorp, 28th May 1833: *ibid.*, f. 134.

20 Chadwick, *Victorian Church*, vol. I, pp. 57–8, footnote. On Phillpotts' speech, see Nockles, 'Continuity and change', vol. I, p. 16.

21 Van Mildert to Thorp, 25th June 1833: Thorp Correspondence, vol. I, f. 135. Cf. Van Mildert to Bruce Knight, 24th June 1833, in Ives, *Memoir*, pp. 184–5.

22 Van Mildert to Joshua Watson, undated, in Churton, *Memoir*, vol. II, pp. 24–5.

23 In a letter to an unnamed friend, quoted by Ives, *Memoir*, p. 135.

24 W. Van Mildert, *Speech of the Right Reverend William, Lord Bishop of Durham, in the House of Lords, on Wednesday, July 17, 1833, on the Second Reading of the Church Temporalities (Ireland) Bill*, extracted from the *Mirror of Parliament*, Part CCXXXVI. London (1833), pp. 3–4.

25 *Ibid.*, p. 9.

26 Van Mildert to Peel, 18th Feb. 1835: British Library Ms. Add. 40415, ff. 4–9.

27 Van Mildert, *Speech . . . on a Bill for the removal of certain disqualifications of the Roman Catholics*, pp. 9–10.

28 H. Bathurst, *Memoirs of the late Dr. Henry Bathurst*, London (1837); quoted in Norman, *Church and Society*, p. 106.

29 Joshua Watson to a young clergyman 'who was inveighing against the choice of bishops by the State'; Churton, *Memoir*, vol. II, pp. 154–5. Froude to Newman, 30th July 1833; Newman, *Letters and Diaries*, vol. IV, pp. 16–17.

30 Keble to Newman, 8th Aug. 1833: *ibid.*, pp. 22–3. Nockles, 'Continuity and change', pp. 24–30, examines the conception of Establishment put forward by Keble and Froude.

31 Archbishop Whately of Dublin supported the Bill. The Bishop of Ferns and Leighlin published a pamphlet 'in favour of the church quietly submitting to parliamentary authority' (Nockles, 'Continuity and change', vol. I, p. 17); for Newman's attack on the pamphlet see *Letters and Diaries*, vol. IV, pp. 163–6.

32 Newman to J. W. Bowden, 31st Aug. 1833: *ibid.*, p. 33.
33 Best, *Temporal Pillars*, p. 346. 'To have founded a university after the manner of a great mediaeval churchman would have been no mean achievement in any age: to have done so in 1831–3 when the radical wolves "Hume and Co." were howling at the door of the ecclesiastical sheepfold was something of a miracle': Hughes, 'Bishops and Reform', p. 460.
34 Van Mildert to Joshua Watson, undated, in Churton, *Memoir*, vol. II, p. 25. Churton adds: 'The occasion seems to have been such as to remove his apprehensions in the particular instance to which he alludes, as Joshua Watson in his reply congratulates him on the unexpected ally whom he found in the Primate.'
35 Augusta Lady Castletown to her father Archy Douglas, 25th Oct. 1833: 'Poor Mrs. Van Mildert, she has had a stroke . . .': in Adams, *Douglas Family*, p. 393. Durham University Library Add. Ms. 274.2207V21P8 has three copies of the prayer; f. 67 seems to be the original. The handwriting makes plain the stress under which Van Mildert wrote it. Jane had been 'considerably shaken' by illness in February: Van Mildert to Thorp, 15th Feb. 1833: Thorp Correspondence, vol. I, f. 108.
36 Van Mildert to Thorp, 18th, 19th Feb. 1834: *ibid.*, ff. 166b, 167. Thorp to Jenkyns, 7th March 1834: Jenkyns Papers, IVA.
37 Van Mildert to Bruce Knight, 24th Nov. 1834: in Ives, *Memoir*, p. 139. Van Mildert to Thorp, 7th March 1835: Thorp Correspondence, vol. II, f. 189. 'Mrs. V:M: continues . . . as well as for some time', Van Mildert to John Burder (mutilated fragment), 15th Dec. 1834, in 'William Van Mildert, Bishop of Durham 1826 to 1836', scrapbook in Durham University Palaeography Department, f. 5c.
38 See Gilley, *Newman*, p. 111, for Newman's personal role in creating 'the "myth" of July 14th'.
39 Best, *Temporal Pillars*, p. 346.
40 Van Mildert to Singleton, 6th Feb. 1835: British Library Ms. Add. 40314, f. 62.
41 '. . . in which I have had lately full employment'. Van Mildert to Cornelius Ives, May 1835, in Ives, *Memoir*, pp. 141–2.
42 Van Mildert's speeches on the 1829 Roman Catholic Relief Bill, p. 30.
43 Newman told C. P. Golightly that Lyall, Archdeacon of Colchester and Rose's co-editor on the *Theological Library*, was at the Hadleigh conference: Newman to Golightly, 30th July 1833. Froude thought Lyall 'a most agreable [sic] man and clever and I should not think a mere conservative in heart, tho no Apostolical'. Froude to Newman, from Hadleigh, 30th July 1833; Palmer to Newman, (27th Oct. 1833): Newman, *Letters and Diaries*, vol. IV, pp. 13, 17, 71.
44 Joshua Watson to Norris, 24th Oct. 1833: in Churton, *Memoir*, vol. II, pp. 26–7.

45 Newman to Palmer, 24th Oct. 1833. For Rose's origination of the Address idea see Rose to Newman, 14th Oct. 1833, but also Rose to Newman, 10th March 1834: *Letters and Diaries*, vol. IV, pp. 67–70, 160, 207.

46 Joshua Watson to Lyall, Nov. 1833: Churton, *Memoir*, vol. II, p. 31.

47 Norris to Joshua Watson, undated: *ibid.*, p. 29.

48 Newman, *Letters and Diaries*, vol. IV, pp. 10–12. Cf. Newman to Froude, 8th Nov. 1833: 'The address is down [done] today – such a composition I never saw – we have re-written each other's, (London and Oxford) three times – but now we here have made a few alterations nostro periculo and have printed it off.'

49 *Ibid.*, p. 140, note 2. See Nockles, 'Continuity and change', vol. II, p. 436.

50 'And while we most earnestly deprecate that restless desire of change which would rashly innovate in spiritual matters, we are not less sollicitous to declare our firm conviction that, should any thing from the lapse of years or altered circumstances require renewal or correction, your Grace ['and our other Spiritual Rulers' added at the end of November 1833] may rely upon the cheerful cooperation and dutiful support of the Clergy in carrying into effect any measures, that may tend to revive the discipline of ancient times, to strengthen the connexion between the Bishops, Clergy, and People, and to promote the purity, the efficiency, and the unity of the Church.' Newman, *Letters and Diaries*, vol. IV, p. 91, and note 3.

51 Rose to C. Wordsworth, 30th Nov. 1833: Lambeth Palace Library Ms. 1822, ff. 215–16. Thomas Sikes had 'hard work' persuading Strong to 'take up the Address'; T. Mozley to Newman, *Letters and Diaries*, vol. IV, p. 154, n. 1.

52 Newman to Bowden, 9th Feb. 1834: *ibid.*, p. 188. Van Mildert to Bruce Knight, 18th Dec. 1833, in Ives, *Memoir*, pp. 136–7. Van Mildert had probably been asked to receive and transmit the Durham clergy's collected signatures, as Phillpotts did in Exeter.

53 By Joshua Watson, according to Churton: *Memoir*, vol. II, p. 34. See Webster, *Joshua Watson*, p. 103; Newman to Bowden, 30th Jan. 1834: *Letters and Diaries*, vol. IV, p. 183.

54 Wordsworth to Joshua Watson, 12th Nov. 1833: British Library Ms. Add. 46137, f. 169.

55 Froude to Newman, 17th Nov. 1833: *Letters and Diaries*, vol. IV, p. 112; also pp. 11–12, 140, 151.

56 In 1840 Newman replied with the unsanctioned dedication of a volume of sermons, complimenting Watson's 'long and dutiful ministry, and patient service to his . . . mother' the Church: Webster, *Joshua Watson*, p. 104; Churton, *Memoir*, vol. II, pp. 243, 26. Newman to Watson, 12th July 1835: Lambeth Palace Library Ms. 1562, f. 24. Newman, *Letters and Diaries*, vol. IV, p. 265, gives an anecdote of Watson introducing Bowden to Rose 'upon the principle that "all

Newman's friends should know each other"'. See also Keble's affectionate references to Watson (pp. 181, 183, 226).

57 Blomfield to Howley, 11th Dec. 1832: Diocesan Letter-books of C. J. Blomfield, Bishop of London, vol. v, pp. 25–7.

58 Howley, Blomfield, Kaye of Lincoln and Monk of Gloucester.

59 Churton, *Memoir*, vol. ii, pp. 28, 47–8. The wording leaves it unclear whether the writer was Watson or Van Mildert, but the Commission met in London and Van Mildert was at Auckland.

60 Van Mildert's 1831 *Charge*, in Ives, *Memoir*, p. 564.

61 Van Mildert to Peel, 18th Feb. 1835: British Library Ms. Add. 40415, ff. 4–9.

62 Peel to Van Mildert, Most Private, 23rd Feb. 1835: *ibid.*, ff. 136–42. Peel clearly found this letter difficult to write; it is so much edited that he had to have it fair-copied, and parts of the draft are illegible.

63 Van Mildert to Peel, 28th Feb. 1835: *ibid.*, ff. 275–6.

64 Van Mildert to Thorp, 13th March 1835: Thorp Correspondence, vol. ii, ff. 189–90.

65 He suggested prebends of Durham for Carlisle and Chester, Christ Church for Oxford, Westminster and St Paul's for the rest, perhaps supplemented by the Deaneries of Windsor, Westminster and St Paul's. Van Mildert to Howley, 2nd April 1835: British Library Ms. Add. 40419, ff. 143–6. Chadwick, *Victorian Church*, vol. i, pp. 104–5, gives a convenient summary of the report's provisions and of High Church reactions to it.

66 Van Mildert's last letter to Joshua Watson, 28th Jan. 1836: in Churton, *Memoir*, vol. ii, p. 48.

67 Best, *Temporal Pillars*, pp. 315, 431–3; see also Chadwick, *Victorian Church*, vol. i, p. 138. Selwyn, Lady Margaret Professor of Divinity and brother to the Bishop, was a spiritual heir after Van Mildert's own heart. Another, much cheekier, possible taking of Van Mildert's name in vain was the gift of £20 by 'W.V.M.' to help build a 'Scotch Church' at South Shields, reported by *The Times*, 16th March 1836, p. 6, col. 2; in Cochrane, 'Van Mildert', p. 426. Van Mildert, while not unsympathetic to needy individual Dissenters, refused on principle to 'contribute towards the expense of Dissenting places of worship': Ives, *Memoir*, p. 151.

68 Churton, *Memoir*, vol. ii, pp. 43–4.

69 'If Durham is to be brought down [below £10,000] . . . it must undergo retrenchments, which will . . . alter it's character in point of state & representation'; Van Mildert to Howley, 2nd April 1835: British Library Ms. Add. 40419, ff. 143–6. For Van Mildert's views on 'pomp and ceremony' in general and in 'matters of religion', see his 1828 sermon on the consecration of St Paul's Chapel, Ryton: in Ives, *Memoir*, p. 289.

70 Churton, *Memoir*, vol. ii, pp. 44–5. The arrangement with Howley may

well have been that Van Mildert would exchange Churton something from his own preferment at the first opportunity.

71 Van Mildert to Bruce Knight, 8th Dec. 1835, in Ives, *Memoir*, p. 140.

72 *Durham Chronicle*, 5th Feb. 1836, p. 3, cols. 2–3.

73 Ives, *Memoir*, pp. 143–4; *Durham County Advertiser*, Friday 26th Feb. 1836, p. 2, cols. 4–5, p. 3, col. 3. Ives attributes the *Advertiser* obituary to T. L. Strong. The account in Ives' *Memoir* is probably also by Strong: Churton, *Memoir*, vol. II, p. 49.

74 Ives, *Memoir*, pp. 144–5. The alterations to the Chapel cost Van Mildert an estimated £1,500; they included another abortive hot-air central heating project: J. Raine, *A Brief Historical Account of the Episcopal Castle, or Palace, of Auckland* (1852), pp. 95–6; quoted by Cochrane, 'Van Mildert', pp. 190–3.

75 *Durham Chronicle*, 4th March 1836, p. 4, col. 3.

76 *The Times*, 24th Feb. 1836.

77 Lord Denman's Charge to the Grand Jury at Durham, quoted by Ives, *Memoir*, p. 146. For Van Mildert's opinion of Denman see Hughes, 'Bishops and Reform', p. 473.

78 Ives reprints the deep purple tribute from Thorp's Archidiaconal Charge: *Memoir*, pp. 146–7.

79 Canon Ilderton, Rector of Ingram, to an unidentified newspaper, Jan. 1890: 'William Van Mildert, Bishop of Durham 1826 to 1836', scrapbook in Durham University Palaeography Department.

80 Diary entry for 30th July 1833: Hughes, *Losh*, vol. II, p. 156.

81 Van Mildert to Howley, 27th Oct. 1818: Lambeth Palace Library Ms. 2184, f. 201.

82 Van Mildert to Thorp, 7th April 1834: Thorp Correspondence, vol. I, f. 172. One consequence of the downgrading of the Palatine See was that Van Mildert's successor Maltby, having no further use for Durham Castle, presented it to the University; something often credited to Van Mildert.

Bibliography

This is not intended as a survey of the extensive literature on the late eighteenth- and early nineteenth-century Church of England. Works listed are mostly those referred to in the text and footnotes. Place of publication is London unless otherwise stated.

1. PUBLISHED WORKS OF VAN MILDERT

[W. Percy, Van Mildert *et al.*], *Poems by A Literary Society, comprehending Original Pieces in the Several Walks of Poetry* (1784)

The Excellency of the Liturgy, and the Advantages of being Educated in the Doctrine and Principles, of the Church of England. A Sermon, preached in the Parish Church of St. Mary Le Bow . . . (1797)

Cautions against Innovation in Matters of Religion. A Sermon, preached in the Parish Church of St. Mary Le Bow . . . (1798)

A Letter to the Society for Promoting Christian Knowledge. Occasioned by two recent publications respecting the British and Foreign Bible Society, by a Member of the Society [attributed to Van Mildert] (1805)

An historical review of the rise and progress of Infidelity, with a refutation of it's principles and reasonings; in a series of Sermons preached for the Lecture founded by the Hon. Robert Boyle (1806; 2nd edition 1808, 3rd 1820, 4th 1831)

To THE INHABITANTS of THE PARISH OF FARNINGHAM in the County of Kent (privately printed, 5th March 1810)

A Sermon on Psalm lvii.1. Preached before the Honourable Society of Lincoln's Inn, on the Occasion of the Assassination of the Right Honourable Spencer Perceval (1812)

An Inquiry into the general principles of Scripture-Interpretation, Oxford (1815; 2nd edition 1815; 3rd 1831)

A Sermon Preached Before The Corporation of Trinity House, in the Church of St. Nicholas, Deptford (1816)

A Sermon Preached in the Cathedral Church of St. Paul, June 8, 1820, at the Yearly Meeting of the Children Educated in the Charity Schools in and about the Cities of London and Westminster (1820; reprinted 1850 as *True and False Knowledge Compared: A Sermon*)

A Charge delivered to the clergy of the Diocese of Llandaff at the primary visitation in August MDCCCXXI, Oxford (1821)

A Sermon Preached before The Incorporated Society for the Propagation of the Gospel in Foreign Parts, at their Anniversary Meeting, in the Parish Church of St. Mary le Bow (1822)

The Works of the Rev. Daniel Waterland, D.D., formerly Master of Magdalene College, Cambridge, Canon of Windsor, and Archdeacon of Middlesex. To Which is Prefixed a Review of the Author's Life and Writings, by William Van Mildert, D.D., Lord Bishop of Llandaff, 10 vols., Oxford (1823; 2nd edition 1843; 3rd 1856; extracts, *A Review of the Doctrine of the Eucharist: with Four Charges to the Clergy of Middlesex Connected with the Same Subject*, reprinted 1896)

Substance of A Speech, delivered in the House of Lords, on Tuesday, May 17, 1825, by William, Lord Bishop of Llandaff, on a Bill for THE REMOVAL OF CERTAIN DISQUALIFICATIONS OF the Roman Catholics (1825)

A Charge delivered to the Clergy of the Diocese of Durham, MDCCCXXVII, Oxford (1828)

[Speeches on the Bill for the Repeal of the Corporation and Test Acts, reprinted from the Mirror of Parliament] (1828); mentioned by Ives, *Memoir*, p. 86.

A Sermon Preached at The Consecration of St. Paul's Chapel, in the Parish of Ryton, Durham (1828)

Substance of SPEECHES delivered in the HOUSE OF LORDS, on the subject of THE ROMAN CATHOLIC RELIEF BILL, on April 3d, 7th, & 8th, 1829. By WILLIAM, Lord Bishop of Durham (1829)

A Sermon for the Sons of the Clergy in the Diocese of Durham, preached at St. Nicholas' Church, Newcastle, Oxford (1830)

A Charge delivered to the Clergy of the Diocese of Durham, Oxford (1831)

Sermons preached before the Honourable Society of Lincoln's Inn, from the year 1812 to the year 1819, Oxford (1831)

Speech of the Right Reverend William, Lord Bishop of Durham, in the House of Lords, on Wednesday, July 17, 1833, on the Second Reading of the Church Temporalities (Ireland) Bill, extracted from the *Mirror of Parliament*, Part CCXXXVI (1833)

Memorial edition of Van Mildert's Works: one volume of *Sermons on several Occasions, and Charges, by William Van Mildert, D.D., Late Bishop of Durham. To which is prefixed a memoir of the Author* by C. Ives, with the Boyle Lectures, Bampton Lectures and Lincoln's Inn Sermons, 6 vols. in all, Oxford (1838)

2. UNPUBLISHED PAPERS

Van Mildert Manuscripts: Durham University Library; some on deposit from Van Mildert College.

Letterbook of Shute Barrington, 1802–18: Durham University Library.

Diocesan Letter-books of C. J. Blomfield, Bishop of London: Lambeth Palace Library.

Chapter Book, Batells Book, Van Mildert's private account book: Christ Church archives, Oxford.

Durham Acta Book: Diocesan Registry.

Archives of Dean and Chapter of Durham: Dean and Chapter Registry.

Farningham Parish Records: Kent County Archives, Maidstone.

Papers of 2nd Earl Grey: Grey of Howick Mss., Durham University Library.

Horsley Papers: Lambeth Palace Library.

Howley Papers: Lambeth Palace Library.

Jenkyns Papers: Balliol College Library, Oxford.

Liverpool Papers: British Library.

Llandaff Acta Book: National Library of Wales, Aberystwyth.

Norris Papers: Bodleian Library.

Peel Papers: British Library.

Notebooks of Beilby Porteus: Lambeth Palace Library.

Batells Book 1779–91: The Queen's College archives, Oxford.

Strong Papers: Bodleian Library.

Thorp Correspondence: Durham University Library.

Papers of Christopher Wordsworth: British Library, Lambeth Palace Library.

3. PRINTED WORKS AND UNPUBLISHED THESES

Adams, P. W. L., *A History of the Douglas family of Morton in Nithsdale (Dumfriesshire) and Fingland (Kirkcudbrightshire) and their descendants*, Bedford (The Sidney Press, 1921).

Allen, W. O. B. and McClure, E., *Two Hundred Years: the History of The Society for Promoting Christian Knowledge, 1698–1898* (SPCK, 1898).

Aspinall, A., ed., *The Letters of King George IV, 1812–1830* (Cambridge University Press, 1938); *The Correspondence of George Prince of Wales 1770–1812*, 8 vols. (Cassell, 1971).

Best, G. F. A., 'The mind and times of William Van Mildert', in *Journal of Theological Studies*, New Series, vol. XIV, part 2 (October 1963), pp. 355–70; *Temporal Pillars: Queen Anne's Bounty, the Ecclesiastical Commissioners and the Church of England* (Cambridge University Press, 1964).

Black, S. B., *The Children of Farningham and their Schools 1800–1900*, Kent (Darenth Valley Publications, 1982).

Bradshaw, A., 'William Van Mildert's visit to the Netherlands in 1792', in *Durham University Journal*, vol. LXXI, no. 1 (December 1978), pp. 45–53.

Braine, R. K., 'The life and writings of Herbert Marsh (1757–1839)', Cambridge (Ph.D. thesis, 1989).

Brilioth, Y., *The Anglican Revival* (Longmans, 1925).

Brown, F. K., *Fathers of the Victorians* (Cambridge University Press, 1961).

Brown, P. A., *The French Revolution in English History* (Crosby Lockwood & Son, 1918).

Burgon, J. W., *Lives of Twelve Good Men*, 2nd ed., 2 vols. (John Murray, 1889).

Carpenter, S. C., *Church and People, 1789–1889* (SPCK, 1933).

Chadwick, O., *The Victorian Church*, 2 vols. (Black, 1966).

Church, R. W., *The Oxford Movement: Twelve Years 1833–1845* (Macmillan, 1892).

Churton, E., *Memoir of Joshua Watson*, 2 vols., Oxford (J. H. Parker, 1861).

Clark, J. C. D., *English Society 1688–1832: Ideology, social structure and political practice during the ancien regime* (Cambridge University Press, 1985); *Revolution and Rebellion: State and Society in England in the Seventeenth and Eighteenth Centuries* (Cambridge University Press, 1986).

Clarke, C. P. S., *The Oxford Movement and After* (Mowbray, 1932).

Lowther Clarke, W. K., *A Short History of the S.P.C.K.* (SPCK, 1919); *A History of the S.P.C.K.* (SPCK, 1959).

Clarkson, L., *Death, Disease and Famine in Pre-industrial England*, Dublin (Gill & Macmillan, 1975).

Cochrane, R. A., 'William Van Mildert, bishop of Durham 1826–1836', Durham (M.Litt. thesis, 1950).

Coleman, B. H., 'Anglican church extension and related movements c. 1800–1860 with special reference to London', Cambridge (Ph.D. thesis, 1968).

Warre Cornish, F., *A History of the English Church in the Nineteenth Century*, 2 vols. (Macmillan, 1910).

Culler, A. D., *The Imperial Intellect – a study of Newman's educational ideal*, New Haven (Yale University Press, 1955).

Dahm, J. J., 'Science and apologetics in the early Boyle Lectures', in *Church History*, vol. 39 (1970), no. 2, pp. 172–86.

Daubeny, C., *A Guide to the Church, in Several Discourses* (T. Cadell and W. Davies, 1798).

De Jong, J. A., *As the Waters Cover the Sea: Millennial Expectations in the Rise of Anglo–American Missions 1640–1810*, Amsterdam (1970).

Evans, M., ed., *Letters of Radcliffe and James* (Oxford Historical Society, 1888).

Faber, G., *Oxford Apostles: A Character Study of the Oxford Movement* (Faber, 1933).

[W. C. Farr, ed.], *Merchant Taylors' School: Its Origin, History, and Present Surroundings*, Oxford (Blackwell, 1929).

Gash, N., *Mr. Secretary Peel – the life of Sir Robert Peel to 1830* (Longman, 1961); *Peel* (Longman, 1976).

Gilbert, A. D., *Religion and Society in Industrial England* (Longman, 1976).

Gillespie, C. C., *Genesis and Geology*, New York (Harper & Row, 1959).

Gilley, S., 'Christianity and Enlightenment: an historical survey', in *History* of European Ideas, vol. i (1981), no. 2, pp. 103–21; 'Nationality and liberty, protestant and catholic: Robert Southey's *Book of the Church*', in S. Mews, ed., *Religion and National Identity, Studies in Church History*, vol. 18, Oxford (1982); *Newman and his Age* (Darton, Longman and Todd, 1990).

Green, V. H. H., *Religion at Oxford and Cambridge* (SCM Press, 1964); *A History of Oxford University* (Batsford, 1974).

Halévy, E., *A History of the English People in the Nineteenth Century*, 6 vols. (Ernest Benn, 1949–52).

Hardy, C. E., *John Bowes and the Bowes Museum*, Newcastle (Frank Graham, 1978).

'Substance of the Speech of the Earl of Harrowby, on moving for the Recommitment of a Bill for the better Support and Maintenance of Stipendiary Curates', in *Quarterly Review*, vol. x, no. xix (October 1813), pp. 41–57.

Havens, A. S., 'Henry Jenkyns on the Thirty-nine Articles: a study in nineteenth-century Anglican confessionalism', Durham (M.A. thesis, 1982).

Heesom, A. J., *The Founding of the University of Durham*, Durham (Cathedral Lecture, 1982); 'Who thought of the idea of the University of Durham?' in *Durham County Local History Society Bulletin* (1982).

Hobsbawm, E. J., *The Age of Revolution 1789–1848* (Weidenfeld & Nicholson, 1962).

Hodgkin, R. H., *Six Centuries of an Oxford College*, Oxford (Blackwell, 1969).

Horne, G., *A Charge intended to have been delivered to the Clergy of Norwich, at the Primary Visitation of George, Lord Bishop of that Diocese*, Norwich (Yarington & Bacon, 1791).

Horsley, S., *The Charges of Samuel Horsley, late Lord Bishop of St. Asaph; delivered at his several Visitations of the Dioceses of St. David's, Rochester, and St. Asaph*, Dundee (1813).

Hughes, E., 'The Bishops and Reform 1831–3', in *English Historical Review*, vol. lvi (July 1941), pp. 459–90; ed., *The Diaries and Correspondence of James Losh*, 2 vols., Durham (Surtees Society, 1962–3).

Huish, R., *Memoirs of Caroline, Queen of Great Britain*, 2 vols. (1821).

Hunt, J., *Religious Thought in England in the Nineteenth Century* (Gibbings, 1896).

Jacob, M. C., *The Newtonians and the English Revolution 1689–1720*, Sussex (The Harvester Press, 1976).

Jebb, H. H., *A Great Bishop of One Hundred Years Ago, being a sketch of the life of Samuel Horsley, LL.D., formerly Bishop of St. David's, Rochester, and St. Asaph and Dean of Westminster* (Edward Arnold, 1909).

Jones, W., ed., *The Works of the Right Reverend George Horne, D.D., Late Lord Bishop of Norwich; to which are prefixed Memoirs of his Life, Studies, and Writings*, 2nd ed. (F. C. & J. Rivington, 1818).

[B. Kennicott], *A Word to the Hutchinsonians: or Remarks on Three extraordinary*

Sermons Lately preached before the University of Oxford, by The Reverend Dr. Patten, The Reverend Mr. Wetherall, and The Reverend Mr. Horne, By A Member of the University (1756).

Ker, I. and Gornall, T., eds., *The Letters and Diaries of John Henry Newman*, 5 vols., Oxford (Clarendon Press, 1978–81).

McManners, J., *The French Revolution and the Church* (SPCK, 1969).

Magrath, J. R., *The Queen's College*, Oxford (Clarendon Press, 1921).

Mallet, C. E., *A History of the University of Oxford* (Methuen, 1927).

Mathieson, W. L., *English Church Reform 1815–1840* (Longman, 1923).

Maynard, W. B., 'The ecclesiastical administration of the Archdeaconry of Durham 1774–1856', Durham (Ph.D. thesis, 1973).

Newman, J. H., *Lectures on the Prophetical Office of the Church, viewed relatively to Romanism and Popular Protestantism* (Rivington, 1837).

Nockles, P. B., 'Continuity and change in Anglican High Churchmanship in Britain, 1792–1850', 2 vols., Oxford (D.Phil. thesis, 1982).

Norman, E. R., *Church and Society in England 1770–1970* (Oxford University Press, 1976).

Overton, J. H. and Relton, F., *The English Church from the Accession of George I to the end of the Eighteenth Century* (Macmillan, 1906).

[Park, J. A.], *Memoirs of William Stevens, Esq.* (1812).

Pascoe, C. F., *Two Hundred Years of the S.P.G.: An Historical Account of the Society for the Propagation of the Gospel in Foreign Parts, 1701–1900* (SPG, 1901).

Port, M. H., *600 New Churches, a Study of the Church Building Commission, 1815–1856, and its Church Building Activities* (SPCK for the Church Historical Society, 1961).

Porteus, B., *A Charge delivered to the Clergy of the Diocese of London, at the Visitation of that Diocese in the year MDCCXCIV* (F. & C. Rivington, 1794); *A Charge delivered to the Clergy of the Diocese of London, in the years 1798 and 1799* (1799).

Reardon, B. M. G., *Religious Thought in the Victorian Age: A Survey from Coleridge to Gore*, New York (Longman, 1980).

Rudwick, M. J. S., *The Meaning of Fossils* (Macdonald, 1972).

Smith, G., *The Life of William Carey: Shoemaker and Missionary* (John Murray, 1885).

Soloway, R. A., *Prelates and People: Ecclesiastical Social Thought in England 1783–1852* (Routledge and Kegan Paul, 1969).

Stephen, W., *History of the Scottish Church*, 2 vols., Edinburgh (David Douglas, 1894, 1896).

Stevenson, J., *Popular Disturbances in England 1700–1870*, New York (Longman, 1979).

Stone, L., ed., *The University in Society*, 2 vols. (Princeton University Press, 1974).

Storr, V. F., *The Development of English Theology in the Nineteenth Century*, London (Longmans, 1913).

The Clerical Guide, or, Ecclesiastical Directory, 2nd ed. (corrected), (F. C. & J. Rivington, 1822); *The Clerical Guide, and Ecclesiastical Directory*, New Edition (J. G. & F. Rivington, 1836).

The Georgian Era: Memoirs of the most eminent persons who have flourished in Great Britain, from the accession of George the First to the demise of George the Fourth, 4 vols. (Vizetelly, Branston & Co., 1832).

Thompson, E. P., *The Making of the English Working Class* (Penguin Books, 1968).

Varley, E. A., 'A study of William Van Mildert, Bishop of Durham, and the High Church movement of the early nineteenth century', Durham (Ph.D. thesis, 1985); *The Last of the Prince Bishops*, Durham (Cathedral Lecture, 1986).

Virgin, P., *The Church in an Age of Negligence: Ecclesiastical Structure and Problems of Church Reform* (James Clarke, 1989).

Ward, W. R., *Victorian Oxford* (Cass, 1965); *Religion and Society in England 1790–1850*, New York (Schocken Books, 1973).

Watson, R. S., *The History of the Literary and Philosophical Society of Newcastle-upon-Tyne (1793–1897)* (Scott, 1897).

Webster, A. B., *Joshua Watson: The Story of a Layman, 1771–1855* (SPCK for the Church Historical Society, 1954).

Welbourne, E., *The Miners' Unions of Northumberland and Durham* (Cambridge University Press, 1923).

Duke of Wellington, ed., *Despatches, correspondence, and memoranda of Field Marshal Arthur, Duke of Wellington, K.G., 1819–32 (in continuation of former series)*, 8 vols. (John Murray, 1867–80).

Whiting, C. E., *The University of Durham 1832–1932* (The Sheldon Press, 1932).

Wilberforce, R. I. and S., *The Life of William Wilberforce*, 5 vols. (John Murray, 1838).

Wilde, C. B., 'Hutchinsonianism, natural philosophy and religious controversy in eighteenth century Britain', in *History of Science*, vol. xviii (1980), pp. 1–24.

Woodforde, J., *The Diary of a Country Parson*, ed. J. Beresford, 5 vols. (Oxford University Press, 1924).

Index